WAYS OF
IMPERFECTION

WAYS OF
IMPERFECTION

*An Exploration of
Christian Spirituality*

Simon Tugwell, o.p.

Templegate Publishers
Springfield, Illinois

First published in the United States in 1985

Templegate Publishers
302 East Adams Street
P.O. Box 5152
Springfield, IL 62705

http://www.templegate.com

Cover: Detail from *The Adoration of the Magi*, by Sandro Botticelli,
1475, Uffizi, Florence

This book was manufactured in the United States

Contents

Preface

'Spirituality' seems to be in vogue these days. Yet it is in some ways a tricky notion. The confident modern usage of the word is, in fact, *very* modern, which makes it unclear quite how we should set about identifying the 'spirituality' of earlier christian writers.[1] If we simply look for things which seem to anticipate later, more obviously 'spiritual' writers, not only shall we probably distort the message of the earlier writers, but we shall also strengthen the rather monochrome picture of 'spirituality' which so inhibits our awareness of the diversities which are legitimate within the christian life.

The earliest known use of the Latin word *spiritualitas*[2] remains very close to what St Paul meant by 'spiritual' (*pneumatikos*): christians, by virtue of their baptism, are meant to be 'spiritual' in the sense that they are meant to be 'led by the Spirit' and to 'live by the Spirit'.[3] The 'spiritual' life of the christians is contrasted, not with some other facets of the christian life, but with an 'unspiritual', carnal, life.[4] In the thirteenth century it was still possible to identify the 'spiritual life' as being, precisely, the life of grace,[5] but already 'spirituality' was beginning to be divorced from the christian life as a whole.[6] By the end of the middle ages it was often regarded as a special way of being a christian, or a special interest which some christians might have, but which was not applicable to the general run of believers.[7] Some christians are 'spiritual', others, by implication, are not, and the criterion is not fidelity to the gospel, but a particular intensity of 'interiority', or something of the kind.[8] A theological protest was made against this quite unjustified restriction of 'spiritual' words,[9] but it did not make much difference.

The standard modern notion of 'spirituality', as expounded, for instance, in Jordan Aumann's admirably clear textbook,[10] tends to obscure the fact that there has, down the ages, been a fair amount of controversy and disagreement about what it means for us to live by the Spirit, and suggests a scheme into which it is difficult to fit many christian writers who might still be able to shed light on our own attempts to live a serious christian life.

The great French Jesuit, Jean-Pierre de Caussade (1675–1751), claimed that what he was proposing was 'a way of viewing things',[11] and this is how I intend to delimit the subject matter of 'spirituality'.

It is not just concerned with prayer and contemplation and spiritual exercises, it is concerned with people's ways of viewing things, the ways in which they try to make sense of the practicalities of christian living and to illuminate christian hopes and christian muddles.

The essays in this book fall far short of offering a history of christian spirituality. Many important authors are omitted entirely or discussed only from a very limited point of view; in particular the great Spanish spiritual writers of the sixteenth century, whose influence on subsequent spirituality has been almost tyrannical, do not feature here. In fact the period since the end of the fourteenth century is represented only by Caussade and Thérèse of Lisieux. Yet the selection of authors and topics treated here is not completely random. They represent a variety of themes which have reappeared with a certain persistence in the history of the church. And the omission of some of the generally accepted 'great figures' allows the supposedly lesser lights to be seen more clearly and this, I hope, will contribute to a more balanced vision of the development of christian spirituality. In any case, it is nice sometimes to see the stars, which we can only do when the sun is not shining.

In its general outline this book grew out of a series of articles published in *Doctrine and Life* between January 1982 and July/August 1983. Some of the articles have been taken over with few alterations, and I am grateful to the editor for permission to use them here. But most of the material has been fairly thoroughly revised.

In the notes I have tried to give references to the texts I have used in such a way that they will be useful regardless of the different editions which may be available to the reader; I have therefore not given detailed bibliographical information about most of the authors cited. I have supplied bibliographies for most of the chapters in connection with the major texts being discussed in those chapters, and wherever it has been necessary for some reason or another to give references to particular editions. I have also made no attempt to list all existing translations; instead I have confined myself to mentioning translations which I can, with varying degrees of enthusiasm, actually recommend. In general the bibliographies are attached to individual chapters, but there is a single bibliography for chapters 9-11 together. In the Index references to pages carrying bibliographical information are highlighted.

Except where the contrary is stated, all translations in this book are my own.

Oxford
1 June 1984   SIMON TUGWELL, O.P.

Notes

[1]Gustavo Vinay raised the question in *Studi Medievali* 2 (1961), pp. 705–9, prompting Jean Leclercq to reply with a brief history of the word 'spirituality' in the same journal 3 (1962), pp. 279–96.

[2]Pseudo-Jerome, *Epist.* 7:9 (PL 30 [1846 edn]:114D–115A).

[3]Rom. 8:14, Gal. 5:25.

[4]Rom. 8:4, 1 Cor. 3:1.

[5]*Spiritualis uita, scilicet uita gratie*: sermon of Jordan of Saxony, ed. A. G. Little and Decima Douie, *English Historical Review* 54 (1939), p. 13:17.

[6]A disjunction between 'spiritual exercise' and christian practice as a whole is already apparent in Guigo II in the twelfth century; cf. below, chapters 9–11.

[7]Domenico Cavalca in the 1330s appears to identify *vita spirituale* with religious life (*Frutti della Lingua*, ch. 22). In 1558 Luis of Granada warned Bartholomew of the Martyrs, whom he had just commanded to accept the archbishopric of Braga, 'not to desire that everyone should have a spiritual life': Luiz de Sousa, *Vida do ven. D. Fr. Bartolomeu dos Martyres* I, ch. 8 (Paris 1760, I, p. 39). Cf. A. Huerga in *Historia de la Espiritualidad* II (Barcelona 1969), p. 111.

[8]St Teresa of Avila, for instance, uses *espíritu* and *espiritual* in a very restrictive sense, which allows for a complete dichotomy between being 'virtuous' and being 'spiritual': e.g. *Life* 13:16–19.

[9]Cf. the lively critique of the pietistic appropriation of words connected with 'spirit' in Juan de la Cruz, o.p., *Diálogo sobre la Necesidad de la Oración Vocal*, ed. V. Beltrán de Heredia (Madrid 1962), pp. 270ff. A translation of this work is in preparation for the series *Dominican Sources*.

[10]Jordan Aumann, *Spiritual Theology*. Huntingdon (Ind.) and London 1980. Cf. my review of this work in *New Blackfriars* 62 (1981), pp. 44–5.

[11]J. P. de Caussade, *Lettres Spirituelles*, ed. Michel Olphe-Galliard, I (Paris 1962), p. 64.

General Abbreviations

MOPH   Monumenta Ordinis Praedicatorum Historica (Rome).
PG   Migne, *Patrologia Graeca.*
PL   Migne, *Patrologia Latina.*
PLS   A. Hamman, *Patrologiae Latinae Supplementum.*
SC   Sources Chrétiennes (Paris).

Other abbreviations are listed with the bibliographies at the end of chapters.

1

The Apostolic Fathers

The church has known many different moods in the course of her history. Sometimes she appears to be very confident of herself and of the value of her message, sometimes she seems rather to be a bit confused and unsure of herself; sometimes she boldly tells everyone exactly what they ought to be doing, sometimes she gives the impression of groping in the darkness. And it is not necessarily in her 'best' moments, when she is most confident and clear, that she is most true to herself. There is a kind of unsatisfactoriness written into her very constitution, because she is only a transitional organisation, keeping people and preparing them for a new creation, in which God will be all and in all, and every tear will be wiped away.[1] When she speaks too securely, she may obscure the fact that her essential business is with 'what no eye has seen, no ear has heard, nor has it entered the heart of man'.[2] The blunt truth is, as St John says, that 'we have not yet been shown what we shall be'.[3] A time of confusion like our own, when people become disillusioned with the church and with christianity, should be a salutary, educative time, when we face the facts.

Christianity *has* to be disappointing, precisely because it is not a mechanism for accomplishing all our human ambitions and aspirations, it is a mechanism for subjecting all things to the will of God. The first disciples were disappointed because Jesus turned out not to be the kind of Messiah they wanted. Even after the resurrection St Luke shows us how the apostles were still dreaming of a political restoration of the kingdom of Israel.[4] They had to be disappointed. When people turn away from the church, because they find more satisfaction elsewhere, it is important not to assume that we, as christians, ought to be providing such satisfaction ourselves; it is much more urgent that we take yet another look at just what it is that we have genuinely been given in the church. We may indeed say that christianity does direct us towards the fulfilment of all our desires and hopes; but we shall only say this correctly if we understand it to mean that a great many of the desires and hopes we are conscious of will eventually turn out to be foolish and misconceived. It is God who knows how to make us happy, better than we know

1

ourselves. Christianity necessarily involves a remaking of our hopes. And our disappointments are an unavoidable part of the process.

In the early church, almost from the outset, we find evidence of christians who were becoming disillusioned. In the motley collection of writings which are generally designated by the term 'the Apostolic Fathers', we see how various christian teachers responded to this situation, and the one thing they all have in common is what we may call a 'spirituality of imperfection'. Forced by their circumstances, they develop an understanding of christianity which makes positive sense of the uncertainties and inadequacies of life in the church. It is likely that they have a great deal to say to our own age, because in many ways the temptations of today are remarkably like the temptations of their time.

The writings of the Apostolic Fathers cover the period, more or less, between the last decades of the first century A.D. and the middle of the second century. They reflect a variety of very different situations in different christian communities. Clement, writing from Rome in about 95, addresses himself to the church in Corinth, which was torn by schism; the Didache and the letter ascribed (falsely) to Barnabas may come from Palestine or Syria or from Egypt, and the major problem they deal with is posed by the temptation to adopt Jewish practices. Ignatius flashes across the scene on his way to be martyred in Rome early in the second century. Hermas was called to intervene in a crisis in the Roman church, probably towards the middle of the second century, precipitated by the relentless perfectionism of some teachers in the church who disallowed the possibility of any further repentance for christians who had fallen into sin.

In this period the church was still feeling her way towards an understanding of herself. As yet she had no official canon of christian scriptures, though at least some of the New Testament writings may have been known to some of the Apostolic Fathers. There were traditions of sayings of Jesus and a certain number of ethical and doctrinal traditions, but there was still a great deal to be explored. The organisation of the church was in some places still very rudimentary and teaching was supplied mainly by freelance teachers, who were, it was hoped, inspired by God, but who had no hierarchical status of the kind we have since become used to. What later emerged as the orthodox faith of the catholic church still had to struggle against a number of alternative versions of christianity; it is only with hindsight that we can pick out the orthodox writers. In some places it is quite likely that groups whom we regard as heretical were in fact the most numerous party among those calling themselves christians.[5]

In such a situation it is not surprising that some people wanted

more certainty than the church could offer them. Hermas retorts
by declaring that it is a hallmark of the true prophet that he does
not answer questions. It is a sign of lack of faith to demand answers,
and it is the false prophets who provide them, like pagan
soothsayers. The true prophet, in Hermas' view, does not offer any
kind of personal service, he speaks only in the full assembly of the
church, and he says simply what the Holy Spirit bids him say.[6]

According to St Ignatius of Antioch, what is special about christianity is precisely 'the presence of the Saviour, our Lord Jesus Christ,
his passion and resurrection'.[7] He is our true life, and apart from
him we are only ghosts, masquerading as human beings but lacking
substance.[8] Faith is the beginning of life, but this has to be fulfilled
in charity,[9] and this is a practical matter, involving generosity to
others,[10] patient endurance of insults, gentleness,[11] and, above all
else, belonging to the church, in communion with the bishop and his
clergy.[12] To those who want documentary proof from 'the archives'
(presumably meaning the Old Testament) Ignatius can only say,
'My archives are Jesus Christ.'[13] Against those who are primarily
interested in 'higher things' – Ignatius' polemical intent is unmistak-
able – he says that he too knows his way around heavenly things,
but that is not what makes him a christian.[14] The really divine life
consists of the combination of faith and charity, which together 'are
God'.[15] Maybe individual teachers could provide more excitement
for their devotees, but the authentic 'imprint and teaching of immortality' is found only in the unity of the church.[16] No one who is
'outside the sanctuary' (who does things in separation from the
bishop, that is) can share in the bread of God, which is the antidote
to death.[17] What God offers, and indeed what he is, is unity, so it
is only in the unity of the church that we can be one with him.[18] The
bishop may be much less impressive than the heretical purveyors of
'big talk', but that is all the more reason to revere him.[19]

Unity is one of Ignatius' favourite themes,[20] and he at least hints
at a kind of mystical doctrine of unity which foreshadows that of
the neo-Platonists. God is One, in the mystery of his own being;
but from his primordial Silence there comes a Word, and the Word
is himself One, coming from the One without being separated from
the One.[21] And he comes into our world, taking to himself the
reality of our flesh, and dying and rising again in that flesh, so
forging a unity between flesh and spirit.[22] His disciples must enter
into this unity, by responding both to his words and deeds and to his
silence, and this means reproducing in themselves the conjunction of
silence and word, of faith and charity, of flesh and spirit.[23] And this
is what takes place in the structured unity of the church, with its
bishops, presbyters, deacons and laity. What Ignatius celebrates
and prays for in the churches is precisely the threefold unity 'of the

flesh and spirit of Jesus Christ, who is our utter life; of faith and love, than which nothing is better; and, most important of all, of Jesus and the Father'.[24]

Any desire for a more purely 'spiritual' religion meets with Ignatius' disapproval. It was evidently being claimed in some circles that spiritual people could have no further truck with the flesh (which meant, of course, making light of the public structures of the church and of the demands of practical charity). Ignatius turns their slogan against themselves: indeed the spiritual man can do nothing carnal, because whatever he does, even in the flesh, is spiritual, because he does it all in Christ.[25] But, lest we should think that doing things in Christ means achieving some kind of 'spiritual' self-awareness, Ignatius makes it clear that what he means by doing things in Christ is quite precisely doing things in union with the bishop.[26] The criterion is not whether we can feel ourselves to be spiritual, but whether we operate within the unity of the church.

And if this does not appear to be getting us anywhere, that is quite in order. 'Nothing that appears is good.'[27] The key to our redemption, and indeed to our reality, is what Ignatius calls 'the passion of my God',[28] and we are all required to 'volunteer' to share this passion,[29] even though only a few will actually be martyred. It is only when he has disappeared from the world to be 'in the Father' that Christ fully 'appears';[30] it is then that he becomes the 'perfect man'[31] who strengthens us and makes us real. So Ignatius longs for his martyrdom, when he will 'truly be a disciple of Jesus Christ, when the world will no longer even see my body'.[32] It is then that he will become a 'word of God'; otherwise he is just a 'noise'.[33] This probably sheds light on why Ignatius (who was himself a bishop) says that the bishop should be particularly revered when he is silent.[34] The silence of the bishop bears witness to the reality of God, both in the mystery of his divine silence and in the silence of his passion.[35] The church is the place where all things pass over into reality by being plunged into the hidden reality of God, so that the outer and inner become one, the word and the silence are reunited. Ignatius reckons that he will become truly human only at his matyrdom,[36] when the world sees him no more, and that dramatically focuses the direction in which the whole church has to move. Here and now it mediates the reality of life which there is in Christ only in so far as it resists the temptation to become either too 'spiritual' or too apparent. The key to the church's function is the conjunction of the flesh, with all its frailty and tediousness, with the hidden, imponderable reality of the spirit.

Clement is a much less brilliant writer than Ignatius, but he too is concerned to celebrate the church and to protect it against the temptation of more exciting religion outside the church. The schism in Corinth had, it seems, been started because some of the more gifted members of the community, both intellectually and charismatically, had rebelled against the official leaders who derived their authority, through the apostolic succession, from Christ himself.[37] The situation, in fact, is not unlike that which St Paul had to deal with in his letters. The volatile Corinithians were liable to become too spiritual to be charitable, so St Paul had to remind them that there was a much more important sense to be given to the word 'spiritual', centred on charity and mutual respect and support.[38] Similarly Clement insists that the essential gift of God is not to be identified with any spectacular powers that individuals might happen to possess, but with order and peace. He draws an attractive picture of the harmoniousness of the whole cosmos to illustrate the 'objective given from the beginning, namely peace',[39] and reinforces it with a reminder of the orderliness of an army and the disciplined regularity of the Old Testament cult.[40] He also alludes to the dire penalties paid by those who offered unlawful worship in the Old Testament.[41]

In Clement's view, it is mistaken to look for glory or greatness simply on the basis of our own achievements; what counts is faith, which means a readiness to abide by God's will.[42] We must be 'content with the provisions Christ gives us for the journey', even if they do not satisfy our vanity.[43] Our words have value only in so far as they proceed from obedience to the will of God.[44] Our only hope is in Christ,[45] and 'it is better to be found small and in line within the flock of Christ than to be very impressive and be pitched out from hope in him'.[46]

Barnabas and the compiler of the Didache start with a rather different problematic, but their message is of a similar kind. They imply a church with a much less developed structure than we find in Clement and Ignatius. The Didache shows us a church only just beginning to have bishops and deacons, and they do not seem to have gone down very well at first in a community that was used to being served by apostles (wandering preachers who were not allowed to settle down),[47] prophets (who spoke 'in spirit')[48] and teachers.[49] Barnabas himself was almost certainly a teacher in the same sense, and may well have been itinerant. He knows nothing of bishops and other territorial clergy.

Both Barnabas and the Didachist are convinced that, through Christ, God has revealed his will and his truth to us, he has shown us the 'way of life'.[50] But this revelation is not a lump sum on which we can presume. The word of God has to be cultivated. The Didachist exhorts people to seek out the company of the saints every day, in order to lean on their words.[51] Barnabas is particularly convinced that, since the days are evil and subject to the power of the enemy, 'we ought to be careful and seek out the Lord's decrees'.[52] We must keep guard over our life and be as accurate and perceptive as we can be in our attention to God's word, otherwise the evil one will 'slip in some error and sling us out from our life'.[53]

The Didachist believes that we can still expect new teaching from God through his prophets and teachers.[54] And, in the absence of any complete system of accepted doctrine, this meant that it was of paramount importance to be on guard against teachers of error.[55] And, as both Barnabas and the Didachist indicate, the fundamental safeguard is the collective study in the church of God's word. It is in coming together frequently that christians can be most certain of not being beguiled by untruth.[56]

For Barnabas the temptation of error is typified by the temptation to adopt Jewish practices. It is unlikely that he was concerned only with converts from Judaism; most probably he is dealing with christians from all kinds of backgrounds, who were looking for a religion that would give them more immediate and more tangible results.[57] In his view the whole cultic and religious system of Judaism was due to a dreadful mistake. The Israelites rejected the covenant as soon as it was given to them[58] because they were misled by a 'wicked angel'.[59] As a result they misunderstood all the commandments. What God wanted was spiritual circumcision, but they practised only bodily circumcision.[60] What God wanted was the avoidance of certain spiritual vices, but they took him to mean that they had to avoid eating certain kinds of animal.[61] But their most serious mistake was that they imagined that they were much more advanced along the way than was the case: they thought they could celebrate the sabbath, but the commandment requires that the sabbath should be celebrated 'with clean hands', and we do not yet have clean hands. Barnabas regards it as quite crucial that we should appreciate that we are not yet justified, we are still sinners. We cannot celebrate the sabbath until the end of time, when we will be made clean.[62] So Barnabas even reinterprets the story of the creation of man to direct our attention to what is still in the future: man, according to Genesis, is supposed to rule the fish and the beasts and the birds, but that we cannot do; therefore we are not yet man, as presented in the bible. We must grow to that point.[63]

What we can do now is try to see clearly just where we have got to, and not act as if we had got further. That means that our task now is to avoid complacency; if we supposed that we were already made righteous, the only result would be that we should 'go to sleep over our sins'.[64] Instead we ought to be doing whatever good we are capable of, in order to atone for our sins. And one kind of good deed which Barnabas seems to favour is speaking God's word to one another.[65] Christ dwells in us now quite precisely as 'prophesying' in us,[66] and the proper effect of our baptism is that our words bear fruit in other people.[67]

What we have in the church, then, is not so much an achievement of perfection or sanctity, as a promise and a way to follow. We have a new beginning.[68]

The Didachist is much less systematic in his account of things, but he too is concerned that christians should dissociate themselves from Judaisers – he rather quaintly says that they should not fast on the same day as the Judaisers.[69] But it is probable that the underlying problem is much the same as in Barnabas. By judaising a person could associate himself with a religious system which gave clear and immediate indications of what was required, with the prospect of being able, with any luck, to assure himself, as the Pharisee in our Lord's parable does,[70] that he is doing very well. It is presumably against this kind of perfectionism that the Didachist appends a rather surprising rubric to his ethical catechesis: 'If you can carry the whole yoke of the Lord, you will be perfect; if you cannot, do what you can.'[71] Although commentators have suggested various sophisticated ways of interpreting this, it should be taken at its face value.[72] Since the Didachist assumes that whenever christians come together for prayer they should begin by confessing their sins,[73] and since he regards perfection as something to be prayed for in the eucharist, as an eschatological reality,[74] it is probable that he reckoned that it was unrealistic to expect people to be able to observe fully all the ethical requirements contained in his teaching. What mattered was that people should do their best. Rather than redefine the rules, to allow anyone to declare himself perfect, the church needed to provide a vision of life in which imperfections could be endured.

In Rome there was evidently a perfectionist school of thought, according to which there is no possibility of any further repentance after baptism.[75] As a result of this kind of doctrine, it seems that a fair number of people had simply left the church in despair. Hermas was commissioned, in a vision of the Church, to assure people that christians who had fallen away *could* repent,[76] and his preaching apparently resulted in a considerable revival of hope. The church was rejuvenated like an elderly invalid 'who had already despaired of himself because of his infirmity and poverty' and then suddenly receives an inheritance and leaps out of bed to resume his life.[77]

As an alternative to the rigorism of his opponents, Hermas proposes a much more nuanced account of what it means to be a christian. Simply denying the possibility of repentance he comes to regard as an extreme form of wickedness.[78] What is necessary is rather to warn people of situations which may make it impossible or extremely difficult for them to repent. And the heart of the matter seems to be one's attitude to the faith and to the church. Dithering is singularly unhelpful, but a whole-hearted believer stands a very good chance of salvation, even if he does commit some sins, because his sins will not do very much damage. Even someone who has failed signally to keep the commandments, but has nevertheless remained deeply loyal to the church and has cultivated christian company and has never blasphemed the name of Christ, is likely to turn out all right in the end.[79]

Hermas' doctrine is complicated by his belief in very powerful spiritual agencies, which seem to be able, at least in some cases, to control human beings. In one passage Hermas says that even the most determined sinner will not be able to avoid being a little bit virtuous if a 'good angel' gets hold of him, and conversely, if a 'bad angel' gets hold of you, however excellent your moral record, you will not be able to avoid 'sinning a bit'. What we can do is make sure that we do not put our trust in the wrong 'angel'. However much he pushes us around, we must retain our conviction that he has no good to offer us. And, since the good spirit is a delicate, sensitive being, we must avoid crowding him out with undesirable company.[80] If we make life too difficult for him, he will simply move out.[81] And so we should cultivate the things that he likes, such as truthfulness, patience, whole-heartedness and cheerfulness, and avoid the things he dislikes, especially bitterness and sullenness.[82]

Over against the programme of perfectionism, whose harmful results he could see, Hermas suggests rather a programme of survival. We shall, in all probability, sin from time to time; but shall we survive our sins? If we remain loyal to the faith and to the church, there is a good chance that we shall survive. If we are disloyal, then even our good qualities are unlikely to benefit us much in the end. If we deny our faith in full deliberateness, there is very little chance of our being able to repent.[83]

All of this is, of course, far removed from the schemes of spiritual exercises and the guides to the higher reaches of 'contemplation' that have come to be the stock in trade of spiritual writers. But maybe the questions aired by the Apostolic Fathers are really more fundamental. And they can alert us to the danger of being too competent in our spirituality, too sure of the geography of the higher realms. We do not know what we are to be, but we believe, as christians, that it is in the church that we stand the best chance of receiving whatever the final gift will be. The way of life which is shown to us in the church is not nearly as well defined as some alternatives that we might fancy, but we remain on the way, not by knowing exactly what it involves, but by remaining in the church, in tolerant communion with our fellow christians, even if they are not as brilliant and mystical as some other people.

Bibliography and Abbreviations

Editions used
J. B. Lightfoot, *The Apostolic Fathers*. London 1885–90.
Robert Joly, *Hermas: Le Pasteur* (SC 53bis). Paris 1968.
P.Th. Camelot, *Ignace d'Antioche: Lettres* (SC 10). Paris 1969.
Annie Jaubert, *Clément de Rome: Épître aux Corinthiens* (SC 167). Paris 1971.
Pierre Prigent and R. A. Kraft, *Épître de Barnabé* (SC 172). Paris 1971.
Willy Rordorf and André Tuilier, *La Doctrine des Douze Apôtres (Didachè)* (SC 248). Paris 1978.

Recommended translations
J. B. Lightfoot, *The Apostolic Fathers* (several edns).
Kirsopp Lake, *The Apostolic Fathers*. Loeb Classical Library, first publ. 1912–13.

Other editions referred to
J. H. Srawley, *The Epistles of St Ignatius*. London 1900.
J. A. Fischer, *Die apostolische Väter*. Munich 1956.
R. M. Grant, *Ignatius of Antioch*. London, Camden (N.J.) and Toronto 1966.
D. Ruiz Bueno, *Padres Apostólicos*. Madrid 1967.

Abbreviations
References are given to the SC editions, but are easily applied to other editions. The abbreviations for the different writers and works are obvious.

Notes

[1] 1 Cor. 15:28, Apoc. 21:4.
[2] 1 Cor. 2:9.
[3] 1 John 3:2
[4] Acts 1:6. Cf. St John of the Cross, *Ascent of Mount Carmel* II 19:9-10.
[5] Cf. Walter Bauer, *Rechtgläubigkeit und Ketzerei im ältesten Christentum*. 2nd edn. Tübingen 1964. (English tr. *Orthodoxy and Heresy in Earliest Christianity*. Philadelphia 1971, London 1972.)
[6] Hermas 43 (*Mand.* XI). Cf. J. Reiling, *Hermas and Christian Prophecy*. Leiden 1973.
[7] Ignatius, *Phld.* 9:2.
[8] *Eph.* 3:2, *Phld.* 6:1, *Sm.* 2 etc.
[9] *Eph.* 14:1.
[10] *Sm.* 6:2.
[11] *Eph.* 10.
[12] E.g. *Eph.* 4:1, *Magn.* 13; the theme is all-pervasive in Ignatius.
[13] *Phld.* 8:2.
[14] *Tr.* 5.

[15]*Eph.* 14:1.

[16]*Magn.* 6:2.

[17]*Eph.* 5, 20:2.

[18]*Tr.* 11:2 etc.

[19]*Eph.* 6:1, 10:2. For this interpretation of the 'silent bishop', cf. L. F. Pizzolato, 'Silenzio del Vescovo', *Aevum* 44 (1970), pp. 205–18; Peter Meinhold, *Studien zu Ignatius von Antiochien* (Wiesbaden 1979), pp. 19–36.

[20]He draws attention to this himself in *Phld.* 8:1.

[21]*Magn.* 7:2, 8:2.

[22]E.g. *Eph.* 7:2, *Magn.* 1:2. Cf. Sergio Zañartu, *El Concepto de Zwή en Ignacio de Antioquia* (Madrid 1977), pp. 184–5.

[23]*Eph.* 15.

[24]*Magn.* 1:2. In spite of the translators and commentators, I take all three pairs of genitives in the same sense. 'Unity *of* flesh and spirit' is supported by Lightfoot and Srawley in their translations, and by Zañartu (op. cit., p. 117[19]), against 'union *with*', proposed by Bauer (cf. William F. Arndt and F. Wilbur Gingrich, *A Greek-English Lexicon of the New Testament*. Chicago and Cambridge 1957, s.v. ἕνωσις) and adopted by Camelot and Ruiz Bueno in their translations, and by Virginia Corwin, *St Ignatius and Christianity in Antioch* (London 1960), p. 261. 'Union *in* faith and love' is preferred by Srawley, Camelot and Ruiz Bueno. 'Union *with* Jesus and the Father' is apparently almost universally adopted, but 'union *of* is accepted by J. A. Fischer and R. M. Grant in their translations.

[25]*Eph.* 8:2.

[26]*Eph.* 3:2–4:1; cf. *Pol.* 5:2.

[27]*Rom.* 3:3. This is probably derived from a Gnosticising slogan. Cf. *Martyrium Petri* 8, 'Separate your souls from everything that appears, since it is not true.' Origen, *On Prayer* 20:2, cites Ignatius' phrase in connection with Matt. 6:5.

[28]*Rom.* 6:3.

[29]*Magn.* 5:2.

[30]*Rom.* 3:3. There is a suggestive parallel in the Hermetic books, treatise 5, entitled 'God who does not appear is the most manifest of all'.

[31]*Sm.* 4:2, on which see A. Orbe, *Estudios Valentinianos* IV: *La Teologia del Espiritu Santo* (Rome 1966), p. 160[21].

[32]*Rom.* 4:2.

[33]*Rom.* 2:1. There is some uncertainty about the text here; I follow that given by Lightfoot. Cf. Orbe, op. cit., p. 167. For the contrast between 'word' and 'noise', cf. Irenaeus, *Adv. Haer.* I 14:4, Hermetic books 12:13.

[34]*Eph*, 6:1.

[35]The meaning of *Eph.* 6:1 has been much disputed. Henry Chadwick, 'The Silence of Bishops', *Harvard Theological Review* 43 (1950), pp. 169–72, proposed an interpretation linking the bishop's silence with the silence of God (cf. *Eph.* 15:1, *Magn.* 8:2), but this has been challenged by, for instance, Pizzolato, art. cit. It is also possible to connect the bishop's silence with Christ's silence in his passion (cf. *Eph.* 19:1; *Odes of Solomon* 31:8–12; *Gospel of Peter* 4:10). Ignatius certainly suggests that there is a special significance in the fact that he is going to his martyrdom as a bishop (*Rom.* 2:2 – following immediately after an important passage playing on 'silence' and

'word'). I take it that the bishop's silence includes a reference to both the divine mystery and the passion.

[36]*Rom.* 6:2.

[37]Apostolic succession: 1 Clem. 42. On the schism: 23:2, 48:5–6, with the comments of Hans von Campenhausen, *Ecclesiastical Authority and Spiritual Power* (London 1969), p. 86.

[38]1 Cor. 3:1, 3.

[39]1 Clem. 19:2, 20.

[40]1 Clem. 37, 40.

[41]1 Clem. 4:12, 41:3.

[42]1 Clem. 32:3–4.

[43]1 Clem. 2:1.

[44]1 Clem. 32:3, 34:1–5, 37.

[45]1 Clem. 36.

[46]1 Clem. 57:2.

[47]Did. 11:5. Compulsory itinerancy reappears in Manichaean monasticism: A. Vööbus, *History of Asceticism in the Syrian Orient* I (Louvain 1958), p. 117[34].

[48]Did. 11:8.

[49]Did. 15.

[50]Did. 1:2. 10:2; Barn. 5:3–4, 19.

[51]Did. 4:2.

[52]Barn. 2:1.

[53]Did. 16:1; Barn. 2:10.

[54]Did. 11:2.

[55]Did. 11.

[56]Did. 16:2; Barn. 4:10.

[57]Barn. 3:6. The word προσήλυτοι implies that Barnabas is not addressing people who were originally Jews. On the general difficulty of believing that christianity is 'the real thing', by comparison with more obviously full-blooded religions, cf. C. S. Lewis, 'Religion: Reality or Substitute?', *Christian Reflections* (Fount paperbacks 1981), p. 56.

[58]Barn. 4:7–8, 14:1–3.

[59]Barn. 9:4.

[60]Barn. 9.

[61]Barn. 10.

[62]Barn. 15, cf. 4:10 with Prigent's note in the Sources Chrétiennes edn.

[63]Barn. 6:18–19.

[64]Barn. 4:13.

[65]Barn. 19:10.

[66]Barn. 16:9.

[67]Barn. 11:8.

[68]Barn. 6:11.

[69]Did. 8:1. The 'hypocrites' referred to must be Judaising christians, not Jews: cf. Willy Rordorf and André Tuilier in the Sources Chrétiennes edn, p. 37.

[70]Luke 18:11; cf. St Paul's comments in Phil. 3:6.

[71]Did. 6:2.

[72]For different interpretations see Jacques Liébaert, *Les Enseignements*

Moraux des Pères Apostoliques (Gembloux 1970), p. 115. The view that the text should be taken at its face value is supported by the similar doctrine found in *Liber Graduum* (Patrologia Syriaca III. Paris 1926), II and XXIV.

[73]Did. 4:14.

[74]Did. 10:5. It should be noted that there seems to be a tension between this verse and Did. 16:2, which makes perfection necessary for survival in the last days.

[75]Herm. 31:1 (*Mand.* IV 3:1). The background to this rigorist doctrine should perhaps be sought in Hebrews 6:4.

[76]Herm. 6 (*Vis.* II 2).

[77]Herm. 20–1 (*Vis.* III 12–13).

[78]Herm. 72:5 (*Sim.* VIII 6:5).

[79]E.g. Herm. 72:4 (*Sim.* VIII 6:4), 74–5 (*Sim.* VIII 8–9), 76:3 (*Sim.* VIII 10:3), 96:3 (*Sim.* IX 19:3), 108:2 (*Sim.* IX 31:2).

[80]Herm. 36 (*Mand.* VI 2).

[81]Herm. 33:3 (*Mand.* V 1:3).

[82]Herm. 27–8 (*Mand.* II, III), 33–4 (*Mand.* V), 40–2 (*Mand.* X).

[83]Herm. 103:5 (*Sim.* IX 26:5) etc.

2

The Desert Fathers

The genuine historical origins of christian monasticism are somewhat unclear,[1] but the myth that it all began in Egypt with St
Anthony (†356) and the other Desert Fathers is true at least to the
extent that it is to them that succeeding generations of monks keep
looking back for inspiration. The writings of Cassian, who made
himself the interpreter of Egypt in the West, and that rather amor-
phous collection of sayings and stories which came to be known as
The Lives of the Fathers provided much of the staple diet of monks
and others who wished to be serious about their christian lives, and
even where there is no explicit reference to the Desert Fathers it is
not hard to recognise their influence. Thus, for example, in the life
of the Irish monk, St Canice, two outstanding examples of monastic
obedience are lifted, without acknowledgment, from the Desert
Fathers.[2] Any number of edifying stories used by medieval preachers
and writers derive from the same source, and it was the example
of these same Fathers which prompted the young Catherine of Siena
to set off at a tender age to become a hermit.[3]

However, if we are to understand the characteristic emphases of
the Desert Fathers, it is important to put them back into their
context and see that they are not founding something entirely new;
to a considerable extent they are reacting to a situation which had
taken shape before them, with roots in very primitive developments
in the church.

As early as St Paul we find the suggestion that celibacy enables
us to concentrate on the Lord, without the distractions of married
life.[4] And there is no doubt that this is one important strand in the
development of christian asceticism. It underlies the romantic
notion of our being 'married to the Lord', which is felt to exclude
the possibility of any other kind of marriage.[5] It also underlies the
more speculative notion that by celibacy and withdrawal from the
normal pressure of social life we can overcome the divisions and
tensions within us and so become 'single' (which may well be one
of the original meanings of the word 'monk').[6]

In some circles the desire to concentrate undistractedly on the
Lord seems to have merged with the belief that Christ has reopened

for us the possibility of living as Adam and Eve were meant to live in paradise. This appears to be the reason or one reason why some ascetics refused to eat any food which depended on artificial means of production, such as agriculture and cooking. Some of them went so far as to eat grass with the wild animals; others, more favoured, were supposedly kept alive, like Elijah, by angelic ministrations.[7] This is also why some ascetics regarded it as improper to engage in any kind of work, work being regarded as part of the condition of fallen man. The goal seems to have been a very literal practice of continual prayer.[8]

Another motive for adopting a life of renunciation seems to have been a desire to devote oneself entirely to the work of the Lord. We may presume that the 'apostles' in the Didache, whom we met in the previous chapter, were necessarily obliged to celibacy and poverty, in view of their continual itinerancy. As the sense of apostolate weakens, for whatever reasons, the perpetual wandering takes on a new significance, as a reminder that we are pilgrims on the face of the earth,[9] with no 'abiding city'[10] until we reach the heavenly Jerusalem. A fascinating text in the Persian father, Aphrahat, interprets the life of ascetic renunciation in terms drawn from the rules given in Deuteronomy 20 for those who wish to enlist in the Lord's army for the holy war.[11]

Whatever particular motives may have been at work in different cases, whatever imagery may have been used to focus different ascetic undertakings, by the time we reach the fourth century there seems to have been a considerable number of people in various places who, in different ways, had committed themselves to a life of renunciation. What they all had in common was a quest for a definition of human life independent of any definitions contained in the ordinary structures of life. It was perhaps in this sense that some monks regarded themselves as 'guarding the walls'.[12] The coming of Christ had reopened the fundamental question, what it means for us to be human beings. It is no longer sufficient to accept from our social milieu the values, aspirations and so on which structure our concept of ourselves; the question has to be pushed to a much further limit: 'What is a human being as such, as envisaged by the Creator?'

It is difficult to avoid the feeling that at least some of the curious practices adopted by some ascetics were intended to be a kind of experiment, designed to extract further evidence of just what it is to be human. It is almost as if they were saying, 'Let us fast for a week and see what happens', or 'Let us fasten ourselves to rocks and see what happens'. It is by pushing human nature to the limits of its endurance that you discover what human nature really is.

It is not surprising that the more dramatically eccentric ascetics aroused the curiosity of their fellow men. What is, at first sight, surprising is that many of them acquired a position of considerable authority and power. The explanation is probably that, by their total renunciation of ordinary human structures, they came to represent a completely different kind of power, which can then be used to challenge the political and economic power which is normally operative in our society. The holy ascetics are at least credited with considerable supernatural power, which they use, in general, to support the poor and the weak, to heal the sick, to cure demoniacs.[13] They are also supposed to be granted privileged access to God, so that they are regarded as bearers of God's truth to the world; their judgment is sought in matters of doctrinal controversy.[14]

When we turn to the monastic literature of Egypt, the figure of the powerful, charismatic holy man appears to be receding into the background. And this is not simply to be explained by the social and geographical circumstances of Egyptian monasticism:[15] Egyptian monasticism is in conscious reaction against charismatic holy men. Although there is evidence that at least some of the Egyptian monks did occupy much the same place in the popular mind as the extravagant wonderworkers we read about, for instance, in the pages of Theodoret's account of the Syrian monks,[16] the Egyptian monks themselves increasingly rejected this model of monasticism.[17]

One of the best pictures of the public holy man that we find in Egyptian sources is, very revealingly, contained in Evagrius Ponticus' account of the demonic temptation to vainglory.[18] What the Egyptian monks came to suspect was that ascetic and thaumaturgical prowess constituted a temptation as well as a public service. And they evidently felt that it was not worth, as they said, pulling your own house down in order to build someone else's.[19]

This is why, in Egyptian monasticism, enormous stress is laid on the virtue of humility. As Evagrius says, 'asceticism with humility is valuable, but asceticism without humility is extremely dangerous'.[20] And another Father said, 'It is better to fail with humility than to succeed with pride.'[21]

Above all else the Egyptian monks emphasised self-knowledge. The one practice which they harp on over and over again is 'paying attention to yourself', and, going with this, they highlight the virtue of 'discernment', by which they mean an ability to diagnose exactly what is going on at any given moment.[22]

This explains why sometimes the Desert Fathers seem to be rather casual about morality. Their concern is not that people should behave correctly according to the rules, but rather that people should be able to see their situation clearly for what it is, and so become free from the distorting perspective which underlies all our sins.

Thus we hear of a fornicating monk, who kept a woman in his cell so indiscreetly that word got round about it. The neighbouring monks resolved to drive the monk away, and abba Ammonas, who happened to be visiting there, was asked to go with them. The offending monk heard them coming and hid his woman in a large jar. Ammonas saw her at once, but 'hid the affair for the sake of God'. He sat down on the jar, and then told the other monks to search the cell. They, of course, found nothing and went away again abashed and apologetic. Ammonas then took the culprit's hand and simply said to him, 'Brother, pay attention to yourself,' and went out.[23]

What is at stake is not isolated or even recurrent instances of sin, but a whole attitude of carelessness, of not facing up to what one is doing. 'Unawareness is the root of all evil', as one monk said.[24]

What the Desert Fathers are afraid of is a purely fanciful spirituality, quite unrelated to human reality. 'If you see a young man going up to heaven by his own will, grab his leg and pull him down again.'[25] Going up to heaven just because you happen to fancy it is not the right way to proceed. Unless there is a solid foundation of absolute realism, any spiritual high-flying will be liable to degenerate into illusion.

A young monk once went to abba Paphnutius, because he was feeling unsettled in the desert; he was tempted by the thought that he was achieving nothing. Abba Paphnutius said to him, 'Go, stay in your cell and make one prayer in the morning and one prayer in the evening and one prayer at night. And when you are hungry, eat, when you are thirsty, drink, and when you are sleepy, go to sleep. And remain in the desert.' The young man was not convinced. We can imagine him wondering to himself, 'What kind of a life is that for an enthusiastic christian?' So he went on to abba John, who emended the advice he had received from Paphnutius, by saying, 'Do not make any prayer at all, just stay in your cell.' Finally the young man went to abba Arsenius, who simply told him to do what the fathers had said.[26]

The point of this is clear enough. Before you can truly pray, let alone achieve any more refined feats of spirituality or service, you have first of all got to make sure that you are really there. And the discipline of simply staying in your cell is intended to bring you face to face with yourself and with your real needs and capacities. Before you can profitably fast or undertake any of the customary austerities in the matter of food and drink and sleep, you have got to face up to your biological needs.

Without this foundation of self-knowledge and realism, any attempt to help other people will founder. This is brought out in a tale of three brothers, which is a typical bit of monastic propaganda.

All three brothers wanted to devote themselves more seriously to living the christian life; one decided to go and look after the sick, one preferred to become a peace-maker, and the third went into the desert. After a time the first two were becoming rather disillusioned. Their attempts to do good were meeting with little success. So they went off to visit the brother who had become a monk. He acted out a little parable: he took a jug of water and poured the water into a bowl and made them look into it. The surface of the water was all ruffled and reflected nothing. A few minutes later, he made them look into it again: this time the surface was smooth and they could see their own faces reflected. So, he explained, unless you become tranquil you cannot know your own faults. The implicit moral is that without such self-knowledge you cannot expect to be able to help others.[27]

If it does sometimes appear that the Desert Fathers are rather inclined to evade the responsibilities of fraternal charity,[28] it is because they are aware that it is all too easy to do more harm than good in one's premature desire to benefit others. Abba Matoes said, 'When I was young, I said to myself that I would do good. But now that I am old, I perceive that I have not one single good deed in me.'[29] In the same vein, abba Poemen advised another monk to settle somewhere 'where you do not do any harm to your neighbour'.[30]

This does not mean that the Desert Fathers simply ignored the dimension of fraternal charity. St Anthony himself taught that life and death depend on our neighbour: 'If we gain our brother, we gain God, if we upset our brother, we sin against Christ.'[31] But fraternal charity was best expressed in very straightforward ways, not in deliberate attempts to help other people. It was regarded as an essential part of desert good manners to offer food to any visitor, and to eat something with him. This was expressly rated higher than fasting.[32] Cassian relates how on one occasion he and his companion visited an old man and he invited them to have something to eat with him. They had already eaten so much (presumably as a result of previous visits) that they could eat no more. But the old man rebuked them, saying that he had already eaten six times that day with different visitors.[33]

The most important way to show fraternal charity was to refrain from interfering with other people, and especially to refrain from criticising them. Even if you see someone tackling a job which you see could be done in a much better way, you should leave him to get on with it unless he actually asks for advice.[34] Even if you see someone sinning, you should humble yourself before God and pass no judgment on him.[35] Isaac of Thebes on one occasion, when he was visiting a monastic community, saw a brother sin and condemned him in his heart; when he returned to his hermit's cell, he found his doorway barred by an angel, who said, 'God has sent me to ask you where he is to put the fallen brother whom you condemned.'[36]

It is the example of forbearance which is expected to convert others. Thus we learn how to deal with pagan priests from a story told about abba Macarius the Great. When he was going with his disciple from Scetis to Nitria, he sent his disciple on ahead; the disciple met a pagan priest and insulted him. The priest beat him up and fled. Shortly after this, Macarius came along, and said to the running priest, 'Bless you, you look worn out!' The pagan priest was amazed at Macarius' courtesy, and promptly became a christian and a monk.[37]

Once, when a monk was excommunicated from the sanctuary because he had sinned, abba Bessarion got up and went out with him, saying, 'I too am a sinner.'[38] The monk's task is to bewail his own sinfulness, not to judge that of others.[39]

Nor should he be severe when others show signs of weakness. Once there was a discussion about the proper way to react when somebody went to sleep in church. Various rigorous lines were proposed, but abba Poemen said, 'If I see that my brother has gone to sleep, I cradle his head in my lap.'[40]

This kind of gentleness is regarded as far less likely to do harm than more aggressive forms of mutual service. Thus, on the whole, the Egyptian tradition disapproves of monks taking it upon themselves to teach one another. If someone asks you what a verse of scripture means, the proper answer is, 'I don't know.'[41] If someone says something you do not agree with, you should not argue with him, but simply say, 'You know best.'[42] If someone wants to be your disciple, you should not give him instructions, but content yourself with setting him an example. And it is up to him to follow your example, if he wants to.[43] (On this point, of course, the hermits' option was different from that of the founders of religious communities, but even there it was only gradually that the notion of obedience developed.)

Even setting an example could be dangerous, so some monks found a way of evading that too. Abba Esaias recalls how once he and six others went to visit abba Sisoes, asking him to say something to them. Sisoes refused, saying, 'Excuse me. I am an uneducated man.' However the old man did tell them how he once went to abba Hor and abba Athre to ask abba Hor to say something to him. Abba Hor likewise refused to give him any advice, but he said, 'Go to abba Athre and do whatever you see him doing.'[44]

It was this habit of passing the buck that contributed to the development of the whole tradition of monastic literature, containing as it did sayings of previous generations of monks. By citing what someone else had said, you could in fact pass on teaching without taking any credit for it to yourself. However, this too was found to have its dangers: some people became collectors of monastic sayings, which they hawked round in order to acquire a name for themselves. So we find abba Felix refusing to utter a word, on the grounds that if he does, it will only go to foster somebody else's vanity.[45] This was probably one reason why eventually the tradition became quite impersonal, finally hardening into Rules, which allowed everybody to escape personal responsibility.[46]

If it was considered improper to interfere with other people, it was considered eminently proper to allow other people to interfere with you. The passage referred to from abba Esaias continues with a striking illustration of how far the monks were prepared to go in giving in to one another. Someone once brought abba Hor and abba Athre a bit of fish, and Athre had already picked up the knife and started cutting it up when Hor called him. He left the knife in the fish and came at once. Sisoes was impressed and asked where the old man had learned such submission. Athre said he had learned it from Hor, and to prove it he took a bit of the fish and cooked it and deliberately spoiled it. Then he took it to abba Hor and said, 'Isn't it good, father?' Hor said, 'Yes, it's excellent.' Then he cooked another bit without spoiling it, and took it to Hor, saying, 'I've spoiled it, father.' And Hor replied, 'Yes, you have spoiled it a bit.'[47]

There are any number of stories one could quote from the Desert Fathers to illustrate their passion for letting other people have their way. This all-round readiness to submit to others was believed to be the royal road to holiness.[48]

Although the casual reader of the literature from the Egyptian desert is likely to come away feeling that the monks were primarily interested in excesses of austerity and in fantastic battles with demons, this is not really the kernel of their message. The austerities, whatever their significance may have been in earlier kinds of asceticism, are not viewed by the main tradition of the Egyptian desert as a way to become superhuman, nor as an ideal in themselves. They are very firmly subordinated to much more fundamental values, such as humility and fraternal charity. Thus in one saying we find Hilarion claiming that, since he put on the monastic habit, he has never eaten meat. Epiphanius caps this with the claim that since he became a monk, he has never let anyone go to bed with a grievance against him, nor has he ever gone to bed having a grievance against someone else. Hilarion admits that this is a far greater way of life than his own.[49]

Similarly the battle with demons is a grimly realistic affair.

Dramatic exorcisms, like any other kind of miracle-mongering, are seen as an occasion for vainglory.⁵⁰ Thus we are told that, though Anthony could foresee the future, he refused to talk about it.⁵¹ And we are warned not to be impressed by anyone who raises the dead, but is not able to control his own temper.⁵²

There is a cautionary tale in the sayings of abba Poemen. He was once visited by a very distinguished foreigner, who came specially to see him. He was ushered into his presence and started talking. But Poemen averted his gaze and refused to speak to him. In dismay, the visitor went out and asked Poemen's disciple what was going on. Poemen then explained, 'He is from above and speaks of heavenly things, but I am of the earth and speak about earthly things. If he had spoken to me about the passions of the soul, then I should have answered him. But if he speaks about spiritual things, I know nothing of them.' The visitor tried again, by saying, 'What shall I do, abba, I am dominated by the passions of my soul?' Abba Poemen said, 'Now you are speaking rightly.'⁵³

That is our business, then. Higher things can look after themselves; we must try to cope with all the disorder there is in our souls. That is where we meet the demons, and it is by trying to face up honestly and realistically to our own thoughts and temptations that we do battle with the demons.

There is, as has been said, an 'anti-mystical strand' in Egyptian monasticism;⁵⁴ the Egyptian monks were probably quite right to react against the rather naive supernaturalism which was found in earlier generations of ascetics. Their concern was to bring us down to earth, rather than to encourage exalted aspirations. 'If you have a heart,' said abba Pambo, 'you can be saved.'⁵⁵ This is the essential thing. It does not matter so much what we do; what matters is that there should be a real human being there to do it. Salvation is offered to real people, not to fictitious saints.

Bibliography and Abbreviations

Editions used

Adamnan, *Vita S. Columbae*, ed. J. T. Fowler. Oxford 1894.

Apophthegmata Patrum (Alphabetic series): Τὸ Γεροντικόν. Athens 1961 (text taken from PG 65:71–440).

Apophthegmata Patrum (Systematic series): partial edn by M. Nau, *Revue de l'Orient Chrétien*. 1907–13.

Athanasius, *Vita Antonii*: uncritical Greek text in PG 26:835–976, repr. in Βιβλιοθήκη 'Ελλήνων Πατέρων καὶ 'Εκκλησιαστικῶν Συγγραφέων, XXXIII (Athens 1963), pp. 11–57; critical edn of the Latin text ed. G. J. M. Bartelink, *Vita di Antonio*. Verona 1974.

Cassian, ed. Jean-Claude Guy, *Institutions Cénobitiques* (SC 109). Paris 1965; ed. E. Pichery, *Conférences* (SC 42, 54, 64). Paris 1955, 1958, 1959.
Cyril of Scythopolis, ed. Eduard Schwarz. Leipzig 1939.
Esaias, ed. René Draguet, *Les cinq recensions de l'Ascéticon syriaque d'Abba Isaïe.* Louvain 1968.
Historia Monachorum, ed. André-Jean Festugière. Brussels 1971.
Jerome, *Vita Hilarionis*, cf. Sulpicius Severus.
Palladius, *Historia Lausiaca*, ed. G. J. M. Bartelink. Verona 1974.
Sulpicius Severus, *Vita Martini*, ed. A. A. R. Bastiaensen and Jan W. Smit, *Vita di Martino, Vita di Ilarione, In Memoria di Paola.* Verona 1975.
Theodoret, ed. Pierre Canivet and Alice Leroy-Molinghen, *Histoire des Moines de Syrie* (SC 234, 257). Paris 1977, 1979.
Vita S. Romani etc., ed. François Martine, *Vie des Pères du Jura* (SC 142). Paris 1968.

Recommended translations
Apophthegmata Patrum: the Alphabetic series tr. Benedicta Ward, *The Sayings of the Desert Fathers.* London 1975; the Systematic series, including much otherwise unedited material, is available in French translation by the monks of Solesmes, ed. L. Regnault, *Les Sentences des Pères du Désert, Nouveau Recueil* (Solesmes 1970), and *Troisième Recueil* (Solesmes 1976).
Athanasius, *Life of St Anthony*, tr. R. T. Meyer. New York 1950.
Historia Monachorum: Benedicta Ward and Norman Russell, *The Lives of the Desert Fathers.* London and Oxford 1981.
Palladius, *Lausiac History*, tr. R. T. Meyer. Westminster, Maryland 1965.

Abbreviations
AP Nau refers to the Systematic Collection of *Apophthegmata Patrum*; AP followed by any other name refers to the Alphabetic Collection.

Notes

[1]Only some of the more important contributions to the study of monastic origins can be mentioned here: M. Harl, 'À propos des Logia de Jésus: le sens du mot μοναχός', *Revue des Études Grecques* 73 (1960), pp. 464–74; Georg Kretschmar, 'Beitrag zur Frage nach dem Ursprung frühchristlicher Askese', *Zeitschrift für Theologie und Kirche* 61 (1964), pp. 27–67; several articles in Colloque de Strasbourg 23–5 avril 1964, *Aspects du Judéo-Christianisme.* Paris 1965; Peter Nagel, *Die Motivierung der Askese in der alten Kirche und der Ursprung des Mönchtums.* Berlin 1966; A. Guillaumont, 'Monachisme et éthique judéo-chrétienne', *Judéo-Christianisme, Recherches de Science Religieuse* (Paris 1972), pp. 199–218; S. P. Brock, 'Early Syrian Asceticism', *Numen* 20 (1973), pp. 1–19; F. E. Morard, 'Μοναχός, moine: Histoire du terme grec jusqu'au IVe siècle', *Freiburger Zeitschrift für Phil. und Theol.* 20 (1973), pp. 332–411; Garcia M. Colombas, *El Monacato Primitivo* (Madrid 1974), I, ch. 1; Robert Murray, 'The Features of the Earliest Christian Asceticism', Peter Brooks, ed., *Christian Spirituality* (London 1975), pp. 63–77.
[2]Charles Plummer, ed., *Vitae Sanctorum Hiberniae* (Oxford 1910), I, p. 153 (the unfinished O comes from AP Mark 1), p. 160 (throwing the child into

the river probably derives from AP Sisoes 10, though the Irish story has been made much more miraculous).

³Raymond of Capua, *Life of Catherine of Siena* 31–3 (English tr. Conleth Kearns. Dublin 1980).

⁴1 Cor. 7:32–3.

⁵E.g. *Acts of Thomas* 14.

⁶Cf. Harl, art. cit.; Robert Murray, *New Testament Studies* 21 (1974), p. 65.

⁷Vööbus, op. cit., II (Louvain 1960), p. 263. This is one among several primitive traits surviving in the *Historia Monachorum*: 1:17, 2:4, 2:9, 6:4, 8:5–6, 8:9, 12:4, 13:8 etc. On Adam's regime, see L. Ginzberg, *Legends of the Jews* (Philadelphia 1937), I, pp. 70–1; Theophilus, *Autol.* II 19.

⁸Vööbus, op. cit., I, pp. 152, 256; II, pp. 147f. *Liber Graduum* III 15, XII 6, XIV 1. *Historia Monachorum* Prol. 5–8, 1:45, 2:4, 8:5, 11:5, 13:4 etc. The later Egyptian tradition emphatically rejects this ideal: e.g. AP John Kolobos 2, Lucius 1, Silvanus 5.

⁹Vööbus, op. cit., I, pp. 85–6, II, pp. 270–1. Acts of Thomas 100, 107, especially in the Syriac version (and cf. A. F. J. Klijn, *The Acts of Thomas* [Leiden 1962], pp. 38, 165–6). *Liber Graduum* II 3, XIX 31. Ps. Ephrem, quoted in Vööbus, *Celibacy, A Requirement for Admission to Baptism* (Stockholm 1951), p. 24¹⁸. A. Guillaumont, 'Le Dépaysement comme forme d'ascèse', *Annuaire de l'École Pratique des Hautes Études, sect. Sciences Religieuses* 76 (1968–9), pp. 31–58. Gerd Thiessen, articles in *Zeitschrift für Theologie und Kirche* 70 (1973), pp. 245–71 and *New Testament Studies* 21 (1974–5), pp. 192–221. K. Niederwimmer, 'Zur Entwicklungsgeschichte des Wanderradikalismus', *Wiener Studien* NF 11 (1977), pp. 145–67. For survivals into Egyptian monasticism: *Historia Monachorum* 13:3, AP Daniel 5 (which gives a fascinating testimony to the transition from wandering to stable monasticism).

¹⁰Hebr. 13:14.

¹¹Aphrahat, *Dem.* VII 18–22 (on which see Robert Murray, 'The Exhortation to Candidates for Ascetical Vows at Baptism in the ancient Syriac Church', *New Testament Studies* 21 [1974], pp. 59–80).

¹²Palladius, *Lausiac History* 18:29. Cf. *Historia Monachorum* Prol. 10, and the comments of Benedicta Ward in the tr. cited above, pp. 12–13. The notion is to be connected with the idea, inherited from Judaism, that the holy man, by his merits, protects the world. Cf. Simon Tugwell, *New Heaven? New Earth?* (London 1976), p. 155¹¹.

¹³Cf. Peter Brown, 'The Rise and Function of the Holy Man in Late Antiquity', *Journal of Roman Studies* 61 (1971), pp. 80–101. Thaumaturgical powers pervade, for instance, Theodoret's *Historia Religiosa* (Syria), texts from Gaul like Sulpicius Severus' *Vita Sancti Martini* and the *Vita Sanctorum Patrum Romani, Lupicini et Eugendi monasteriorum Iurensium abbatum*, and Irish texts like Adamnan's *Vita S. Columbae*. In the *Historia Monachorum* John of Lycopolis in particular is still evidently a very public holy man.

¹⁴Cf. the role of Euthymius and Symeon Stylites in the disputes after the Council of Chalcedon: Cyril of Scythopolis, *Vita Euthymii* 27, 30. Cf. Theodoret, *Hist. Rel.* 2:16, Athanasius, *Vita Antonii* 69.

¹⁵As suggested by Peter Brown, art. cit., pp. 82–3.

[16]Athanasius, *Vita Antonii* 14; *Historia Monachorum* 1; Palladius, *Lausiac History* 21:7. In Jerome, *Vita Hilarionis* 15:2, Anthony is made to ask why sick people from Syria come to him, when they have their own local ascetic in the person of Hilarion. Cf. also AP Macarius 7, 15.

[17]Cf. AP Poemen 9 (Poemen prays to fail in trying to provide miraculous help), Pambo 9 (Pambo is praised for refusing to respond to requests for enlightenment).

[18]Evagrius, *Praktikos* 13.

[19]AP Poemen 127; cf, Macarius the Egyptian 17.

[20]J. Muyldermans, *Evagriana Syriaca* (Louvain 1952), p. 110 (p. 147).

[21]AP Nau 316.

[22]E.g. AP Anthony 8 (cf. Cassian, *Conférences* 2:2), Nau 93. The meaning of 'discernment' (διάκρισις) is brought out by stories like AP Agathon 5, Nikon 1, Nau 50.

[23]AP Ammonas 10.

[24]AP Nau 65.

[25] AP Nau 111 (=244), ascribed to John Kolobos in Barsanuphius and John, Letter 694 (Volos edn) (=693 in the Solesmes French translation).

[26]AP Paphnutius 5.

[27]AP Nau 134.

[28]Cf. Anthony Meredith's remarks on St Basil's 'abandonment' of the Antonian ideal in favour of a form of monasticism in which fraternal charity is to the fore: *Journal of Theological Studies* N.S. 27 (1976), pp. 323–4.

[29]AP Matoes 3.

[30]AP Poemen 159.

[31]AP Anthony 9.

[32]AP Cassian 1, Moses 5.

[33]AP Cassian 3.

[34]AP Macarius of Egypt 26, Esaias X 45, XII 2–5.

[35]AP Poemen 113–14, Paphnutius 1.

[36]AP Isaac of Thebes 1.

[37]AP Macarius of Egypt 39.

[38]AP Bessarion 7.

[39]E.g. AP John Kolobos 21, Moses 2, Pior 3.

[40]AP Poemen 92.

[41]AP Anthony 17, Esaias XIII 1.

[42]AP Matoes 11.

[43]AP Isaac of Kellia 2, Poemen 174.

[44]Esaias VI 6Aab.

[45]AP Felix 1.

[46]On this process, see Philip Rousseau, *Ascetics, Authority and the Church* (Oxford 1978), pp. 189–98. Particularly striking is the reinterpretation of 'discernment' (*discretio*) in Cassian, *Conférences* 2:5, making it more or less equivalent to 'obeying the counsels or conferences of the brethren and the rules of the elders'. We can see even in the *Apophthegmata* the beginnings of a sense that there is a 'proper monastic procedure' (e.g. the reinterpretation of the advice to 'eat when you are hungry' etc. in AP Herakleios 1). AP Poemen 22 illustrates the disadvantages of this development.

[47]Esaias VI 6Acd.

24 WAYS OF IMPERFECTION

[48]In the *Apophthegmata* the praises of obedience are usually sung in terms of obedience to an elder (e.g. AP Rufus 2), but the essential point seems to have been a readiness to abandon self-will (which is the great obstacle between us and God, AP Poemen 54) in favour of anyone at all, even a burglar: e.g. Esaias X 36, XV 73, AP Agathon 30, Theodore of Enaton 1, Macarius of Egypt 18, 40, Nicetas 1, Poemen 17, 158.

[49]AP Epiphanius 4.

[50]Evagrius, *Praktikos* 13.

[51]AP Anthony 29.

[52]AP Agathon 19.

[53]AP Poemen 8.

[54]Andrew Louth, *The Origins of the Christian Mystical Tradition* (Oxford 1981), p. 100.

[55]AP Pambo 10.

3

Evagrius Ponticus

The Desert Fathers, on the whole, were, or at least presented themselves as being, uninterested in theoretical speculation about life.
But their spiritual doctrine was nevertheless systematised in a highly
influential way by one of their number, Evagrius Ponticus († 399).
Although he later fell into disfavour on account of some decidedly
questionable Origenistic theories about the origins of things and
their final destiny,[1] it was recognised in antiquity that his ascetic
doctrine was of immense value and was not invalidated by his
dubious philosophical beliefs.[2]

Although Cassian never mentions him by name, it is certain
that he was deeply influenced by Evagrius, and so, anonymously,
Evagrius has played a considerable role in the development of
western spirituality, a role which scholars have recently come to
appreciate more and more.[3]

Evagrius had a flair for psychology, which enabled him to present
in an unusually coherent and persuasive form the fruits of the
monastic tradition of self-knowledge.

Evagrius accepts the general monastic belief that the arch-enemy
of the soul is in practice a certain kind of thought, for which the
monks used the word *logismos*.[4] The monk's mind becomes befogged
or besotted by these thoughts (both images are found in the literature)[5] so that he cannot concentrate on the actual reality of his own
life. A *logismos* is essentially a train of thought which engages the
mind, so that bit by bit one drifts away from what one is supposed
to be doing into a world of fantasy.

Evagrius suggests that there are basically eight general types of
logismos,[6] and his analysis was taken over by Cassian and was later
adapted to produce the classic list of seven deadly sins.[7]

First comes 'gluttony'. The essence of this is not over-eating, as
Evagrius sees it, nor even a desire for fancy food, though both of
these are harmful. The essence of the problem, as presented by
Evagrius, is anxiety about one's health. The 'thought' of gluttony
makes us imagine ourselves falling ill, being without necessary
supplies, unable to find a doctor. . . . Then it calls to mind other
people who have fallen ill through excessive fasting. Sometimes such

people are even prompted to come and visit us to tell us their troubles. In this way the monk is persuaded to abandon his monastic diet. Notice that the heart of the temptation is a train of thought leading us further and further away from our actual condition, making us solve problems which have not yet arisen and need never arise. Evagrius himself it seems in fact fell ill towards the end of his life because of his abstention from cooked foods. He solved the problem quite realistically by changing his diet.[8] That is the proper way to behave. The healthy procedure is to find a realistic diet and, when necessary, to modify it sensibly, not to insist stubbornly on a diet which has proved unworkable, nor to waste time and energy planning for eventualities which have not yet arisen.

The next 'thought' is that of fornication, and once again Evagrius presents it chiefly as a matter of allowing our fantasies to run away with us. Evagrius knew what he was talking about here. As a young man, he had been a successful deacon in Constantinople, and he had had to flee from there because of an unadvised love-affair. Afterwards it appears that he had some kind of breakdown, from which he recovered thanks to the ministration of St Jerome's friend, Melania the Elder, who was leading the monastic life at Jerusalem.[9] The 'thought' of fornication fills our minds with desire for 'a variety of bodies' (notice how abstract it all is). This is not a matter of a real human relationship with a real human being. A real relationship which goes wrong does far less damage than these purely imaginary entanglements. And the most sinister aspect of these fantasies is that they persuade us that all our attempts to lead a spiritual life are going to get nowhere. If they persist, they will eventually produce actual hallucinations, Evagrius suggests; we shall start acting out detailed erotic scenes in our imaginations, so that we shall be quite taken up with something totally unreal, instead of trying to cope with what is really there.

Then comes love of money, and once again Evagrius sees the essential problem as being one of futile planning for an unreal future. This 'thought' conjures up in our minds the picture of ourselves living on into a terrible old age, in which we are too weak to work. We shall fall ill in dreadful poverty and shall have to face the embarrassment of begging from others. What we ought to do, of course, is have faith in God and leave the future to him. Hoarding money as a bulwark against the future boils down to lack of faith.[10]

Next we run into the 'thought' of depression, which often follows on from indulging in foolish wants. 'Thoughts' of this kind lead us by the memory to dwell on the good old days, when we were at home with our parents (or whatever cherished memory we have of the past). Then we are suddenly made to realise that all that is gone and we cannot get it back, so we get plunged into depression.

Again the problem has arisen because we got out of step with present reality.

Next comes anger, which can turn even the most gentle person into a savage beast. It particularly prevents us from praying, because we become obsessed with the thought of someone we take to have wronged us.[11] If we allow this kind of anger to persist, it will ruin our bodily health, give us nightmares and, eventually, according to Evagrius, it will make us hallucinate poisonous snakes. Elsewhere he suggests other kinds of bad dream which this 'thought' provokes.[12] Yet again we see how all the trouble comes from failing to perceive the real issue. After all, if someone has wronged us, our christian duty is simply to forgive them, and that should be the end of it. Evagrius suggests that, rather than brooding on our wrongs, we should go out of our way to do something nice for someone whom we think has wronged us.[13]

After anger comes the famous noonday demon, accidie or listlessness. This is a condition in which we cannot settle down to anything; nothing appeals to us, nothing engages our interest. We go wandering round the room, peering out of the window to see whether we are any nearer to supper time. The day seems eighty hours long. And nobody comes to visit us, so we start thinking bitter thoughts about the lack of charity among other people. Then we begin to wonder what the point of it all is anyway; we could perfectly well lead our christian lives elsewhere. Everything that we have to do goes sour on us. The point of this temptation is, of course, to make us abandon our course. And the tragedy is that if we do run away, we take all our problems with us, and shall run into exactly the same difficulties anywhere we go.

The last two 'thoughts' are the most sinister of all: vainglory and pride. Vainglory is simply daydreaming about our own magnificence. The monastic content of it in Evagrius is a daydream about becoming a famous holy man, sought out by hordes of admiring women, and by people seeking miraculous cures and exorcisms. Finally they will come and drag us off to be ordained. . . . Alas, as likely as not, just when our imagined glory is at its height, the demons will play a further trick on us and we shall find that the holy priest we imagined ourselves to be is wrestling with the most humiliating thoughts against chastity.

Pride is the final madness. It consists essentially in supposing that we can do anything without God.

All these 'thoughts' have a common element, in that they all derive from self-love.[14] And they all also involve a wrong notion of God.[15] In fact, they all trap us into living in a false human world, wrongly structured around ourselves, and leading to a wrong God.

And so they are all designed really to ensure that we cannot approach the true God in anything like genuine prayer.[16]

Genuine prayer, however, is what we have to aim at, according to Evagrius. But we must proceed slowly. Pure prayer, which is closely related to that knowledge of God which is our highest goal,[17] cannot reach its full flowering in us until we have progressed through several stages.[18]

First of all, we must try to defeat the 'thoughts' and the passions which they arouse. Evagrius seems to be using the Stoic notion of 'passions', meaning ways in which our human faculties get trapped into pointless and irrational reactions.[19] They are not to be identified with emotions as such.[20] Passions are by definition disordered reactions, so that passionlessness can be stated to be 'the health of the soul'.[21]

It is not emotionlessness which Evagrius wishes to inculcate, but a state of harmony in which all our faculties are doing precisely what they were created to do, so that they do not disturb our equilibrium or hinder the proper clarity which the mind should have.

At the relatively humble level which we have been considering so far, the natural functioning of the soul involves our desiring faculty being directed towards virtue, our aggressive faculty being directed against all the obstacles to virtue, and our rational faculty being aimed in the direction of contemplation of reality.[22]

Evagrius does not dwell very much on the natural operation of our faculty of desire, but it is important to notice its presence in the healthy soul. A healthy soul is not one which grimly does its duty, it is one which is doing what it wants to do. That is why it does not practise self-control.[23] Virtue is natural to us, it is vice which is unnatural.[24] Vice appears to be attractive only because our minds are seeing things awry, because of *logismoi* backed by demons, whose whole purpose is to keep us in the dark and prevent us from attaining to the knowledge of God.

The first prerequisite, then, is that we should come to be aware of the truth, and Evagrius indicates that we all have a capacity for this. The whole undertaking begins with faith,[25] which gives us some kind of knowledge of truth, however opaque. And there is at least a kind of latent faith, even in those who do not believe in God, according to Evagrius.[26] Faith, when actualised, leads us to fear God, which leads us to make some attempt to introduce order into our lives.[27] And it is this attempt which shows us what is wrong with us.[28] And it is here that we need to be attentive. The demons will, for instance, try to get us into a frame of mind in which we think that we are entitled to be annoyed at somebody.[29] If we succumb to this, then we shall devote our attention to the thought of the person with whom we are annoyed. What the ascetic needs to do is to focus his attention instead on the fact that he is annoyed. Instead of seeing some other human being angrily, he tries to see his own anger. He can then begin to fight against it. And at first he has to use any device for restraining anger that he can think of. But gradually we should become more adept at wielding our own powers, even if at first this only means 'using a nail to drive out a nail', that is to say, playing off one passion against another. For instance, pride and unchastity are reckoned to be incompatible, so we can play off the thought of one against the thought of the other.[30]

But more essentially we need to reclaim anger for its proper purpose. It is always a waste of good anger to get annoyed with other human beings.[31] Instead we should turn our anger precisely against our thoughts and against the demons who deploy them.[32] Evagrius suggests that we should address an angry word to any thought which is troubling us, even before praying for help against it, since it is the nature of anger to disperse thoughts.[33]

In this way we shall be using anger in accordance with its true nature, to clear a way through the thoughts which swarm all around us, so that we can gradually come to a clearer perception of what it is all about. Thus we move from a fairly blind lashing out against whatever seems to be getting in our way to a position where we are fighting in the daylight.[34]

The desired goal of this whole exercise is a state in which we are no longer at the mercy of inappropriate reactions. And this is a profound state of balance and harmony. It is interesting that Evagrius mentions as a sign of approaching passionlessness the fact that we are no longer troubled by our dreams.[35] This suggests, in more modern parlance, that the state of virtue is envisaged as one in which our subconscious is not at odds with our conscious purposes.

The fruit of passionlessness is love, and this is the doorway through which we pass to knowledge.[36] All knowledge is thus characterised by charity. Though Evagrius does not elaborate on this, it is an important hint. Once we are freed from our passions, we can see and appreciate things for what they really are.[37] Things are no longer simply viewed from the perspective of deranged fears and fantasies, but in the plain truth. Evagrius, rather mysteriously, says that once we have reached a certain degree of passionlessness, the mind becomes aware of its own native light.[38] This seems to mean that the mind becomes conscious of its own lucidity, enabling it to see things truly.[39]

This leads us into the first stages of contemplation and knowledge. Instead of living in the sticky world of the passions in which we see things largely with reference to ourselves, we can now live in a world of facts. And these, it seems, are to be viewed as essentially a pedagogical device provided by God to lead us to the knowledge of himself.[40]

What Evagrius has in mind is something rather different from the romantic sort of contemplation of nature which has sometimes been recommended in recent times. For Evagrius, the essential thing is that we should come to understand the structure of things, the rationale of things.[41] By contemplating the principles or reasons (*logoi*) of things, we come to some apprehension of the divine Logos who gives all created things their existence and reality.[42]

Evagrius does not seem to regard this as merely an optional development. We shall not reach the knowledge of God unless we pass through the knowledge of created realities.[43]

However, this intermediate stage has its own dangers. We may become too fascinated by something which is less than God, whether it be our own psychological equilibrium or the clear perception of created beings. This is why Evagrius warns us that, just because we have attained to passionlessness, we should not assume that we have yet attained to true prayer. And just because we are capable of perceiving things clearly in themselves, without any disordered reaction to them, it does not mean that we have yet reached our goal.[44] If the demons cannot any longer get at us directly through our passions, they can still occupy our minds with particular thoughts.

Prayer is defined as a 'putting away of thoughts'.[45] Any thought, however devoid of passion, however simple, is necessarily less than God. And the very luminosity of the mind can become a temptation, if we try to conceive of God by some kind of shaping of our mind's light. This would seem to be one of the most insidious of all demonic attacks, because it occurs at a high level of spiritual maturity. Evagrius suggests that there is a way in which a demon can get hold of our brain and fiddle the mind's light so that the person praying sees some kind of vision and identifies what he has seen as being God.[46] But God can never be contained within any particularised vision. God has no shape whatsoever,[47] so the 'thought' of God must be quite unlike any thought which shapes the mind.[48] That is to say, God can never be in any simple way the 'object' of our understanding. He is not 'outside', as objects of knowledge are.[49] He is, in fact, 'substantive knowledge'.[50] Knowledge of God is stated by Evagrius to be 'co-extensive with the substance of the mind'.[51]

Cassian derived from Evagrius the belief that the highest prayer of all is when we are no longer conscious of our prayer.[52] A similar doctrine is in fact found in a comment on the book of Proverbs, whose authorship has recently been reclaimed for Evagrius: when we contemplate, we no more know that we are contemplating than we are conscious of our own sleeping.[53]

It seems, then, that it does not really make much difference whether you call the highest state knowledge of God or ignorance of God. Evagrius speaks in at least two places of an ignorance which has no bounds, which he seems to correlate with knowledge which has no bounds.[54] This surely follows from the insistence that God himself has no bounds, no definition. He can never be contained within anything which we can comprehend intellectually.

We may surmise that this is, in fact, one reason why it is important to approach God by way of creatures. It is the study of the structure of created reality which ensures that our final intellectual helplessness is really concerned with God and not just some diabolical travesty.

Evagrius does not seem to envisage knowledge-ignorance of God as a state at which one arrives once and for all in this life. This is very probably why he can use the word 'prayer' in the way that he does:[55] the highest function of the mind is precisely an aspiration towards God sustained by the rejection of all thoughts, and, for Evagrius, prayer is most essentially just this 'rising of the mind to God'.[56] The more fully we engage in it, the more intense should be our desire.[57]

It is not clear that Evagrius believes in the possibility or desirability of a state of tranquil 'contemplation' of God beyond this continual striving.[58] The putting away of thoughts does not seem to lead to a decisive condition of having put away all thoughts. Indeed Evagrius says, in a rather puzzling text, that singing psalms without distraction is a greater achievement than praying without distraction,[59] presumably because the ability to descend into the world of multiple reality, to which psalmody belongs, requires a greater concentration of the mind than the simple ascent of the intellect to God. And it is worth noting that, in Evagrius' view, God may sometimes implant in our minds some definite knowledge – which will, of course, be knowledge of something less than himself.[60]

Nor does Evagrius suggest that at any stage we get beyond the reach of temptation and demonic attack. If we ever become complacent and abandon the intense awareness of our sinfulness, something has gone seriously wrong.[61] The risk of pride and vainglory leaves us only at death.[62]

Nor do we receive any encouragement from Evagrius to become such full-time contemplatives that we forget about the fraternal dimension of life. There is an interesting series of macarisms towards the end of the *De Oratione*, in which Evagrius stresses the importance of seeing God in all men and of being as concerned for other people's progress as we are for our own.[63] Earlier on in the same work he bids us pray for all our fellows, not just for ourselves.[64]

According to the Origenist belief which Evagrius adopts, human beings are destined literally to become angels,[65] but one essential characteristic of the life of the angels is their function of helping others.[66] So for us to lead the angelic life does not, for Evagrius, mean withdrawing from all concern for others so that we can enjoy a higher spirituality on our own. The nearer we draw to God, the more we should see ourselves as being one with everybody.

We must remember that the whole edifice which Evagrius has built up rests on very solid foundations. If we lose humility, we lose everything, so any kind of mystical pretentiousness or self-satisfaction will be totally ruinous. Similarly any tendency to forget that we owe all our achievements to God will simply result in the final madness, which is pride. If Evagrius leads us to heights which we do not often find in the Desert Fathers, he never loses sight of the basic realism of the desert. Unless there is a very sound foundation, the higher reaches of the spiritual life will be no more than illusion, and a very dangerous illusion too.

Bibliography and Abbreviations

Editions used, Abbreviations
(a) Editions of particular works

[Basil] Letter 8	in all edns of the letters of St Basil. I have used Yves Courtonne, *Saint Basile: Lettres*. Paris, 1957–66.
Gnostikos	in Frankenberg (see below), pp. 546–53.
KG	ed. A. Guillaumont, *Les Képhalaia Gnostica* (Patrologia Orientalis 28, 1). Paris 1958.
Letters	in Frankenberg, pp. 564–635.
Mönchsspiegel	ed. H. Gressmann, *Nonnenspiegel und Mönchsspiegel des Euagrios Pontikos*, Texte und Untersuchungen 39, 4 (1913).
Or.	the edns of the treatise *On Prayer (De Oratione)* in PG 79: 1165–1200 and in Φιλοκαλία, I (Athens 1957), pp. 176–89, are far from satisfactory; in addition I have used several MSS including the important Paris B.N. Coislin 109. The numbering of the chapters varies slightly in different edns and MSS.
Prakt.	ed. Antoine Guillaumont and Claire Guillaumont, *Évagre le Pontique: Traité Pratique* (SC 170, 171). Paris 1971.

(b) Miscellaneous editions

A travers	J. Muyldermans, *A travers la tradition manuscrite d'Évagre le Pontique*. Louvain 1932.
Evagriana Syriaca, ed. J. Muyldermans. Louvain 1952.	
Frankenberg	W. Frankenberg, *Euagrius Ponticus* (Abhandlungen der königlichen Gesellschaft der Wissenschaften zu Göttingen, Phil.–Hist. Klasse, NF XIII, 2). Berlin 1912.

Muséon	various texts are ed. in *Muséon* 44 (1931), 47 (1934), 51 (1938) and 54 (1941).
PG 79	various texts are ed., under the name of Nilus, in PG 79.

Recommended translations

Or., Prakt.	tr. John Eudes Bamberger (Cistercian Studies series). Spencer (Mass.) 1970.
Or.	G. E. H. Palmer, Philip Sherrard and Kallistos Ware, *The Philokalia*, I (London 1979), pp. 55–71.

There are French tr. in the edns cited of [Basil] Letter 8, KG and *Prakt.*
There is an English tr. of Diadochus in *The Philokalia*, ed. cit., I, pp. 253–96.

Notes

[1] For an account of Evagrius' system and his relationship to Origenism, see Antoine Guillaumont, *Les 'Kephalaia Gnostica' d'Évagre le Pontique*. Paris 1962.

[2] Cf. Barsanuphius and John, Letters 600–2. The popularity of the *Praktikos* and *De Oratione* is shown by the large number of surviving MSS.

[3] S. Marsili, *Giovanni Cassiano ed Evagrio Pontico*. Rome 1936; Owen Chadwick, *John Cassian*, 2nd edn (Cambridge 1968), p. 30.

[4] On the monastic use of this word, see Antoine and Claire Guillaumont, ed. *Évagre le Pontique: Traité Pratique ou Le Moine* (Sources Chrétiennes. Paris 1971), I, pp. 56–63.

[5] AP Anthony 1, Poemen 11; Athanasius, *Vita Antonii* 5.

[6] *Prakt.* 6–14. Cf. Guillaumont, ed. cit., I, pp. 63–84.

[7] Books 5–12 of Cassian's *Institutes* are structured round the eight λογισμοί; for the adaptation to seven deadly sins, cf. Gregory, *Moralia* XXXI 45:87 (PL 76:620–1).

[8] Palladius, *Lausiac History* 38:13.

[9] Ibid., 38:2–9.

[10] Abandonment of property is symptomatic of 'taking no thought for the morrow': cf. Athanasius, *Vita Antonii* 3. Hoarding money is a sin against trust in God. AP Nau 30 is a terrifying story of fire descending from heaven upon the tomb of a monk who was found to have some savings hidden under his bed when he died. AP Nau 74, mercifully, draws a different moral: a monk praying anxiously for an anchorite who was found to have fifty gold pieces when he died is reassured by an angel: 'Why are you worrying about the anchorite? Entrust your concern to God's kindness. If everyone was perfect, how would God's kindness be manifested?'

[11] The impossibility of praying properly if we indulge in anger against other people is a recurrent theme in Evagrius: cf. *Or.* 21–2, 46, 48; *A travers*, p. 90 no. 39. In general, anger darkens the mind: *Muséon* 51, p. 201 no. 10. However, the proper use of anger directed against thoughts is important in every phase of the christian life: *Muséon* 44, p. 51 nos. 5–6, 'The contemplative mind is like a dog, using the movement of anger to chase away all passioned thoughts; the practical mind is like a dog, barking down all unrighteous thoughts.'

34   WAYS OF IMPERFECTION

¹²*Prakt.* 54.
¹³E.g. *Mönchsspiegel* 15.
¹⁴*Muséon* 44, p. 379, no. 53.
¹⁵Ibid., no. 49.
¹⁶The demons' ultimate purpose in all they do against us is to prevent spiritual prayer: *Or.* 50.
¹⁷*Or.* 61 links true prayer inseparably with 'theology' (which is the same as the 'knowledge of the Holy Trinity' which is the goal of the christian life, *Prakt.* 1, 3). Cf. also *Or.* 84–6.
¹⁸The three stages are indicated in Evagrius' early letter, found as no. 8 in the collection of St Basil's letters, §4, and in *Prakt.* 1. It should be noticed, though, that pure prayer is required in some sense even in the earlier stages of life: *Prakt.* 42. In spite of the distinction between the two modalities of prayer in the prologue to *De Oratione*, there is no real discontinuity between the 'active' and the 'contemplative' modalities; both are concerned with ridding the mind of extraneous thoughts. In any case, it is clear that the three-fold scheme is not to be taken rigorously; it simply indicates that there are three possible objectives in life, which have a certain autonomy: moral perfection, knowledge of creatures, and knowledge of God. Evagrius' concern is to subordinate the first two to the third.
¹⁹Cf. Chrysippus' examples: 'Often in such a state of blindness we bite keys and kick doors when they do not open immediately, and if we stumble over a stone we attack it vindictively and smash it or throw it somewhere, saying the silliest things while we do all this.' J. von Arnim, *Stoicorum Veterum Fragmenta* III (repr. Stuttgart 1968), no. 478 (p. 129:26–30).
²⁰See the admirable exposition in J. Rist, *Stoic Philosophy* (Cambridge 1969), pp. 25–7. Much confusion has been caused by the fact that Aristotle used the word 'passion' to mean 'emotion' – as was pointed out by St Thomas, *Summa Theologiae* Iᵃ IIᵃᶜ q.59 art. 2 and 5. There is no doubt that the original Stoic doctrine of ἀπάθεια did not exclude proper emotional responses (called, rather confusingly, εὐπάθειαι): the 'opposite' of pleasure (in a bad sense, ἡδονή) is joy (χαρά), defined as 'elation which is in accordance with reason'; similarly fear is contrasted with healthy respect, and lust with wanting (βούλησις), defined as 'an appetite in accordance with reason'. See von Arnim, ed. cit., III, no. 431 (p. 105:16–20).
²¹Evagrius, *Prakt.* 56.
²²*Prakt.* 86.
²³*Prakt.* 68. Cf. St Thomas' contention that self-control is not a true virtue, *Summa Theol.* IIᵃ IIᵃᶜ q.155 a.1. It is also worth noting Hermas' doctrine that there is a good and a bad self-control: it is right to be self-controlled in things that are bad, but wrong to be self-controlled in what is good (38, *Mand.* VIII).
²⁴Cf. the development of this theme in Athanasius, *Vita Antonii* 20.
²⁵*Prakt.* Prol., 84.
²⁶*Prakt.* 81.
²⁷*Prakt.* Prol., 81. Cf. Hermas 16:7 (*Vis.* III 8:7), 26:2 (*Mand.* I 2).
²⁸Cf. *Prakt.* 82.
²⁹*Or.* 24.
³⁰*Prakt.* 58.

[31]Evagrius is categorical that it is *never* right to be angry with another human being: *Or.* 24.

[32]*Prakt.* 24, 86, 93. For this doctrine of the right use of anger, cf. Esaias IX 7; Athanasius, *Vita Antonii* 5, *De Incarnatione* 52; Diadochus of Photike (ed. E. des Places, SC 5bis. Paris 1955), ch. 62; Basil, letter 2:3.

[33]*Prakt.* 42.

[34]*Prakt.* 83.

[35]*Prakt.* 56, 64.

[36]*Prakt.* Prol.; *Mönchsspiegel* 67.

[37]This is genuine 'human thinking': PG 79:1209B.

[38]*Prakt.* 64; PG 79:1228C.

[39]The mind's light appears to consist precisely in its contemplation and knowledge: KG I 74, V 15. The rather splendid imagery is derived from Exod. 24:10, interpreted in connection with the belief that the mind itself is the place of God or the place of prayer (PG 79:1221B). The 'light' appears in the time of prayer (PG 79:1228C) because of the 'judgment' that there is in prayer (*Or.* 12, Letter 25): when we try to turn our minds to God, we discover what is on our minds.

[40]Cf. Basil's notion of this world as God's 'schoolroom': *Hexaemeron* I 6 (16C).

[41]That the λόγοι of things means their raison d'être is suggested by PG 79: 1209A. But this cannot be divorced from the consideration of God's providence (KG IV 89).

[42]*Or.* 52.

[43]Letter to Melania, ed. Gösta Vitestam, *Seconde Partie du Traité qui passe sous le nom de 'La Grande Lettre d'Évagre le Pontique à Mélanie l'Ancienne'* (Lund 1964), pp. 9–11.

[44]*Or.* 56–8.

[45]*Or.* 71.

[46]*Or.* 67–9. 73–4.

[47][Basil] Letter 8:3, *Or.* 68.

[48]PG 79:1228D, *Gnost.* 143, Letter 39.

[49]KG IV 77.

[50]Letter 29, KG II 47, IV 77, 87, V 55–6.

[51]*Prakt.* 3.

[52]Cassian, *Conf.* 9:31.

[53]PG 12:1644. For the ascription to Evagrius, Guillaumont, ed. cit., I, p. 35[4].

[54]*Prakt.* 87, KG III 63.

[55]It is important to bear in mind that 'prayer' was used traditionally to mean 'petition'; the notion of 'contemplative prayer' became current only in the sixteenth century and later. Although Evagrius stretches the word somewhat, his doctrine has to be understood on the basis of the traditional usage. Prayer is the proper acivity of the mind (*Prakt.* 49, *Or.* 83–4), but the text from the *Praktikos* confirms the text quoted in note 11 from *Muséon* 44, p. 51: prayer is combat against demons. And 'prayer' is the appropriate word, because the crucial factor in the struggle is God's help – it is pride which makes us think we can do anything without God. And prayer itself is dependent on God's help (*Or.* 7, 59). If Evagrius seems to be developing

a more 'exalted' doctrine of prayer, it is because he is more conscious that our ascent to God is radically dependent on him. There is an almost exactly parallel development among the later Platonists. Whereas Plotinus has a 'low' view of prayer (cf. J. Rist, *Plotinus* [Cambridge 1967], pp. 199–212 – except that he exaggerates the importance of *Enn.* 5:1:6, which is no more than the commonplace invocation of divine assistance at the beginning of a difficult discussion; cf. the note in H. D. Saffrey and L. G. Westerink, ed., *Proclus: Théologie Platonicienne* I [Paris 1968], p. 131⁴), Porphyry, Iamblichus and Proclus all give prayer a far more important and elevated role in their systems: A. R. Sodano, ed., *Porphyrii in Platonis Timaeum Commentariorum Fragmenta* (Naples 1964), pp. 18–19, Iamblichus, *De Mysteriis* V 26, Proclus, *in Tim.* II 206:26ff. It seems clear that this increased seriousness about prayer is inseparable from the post-Plotinian emphasis on our dependence on God (cf. Andrew Smith, *Porphyry's place in the Neoplatonic Tradition* [The Hague 1974], esp. pp. 109–10). The expanded application of the word 'prayer' relies on its traditional meaning of 'petition'.

⁵⁶*Or.* 36.

⁵⁷*Or.* 119.

⁵⁸Evagrius is very probably influenced by Gregory of Nyssa's doctrine of *epektasis*, on which see the fine comment by Rowan Williams, *The Wound of Knowledge* (London 1979), pp. 55–62.

⁵⁹*Prakt.* 69.

⁶⁰*Or.* 64.

⁶¹*Or.* 78.

⁶²Cf. *Prakt.* 36.

⁶³*Or.* 122–5.

⁶⁴*Or.* 40.

⁶⁵Cf. Antoine Guillaumont, *Les 'Kephalaia Gnostica'*, pp. 114–16. This suggests a strong interpretation of ἰσάγγελος in *Or.* 113.

⁶⁶Guillaumont, op. cit., pp. 106–7.

4

Problems about Grace

The monastic tradition which we have been looking at more or less took it for granted that it is only gradually that we make progress in our christian lives,[1] and that we may never get any further than oscillating between falling and getting up again.[2] As likely as not, our whole life will be one long battle[3] and, when all else fails, we may end up simply saying to God, 'Lord, save me, whether I like it or not; dust and ashes that I am, I love sin.'[4]

The Egyptian monks made little or no attempt to relate this obviously realistic appraisal of the human condition to any systematic doctrine of grace or the sacraments. But in the fourth and fifth centuries the latent doctrinal difficulties erupted into violent controversy.

The problem was caused by a venerable tradition in the church, according to which the new life which we receive in baptism ought, in principle, to result in a radical and immediate change in our whole attitude and behaviour. In Christ we are a 'new creation',[5] circumcised with the true and total circumcision[6] so that we are no longer enslaved to sin:[7] being dead to sin, we can now live for God.[8] What the law of the Old Testament could not do, the grace of Christ has done,[9] cleansing us inwardly in our consciences.[10]

The gift of God entails a corresponding obligation: because we have died with Christ, we must put to death all earthly vices.[11] There are some traces of an early baptismal rite, in which the newly baptised promise to abstain from sin,[12] and this could be taken very strictly to mean that complete sinlessness was expected of them.[13] If people sinned, that showed that they were not genuinely christians.[14]

Although the relationship between the gift and the obligation is not spelled out, the emphasis seems to be on the former. The dramatic change which could be observed in the behaviour of those who became christians was cited as an argument in favour of christianity: where philosophers and lawgivers had signally failed to reform humanity, Christ had succeeded, thereby demonstrating that he is indeed alive and powerful.[15] Sudden and humanly inexplicable conversions to christianity were apparently not uncommon, turning people from 'haters of the word' into willing martyrs for the word.[16] A Manichaean friend of Augustine's became a catholic without warning, after being baptised while he was unconscious.[17] In some circles baptism was regarded as quenching the fire of concupiscence.[18]

We have a dramatic, autobiographical account of the effectiveness of baptism from the pen of St Cyprian. Before his baptism, he was sceptical about the possibility of having his whole character changed by the sacrament. 'How could such a conversion be possible, I asked, that something ingrained in a man's very bodily nature or something that had become habitual through long abuse could so suddenly and speedily be put off?'

> But after the burden of my former life was pushed aside by the assistance of the waters of birth, light from on high flooded into my purged and clean breast; after new birth had made me into a new man by giving me a draught of the Spirit from heaven, it was extraordinary how my doubts were immediately dispelled. Closed doors immediately became open, the darkness became light, what seemed difficult before became easy, what seemed impossible became possible, so that it was clear that my previous life, born of the flesh subject to sin, was of the earth, whereas the new life, animated now by the Holy Spirit, was of God. . . . There is nothing here to be ascribed to human virtue, we are speaking about the gift of God.[19]

Unfortunately sudden and thorough conversions like this could not be relied upon to happen. The simple contention that a sinner, precisely because he is a sinner, is shown up as not being a real believer is expressly rejected by Origen as being manifestly too severe. There must be very few people whose lives are so well run that they never ever sin![20]

But the recognition that people sin after they have been baptised does not result in any abandonment of the belief that baptism is meant to mark a decisive break between the old life of sin and the new life in Christ; instead it makes the church much more insistent on the moral qualifications required of candidates for baptism. Only candidates whose moral behaviour was well attested would be admitted to baptism.[21] The implication of this is explicated by Origen:

> It is the person who is dead to sin . . . who is truly baptised from on high in the Holy Spirit and in water. Notice carefully the order of events in this sacrament. You must first die to sin, if you are to be buried with Christ. It is the dead who are buried. So if you are still alive to sin, you cannot be buried with Christ or

be placed with him in his new tomb, because your old Adam is still alive and cannot walk in newness of life.[22]

This means that baptism must be approached with due caution. As Origen says, 'It is the person who has stopped sinning who receives baptism for the remission of sins. Anyone who comes to baptism as a sinner does not get his sins remitted. So I beg you, do not come to baptism without great care and circumspection.'[23] On this basis Tertullian argues against baptising people too young: 'It is more profitable to delay baptism, in accordance with each individual's character and attitude and age, and this is particularly true of children.' 'Suffer the little children to come to me' he interprets as meaning, 'By all means let them come, but let them come when they are grown up and capable of learning and being taught what it is they are coming to.' Rather ominously he goes on to say, 'Anyone who understands the seriousness of baptism will fear the attainment of baptism more than its postponement.'[24] To make matters even more alarming, Cyril of Jerusalem warns his catechumens that if their attitude is wrong when they come to baptism, not only will it not do them any good, it will ever after ruin their chances of salvation: 'If you get it wrong the first time, the situation is beyond remedy.'[25]

It is clear that the emphasis has been shifted so thoroughly on to the responsibilities consequent upon baptism that the element of grace, of God's gift in the sacrament, has almost disappeared from view. Not surprisingly a great many people preferred not to take the risk of being baptised until they were on their deathbeds. This was evidently so common that St John Chrysostom was afraid that the number of unbaptised believers would be used as an argument against christianity: 'If your philosophy has any power,' they might say, 'what does it mean that so many of you are uninitiated?'[26] We also learn from him that baptism was regarded in the same way that a later generation regarded Extreme Unction: when the priest came to baptise you, you could be really sure you were going to die.[27]

No doubt in some cases it was true to say that people were putting off baptism because they wanted to go on enjoying their sins,[28] but there is no reason to deny that some people deferred baptism because of a genuine fear that they would be unable to live up to the moral standards expected of the baptised.[29] It was precisely because of the assumption that Augustine would sin, and that postbaptismal sin is much graver than prebaptismal sin, that his mother delayed having him baptised.[30]

The Cappadocian fathers, Basil, Gregory Nazianzen and Gregory of Nyssa, all preach firmly against the practice of postponing baptism;[31] all three accordingly reassure us about the possibility of forgiveness if we fall back into sin after baptism.[32] But, in spite of lyrical effusions about the wonders of baptism, their message is rather a grim and moralistic one. St Basil regards it as the hallmark of the baptised christian to be completely unresponsive to the allurements of sin.[33] He speaks of the 'enlightenment', 'purification' and 'rejuvenation' which are imparted by baptism,[34] but, if the *De Baptismo* is genuine,[35] he maintains that we should be disciples of Christ before we approach baptism, and that this already involves 'learning first of all to desist from all sin'.[36] After baptism, at any rate, we are supposed to make something of the 'talent' which we have received – this is one argument against delaying baptism until we are on the verge of death – and if this is difficult, well and good; that is how we earn our reward of glory.[37]

St Gregory Nazianzen says that baptism is a 'gift . . . in the sense that it is given to those who contribute nothing',[38] but in fact he expects us to contribute quite a lot. Baptism destroys our passions[39] and heals us completely,[40] making us perfect[41] and banishing the 'unclean, earthly spirit' from us,[42] so that thereafter the devil can only tempt us from outside.[43] But all the same, we must already have accustomed ourselves to good before baptism, otherwise we shall soon return to our vomit.[44] So Gregory has to exhort his hearers to 'fight a double fight, one to cleanse yourselves before baptism, and one to preserve baptism'.[45]

St Gregory of Nyssa was sceptical about 'instant perfection',[46] and in any case the only perfection he could envisage for the christian was an unending progress towards an ever-receding goal: virtue is as limitless as God himself is.[47] He accordingly denies that baptism causes a perfect elimination of evil from our souls, though it does 'break the continuity of evil'.[48] However baptism ought to result in the death of our passions; but it is our responsibility to see that it does. If we do not kill them off when we are baptised – and Gregory reckons that most people do not – then the 'Egyptians' will come out of the water with us, still very much alive. And in this case, even if we have 'passed through the water', we have not yet reached the 'mystical water'.[49]

Gregory's argument against deathbed baptism is based on that of Basil: the 'talent' given to us is meant to be developed, not buried. But he takes the point much further. If we die immediately after our baptism, even if we escape Hell, we must not expect any reward. It is not the baptised, as such, who are called into bliss, but those who have performed the works of charity.[50] The merely baptised are relegated to the ranks of those who are 'neither rewarded nor punished'.[51]

It would, no doubt, be unfair to say that the Greek fathers had no doctrine of grace,[52] but they did not locate grace where the Augustinian doctrine, which prevailed in the west, located it. They did not readily see grace at work within the conversion of the human will or within human efforts to resist temptation and practise the virtues. Their doctrine therefore leaves largely untouched the problem of sin. The traditional insistence that God does not *force* us[53] was reinforced by the orthodox distaste for the Valentinian gnostics' belief that some people are 'saved by nature' and are thus incapable of damnation;[54] the Greek fathers therefore underline the freedom of our human response and progressively play down the expectation that God's grace will effect a radical transformation in us, at baptism or at any other time.[55]

The result of this, however, is to leave baptism without any clear role in our conversion. It is not terribly surprising, then, that some people took the logical next step and concluded that baptism is indeed useless. Who first had the audacity to say this bluntly is not known, but the council of Side, towards the end of the fourth century, extracted a remarkable confession of faith from an old man called Adelphius:

> He said that those who receive holy baptism obtain no benefit from it; it is only zealous prayer which drives out the indwelling demon. Everyone who is born derives from our first father not only his nature, but also enslavement to demons. When these are driven out by zealous prayer, then the all-holy Spirit descends upon him ... freeing the body from all stirrings of passion and completely turning the soul away from its inclination towards evil.[56]

This was duly condemned as part of the 'Messalian' heresy. How far there ever really was such a heresy it is hard to say; it seems probable that the Messalians were essentially an ascetic movement, growing out of fairly primitive monastic traditions.[57] If some of them were claiming that baptism is ineffective, they were only saying explicitly and tactlessly what might well be regarded as implicit in the doctrine of Gregory of Nyssa.

The orthodox, however, were not amused. In the early fifth century Mark the Hermit wrote several treatises against the Messalians. He regards himself as the champion of grace against 'those who think that they are justified by works'.[58] In his view it is a denial of the whole gospel to maintain that the destruction of sin remains to be achieved, after baptism, by our own works and efforts.[59] Everything is given to us in baptism. Whatever efforts we may make against our own lack of faith, whatever progress we may make in faith and in virtue, we shall discover nothing that we had not already received in advance in baptism. 'As many as were baptised into Christ, it says, put on Christ. And Christ, being perfect God, has given the grace of the Spirit perfectly to those who have been baptised, and this grace receives no increase from us.'[60] After baptism there is nothing preventing us from keeping all the commandments,[61] but all the good that we do derives not just from us, but from the 'treasure of the Spirit', from Christ dwelling in us as a result of our baptism.[62] Our efforts to keep the commandments are not a way to abolish sin, they are an expression of the freedom we have already been given; 'the commandments themselves do not cut off sin (that has been done solely by the cross), they guard the frontiers of the freedom we have been given'.[63]

We can recognise all this as the ancient, strong doctrine of baptismal transformation; and Mark's doctrine of the indwelling of Christ in our hearts and the hidden presence of the Holy Spirit, from which he infers that we ought to dwell in our hearts, guarding them carefully and seeking there the source of life,[64] was to prove extremely fertile in later Byzantine spirituality.[65] But Mark's Messalian interlocutor raises a very real problem: 'If sin is destroyed in baptism, why is it at work again in our hearts?' 'I have been baptised, I call upon God and invoke his grace, with all my will I desire to be rescued and delivered from evil thoughts, but I am powerless. Why is that? Is it not clear that Adam's transgression has left us this inescapable inheritance?'[66]

Mark absolutely refuses to accept that baptism gives us anything less than complete deliverance from sin. He does not deny the reality of postbaptismal sin, but he insists that it is not due to anything left over from our prebaptismal days. If we sin again after baptism, even if we find ourselves enslaved to sin after our baptism, that is due entirely to our own free will; we have *chosen* to surrender our freedom.[67] If we suffer from involuntary evil thoughts, it is because of free choices that we have made previously.[68]

In principle, then, Mark abides by the doctrine that baptism gives us a complete new beginning. If we do not in fact succeed in living the new life in its fulness, that is our fault. 'Holy baptism is perfect with regard to us, but we are not perfect with regard to it.'[69] Baptism does not *force* us.[70] Although it is Christ 'who works in us both to will and to do' (Mark is quoting Philippians 2:13), he does so only in accordance with our own wishes.[71] The gift that is given to us in baptism becomes operative only in proportion to our own faith and obedience.[72] And Mark is very clear that this is strictly our own responsibility. He dismisses the plea that we can only do good if we receive an effective grace from the Holy Spirit as simply an excuse for hedonism; the effectiveness of the Holy Spirit in us depends on our obedience to the commandments, not the other way about.[73] Virtue is essentially only a matter of abstaining from sin, and that is within our own power.[74] If works of virtue do not contribute to our sanctification and do not in any way earn us freedom or the kingdom of heaven, it is because they are simply our duty. 'A slave does not demand freedom as a wage due to him . . . he receives it as a grace.'[75] Obedience to the commandments is a necessary condition for our adoption as God's children, but it is not a sufficient condition; we cannot put God under any obligation to us, and we cannot atone for our past sins. Any reward we may hope to get depends, not on our works, but on whether we do them with faith in Christ, and it is his grace which makes our works significant for our sanctification. Adoption as his children is the gift of his grace.[76]

Mark certainly does not want to deny our dependence on God. Our virtues are brought to birth by prayer, through our union with Christ.[77] All the same, his doctrine does seem to leave our progress in the christian life and our eventual salvation solidly on our own shoulders. His very concern to safeguard the completeness of baptism means that he has to treat grace as a kind of commodity which is given to us once and for all, and thereafter it is up to us to make use of it as we want. He has no word of comfort for those who feel that sense of helplessness to which his Messalian opponents allude.

There seems to be an impasse. On the one hand there is a doctrine which makes baptism all-important, but ineffective unless we make it effective. On the other hand there is a doctrine which denies that baptism makes any significant difference. And the consequences of these two opposed beliefs seem to be curiously indistinguishable from one another.

Notes

[1]Cf. AP Nau 208.
[2]AP Sisoes 38.
[3]AP Theodore of Pherme 2.
[4]AP Nau 582.
[5]2 Cor. 5:17.
[6]Col. 2:11.
[7]Rom. 6:6.
[8]Rom. 6:10–11.
[9]Rom. 8:3.
[10]Hebr. 9:9–14.
[11]Col. 3:3,5.
[12]Pliny, *Ep.* X 96:7; cf. Hippolytus, *Ref.* IX 15:4 and Ps.Clem. *Contestatio* 1:2, which must be modelled on such a rite. In some later rites there is an explicit 'contract' with Christ after the renunciation of Satan (cf. Antoine

Wenger, *Jean Chrysostome: Huit Catéchèses Baptismales*, Sources Chrétiennes no. 50 [Paris 1957], pp. 82, 87). And even without an express formula in the rite, baptism can be interpreted as such a contract: e.g. Gregory Naz., *Or.* 40:8; Cyril of Jerusalem, *Mystagogical Cat.* 1:8.

[13]Justin, *Dial.* 44:4.

[14]*Didascalia* (tr. R. Hugh Connolly. Oxford 1929), p. 38; Justin, I *Apol.* 16:8; Athenagoras, *Leg.* 2:4.

[15]Aristides, *Apol.* 15:3–8; Justin, I *Apol.* 14, *Dial.* 116; Athanasius, *De Inc.* 30.

[16]Origen, *Cels.* I 46.

[17]Augustine, *Conf.* IV 4:7–8.

[18]Cf. Erik Peterson, *Frühkirche, Judentum und Gnosis* (Freiburg 1959), pp. 221–35; P. Prigent, 'Une Trace de Liturgie Judéo-Chrétienne dans le chapitre XXI de l'Apocalypse de Jean', *Judéo-Christianisme: Recherches historiques et théologiques offertes en hommage au Cardinal Jean Daniélou* (Paris 1972), pp. 165–72; Ephrem, *Comm. Diat.* 20:26, 21:10; Ps. Hippolytus, *Paschal Homily* 53; Ps. Clem., *Hom.* 11:26. The belief that baptism quenches concupiscence is probably to be connected with the Jewish expectation that the Messiah would slay the 'evil impulse' (Bab. Talmud, *Suk.* 52a; cf. W. D. Davies, *Paul and Rabbinic Judaism* [London 1970], p. 23), which seems to underlie the text from the apocryphal Gospel of the Egyptians cited by Clement of Alexandria, *Strom.* III 63. The belief that concupiscence has been destroyed is probably one of the sources of encratism, since marriage was regarded as depending on the existence of the 'evil impulse' (Bab. Talmud *AZ* 5a; *Genesis Midr. Rabbah* 9:7).

[19]Cyprian, *Ad Donatum* 3–4.

[20]PG 14:889C.

[21]Origen, *Cels.* III 51; Hippolytus, *Ap. Trad.* 16, 20; Egeria, *Itin.* 45.

[22]PG 14:1038CD.

[23]*Commentary on Luke* 21:4.

[24]Tertullian, *Bapt.* 18. Gregory Nazianzen reckons that children will understand enough to be baptised at the age of three (PG 36:400).

[25]Cyril of Jerusalem, *Procat.* 4,5,7; *Cat.* 17:36. Cf. Clem. Al., *Exc. Theod.* 83, which envisages the possibility of unclean spirits going down with people into the font and getting sealed in and so becoming 'incurable'. The fear of this risk underlies the prebaptismal exorcisms, in so far as they are regarded as testing the candidates to see whether they are pure (as in Hippolytus, *Ap. Trad.* 20). It has also been suggested that the reason why women must loosen their hair and remove their jewels before baptism (Hippolytus, op. cit., 21) is to make sure that there is no place for a demon to lurk, and indeed this interpretation is made explicit in the *Canones Hippolyti* 115. Cf. F. J. Dölger. *Der Exorzismus im altchristlichen Taufritual* (Paderborn 1909), pp. 112–13; W. C. van Unnik, 'Les cheveux défaits des femmes baptisées', *Vigiliae Christianae* 1 (1947), pp. 77–100.

[26]PG 60:24.

[27]PG 49:224. Gregory Nazianzen gives us an amusing picture of the priest trying to reach the dying man through a jostling crowd of friends and relations making a final attempt to secure a remembrance in his will (*Or.* 40:11). It was widely noticed that in times of crisis people came

throning for baptism: e.g. Gregory of Nyssa (PG 46:420A), Augustine (PL 40:722), Cyrillona (*I Carmi di Cirillona*, tr. Costantino Vona [Rome 1963], 6:488ff).

[28]Tertullian, *Paen.* 6; Basil, PG 31:433B; Gregory of Nyssa, PG 46: 425D.
[29]Gregory Nazianzen, PG 36:377ff; Gregory of Nyssa, PG 46:425; Chrysostom, PG 60:23–4.
[30]Augustine, *Conf.* I 11:17–18.
[31]Basil and Gregory of Nyssa devoted sermons specifically to this topic (PG 31:424–44, PG 46:416–32); Gregory Naz., PG 36:372ff.
[32]Basil, PG 31:1089C–1092A; Greg. Naz., PG 36: 357B; Greg. Nyss., PG 46:424A.
[33]PG 31:868D–869A.
[34]PG 31:424C, 429A, 433A.
[35]A good case has been made for the correctness of the ascription of this work to Basil: see Jean Gribomont in P. J. Fedwick, ed., *Basil of Caesarea, Christian, Humanist, Ascetic* (Toronto 1981), I, pp. 44–5.
[36]PG 31:1525C, 1516D.
[37]PG 31:437A, 440BC.
[38]PG 36:361D.
[39]PG 36:360C.
[40]PG 36:368AB.
[41]PG 36:421B.
[42]PG 36:409A.
[43]PG 36:369–72.
[44]PG 36:350D–352A.
[45]PG 36:401D.
[46]*De Virginitate* 23:3.
[47]*Life of Moses*, Preface 5–8.
[48]*Catechetical Oration* 35 (ed. J. H. Srawley [Cambridge 1903], p. 134).
[49]*Life of Moses* II 125–9; cf. *Catechetical Oration* 40 on the need to change our lives if baptism is to be effective.
[50]PG 46:429.
[51]PG 46:428AB.
[52]Cf., for example, Vladimir Lossky, *The Mystical Theology of the Eastern Church*. Cambridge 1957; Werner Jaeger, *Two Rediscovered Works of Ancient Christian Literature* (Leiden 1965), pp. 85–107; Cornelius Ernst, *The Theology of Grace* (Cork 1974), pp. 47–52.
[53]E.g. Barn. 2:6; *Diognetus* 7:4; Irenaeus, *Adv. Haer.* IV 37:1, V 1:1, *Epideixis* 55; Clement of Alexandria, *Quis dives* 10:1–2, 21:2; *Apostolic Constitutions* VI 20:3; Ephrem, *Ep. ad Publium* 23 (ed. S.P. Brock, *Muséon* 89 [1976], p. 293). The problem is, of course, a false one, if we accept St Thomas' account. God moves the will from inside, not as an external constraint, but precisely as its creator; human freedom does not have to be secured by some pretended independence of God's act, it is what it is *because of* God's act (*Summa Theol.* I³II³ᶜ q.9 art. 6, q.10 art. 4, q.109 art. 2; cf. also I³ q.83 art. 1 ad 3). This means that if God causes us to will something, he is to be regarded as creating that particular act of free will in us; by definition he cannot be regarded as 'interfering' with our will, since interference is something which can only be done by one creature to another, not by the

creator to his creature. Cf. Herbert McCabe, 'God, II: Freedom', *New Blackfriars* 61 (1980), pp. 456–69.

[54]Cf. Origen, *Princ.* III 1:8; for the Valentinian doctrine see, for example, Clement of Al., *Exc. Theod.* 56:3.

[55]Chrysostom treats it as frivolous to refuse conversion on the grounds that 'When God wills it he will persuade me and I shall be changed' (PG 51:143).

[56]Patrologia Syriaca III, p. cxcv.

[57]Cf. Robert Murray, *Symbols of Church and Kingdom: A Study in Early Syriac Tradition* (Cambridge 1975), p. 35. On the Messalian question in general, see Jean Gribomont, 'Le Dossier des Origines du Messalianisme', J. Fontaine and C. Kannengiesser, ed., *Epektasis* (Paris 1972), pp. 611–25.

[58]This is the title of one of his treatises; there is a useful translation, based on the Greek MSS, in vol. I of the English *Philokalia*, ed. G. E. H. Palmer, Philip Sherrard and Kallistos Ware (London 1979), pp. 125–46.

[59]*De Baptismo* PG 65:988A.

[60]PG 65:1028BC.

[61]PG 65:992C.

[62]PG 65:1005–8.

[63]PG 65:989–92.

[64]PG: 1005D.

[65]Mark himself develops the point in his *Letter to Nicolas the Solitary* (PG 65:1049; in the English *Philokalia*, p. 159); this text is cited by Nicephorus (PG 147:953–5), on whose fundamental importance in the development of the Hesychastic 'prayer of the heart' see I. Hausherr, *La Méthode d'Oraison Hésychaste* (Rome 1927), pp. 33–8. Mark's doctrine of baptism is cited by Kallistos and Ignatios Xanthopouloi (PG 147:641–4), and it is an important presupposition of the teaching of Gregory of Sinai (cf. PG 150:1293C, 1308AB). Symeon the New Theologian was also influenced by Mark, but in a rather different direction: *Cat.* 22 (ed. Basile Krivochéine, Sources Chrétiennes, no. 104 [Paris 1964], pp. 366–8).

[66]PG 65:992A, 1020C.

[67]PG 65:992B and cf. 988B, 989A.

[68]PG 65:1000C.

[69]PG 65:1005A.

[70]PG 65:988B.

[71]PG 65:1008A.

[72]PG 65:1001BC; *On Those who Think*, 61 (following the numbering given in the *Philokalia*).

[73]Ibid., 59–60, 64.

[74]Ibid., 24–5.

[75]Ibid., 2–3, 20, 24.

[76]Ibid., 18–19, 22, 24, 26, 42–3.

[77]Ibid., 35.

5

The Macarian Homilies

For centuries christians of all sorts have delighted in a collection of fifty spiritual homilies ascribed to 'Macarius'. The Macarian homilies have been recognised as an important source for Byzantine piety, but they were also received enthusiastically in the west. They were among the relatively few books which Jesuit novices were encouraged to read, but they found favour with Protestants too and were an important influence on Lutheran pietism. John Wesley included a substantial selection from the homilies in the first volume of his *Christian Library* and recorded one day in his journal that 'he read Macarius and sang'.[1]

In the twentieth century, however, the works of 'Macarius' have become the subject of considerable scholarly controversy. In the first place, the Macarian corpus has been extended by the discovery of a great many more homilies and letters.[2] Secondly, and more importantly, it has been realised that there is at least a close relationship between the *Asketikon* of the Messalians and the writings of Macarius. This had led several scholars to maintain that Macarius must have been a Messalian and indeed a leader of the Messalians. Some have identified him with a certain 'Symeon', who is mentioned as a Messalian leader, since a few manuscripts of the Macarian homilies name the author as 'Symeon'.[3]

It has already been mentioned that there is a great deal of unclarity about the alleged heresy of the Messalians,[4] and in any case, as we have been reminded by the doyen of modern Macarian studies, Hermann Dörries,[5] the fact that the Messalians used Macarius does not prove that he was a Messalian, any more than we have to believe that Augustine was a Calvinist. It is quite clear that Macarius did not subscribe to the alleged Messalian doctrines which were condemned.

The most we can say with any confidence is that the Macarian writings were composed in the fourth century, by someone who can certainly not be identified with either of the great Macarii of Egyptian monasticism, and who shows definite signs of being influenced by Syrian christianity. He is probably to be situated within the monasticism of Mesopotamia or Asia Minor, possibly within the sphere of St Basil's influence.[6]

Like the Egyptian monks, Macarius believes that christian progress takes time.[7] He disapproves of the brisk slogan apparently being used in some circles, 'On with the new man, off with the old!'[8] And progress is a matter of falling and getting up again, building something up and then being knocked down again.[9] But, unlike the Egyptian monks, Macarius has a great deal to say about grace, and he was clearly drawn into the debate about baptism.

The questions which he raises about baptism – evidently questions which were put to him by his disciples – are closely related to the questions at issue between Mark the Hermit and his Messalian opponents. Why are we not completely transformed once we are renewed in baptism? Is not baptism meant to deprive sin of any power it may have had over us? If there is more to come after baptism, does that not invalidate the claims made for baptism?[10]

Macarius takes it as adequately proved by the facts that the power of sin is not actually broken by baptism. On this, he sides with the Messalians against the belief that baptism breaks the continuity of sin. It may be true to say that sin comes 'from outside', in that it does not constrain our will. It enters us by way of our 'obedience' to it, just as it did in the first place in the case of Eve. But nevertheless it has a 'right' to enter in. It is like a soldier who has left his shield in someone's house: just as he has a right to go in any time he likes to collect his shield, so sin has a right to enter us, because of our own thoughts (*logismoi*), which are patently not perfectly converted and which certainly do come from inside us.[11] Sin needs our consent if it is to take hold of us, but that is precisely the problem: we *do* consent. Our soul is 'shackled' by the power of darkness;[12] 'just as fog occupies the atmosphere, so the power of Satan has filled the hearts of mankind and there is a dark smoke lying over all our choices'.[13] In spite of baptism, then, it is perfectly proper to go on talking about sin being 'mixed' with our souls, so that only God can disentangle them. Sin, unless he intervenes, 'dwells in the limbs of our soul and body'.[14]

God does not *force* our will any more than sin does,[15] so the whole battle centres precisely on the will.[16]

If baptism does not eradicate sin, what does it do? Macarius' answer is plain:

> We receive from it the beginning of the assurance of the Spirit and of our salvation (the apostle says, 'If we hold fast to the beginning of our assurance in him to the end'),[17] and the Spirit we all received in baptism will increase in us, if we make an effort and believe, in proportion to each one's faith, as we make progress

in virtue and persevere in prayers, until he can be perceived and reveals himself, bringing about the perfection of purity and deliverance from the passions, as we progress and walk rightly. . . . But the beginning of this is received very subtly, so that we believe that we have obtained the presence of the Spirit, but do not recognise his working; we are governed by the direction of grace to come gradually into growth and the manifestation of the Spirit.

Macarius uses the image of a newborn baby, which has all the limbs which it will ever have (in that sense it is already complete), but nevertheless it still has to grow up. So it is quite true to say that we receive the 'life of the Spirit' as a result of baptism; baptism is true and valid. But we have still to make progress, and only so will the Spirit grow in us and become manifest as he makes us perfect.[18]

In response to the question why sin can start to work again in someone in whom grace is at work, Macarius says:

When he first tasted grace, his soul revived and enjoyed a heavenly repose quite foreign to this world, so that he would know by experience the sweetness of goodness. But then, if his mind gets a little distracted or something, he is again filled with sin, so that he will be oppressed and learn by experience the bitterness of sin, and then he will seek refuge all the more speedily, seeking that ineffable consolation and repose. Then he obtains it again and revives and rests a little, but then, if he is careless, evil gains access and bitterly oppresses him, as grace gives it leave, so that he may know by experience the sweetness and restfulness and consolation of grace and the bitterness and pain and oppressiveness of sin, so that (if he wishes to be saved) he will the more earnestly flee the one and cleave wholly to grace.[19]

The important thing, in Macarius' mind, is that this weakness which allows sin to go on working in us is 'providential'.[20] It is Christ who gives us freedom or allows us to be oppressed in accordance with his own providential purposes, and it is for our good.[21] If souls which have received grace were simply cosseted in the sweetness and repose of the Spirit, without being subjected to any trials of demonic oppression, they would remain immature, and would be no more 'use', so to speak, to the kingdom of heaven than small children are for the business of this world.[22] Many people want to reach the kingdom without any 'toil and struggle and sweat', but this is impossible.[23] If we did not have to struggle, we should soon become conceited,[24] for one thing, and conceit is the downfall of christians, as it was of the devil.[25] And unless we desire

goodness enough to be prepared to fight for it, we shall not be able
to receive God's good gifts, even if he does give them to us.[26] Above
all, God wishes us to love him with a strong, tested love, and this
is something we cannot obtain without a protracted struggle.[27]

But, however much Macarius stresses the role of our own endeav-
ours, he is explicit that the whole process of our development is the
work of grace. 'As a bee makes a honeycomb secretly in a sieve, so
grace makes love of itself secretly in men's hearts, changing them
from bitterness to sweetness, from roughness to smoothness.'[28]

The first work of grace is simply to enable us to begin to understand what is wrong. 'The whole phenomenal world, from kings to
paupers, is in a state of disturbance and confusion and strife, and
none of them knows why.'[29] 'Human beings do not know themselves
until the Lord reveals them to themselves.'[30] It is only when God,
in his mercy, gives us knowledge of the truth by means of the
scriptures that we can even begin to struggle against evil.[31] It is
only by the divine light of the Holy Spirit that we can begin to sort
out our thoughts (logismoi).[32]

But God does not only give us light, he also works actively in
transforming our attitudes and presuppositions.[33] Grace works in
our souls like a kind of leaven.[34] And, although Macarius speaks
frequently about our growth, he also speaks about the gift of the
Spirit growing in us.[35]

The immediate result of grace is not that everything suddenly
becomes easy for us; on the contrary, the immediate result is an
increase in tension. The straightforward sinner or the completely
perfect saint are both simple creatures, who act without effort;[36] but
once we have begun to be converted from sin without yet having
attained perfection, there are two 'personae' at work in us.[37] It is
now that we enter into that state of inner struggle which is described
by St Paul in Romans 7:14ff, in which we find that there is one law
in our minds and another 'law' in our members.[38]

Macarius rejects the suggestion that sin and grace cannot co-
exist in the same person. To the quotation from 2 Corinthians 6:14,
'What fellowship is there between light and darkness?' Macarius
retorts with John 1:5, 'The light shines in the darkness.' It is only
frivolous people, with but a meagre share in grace, who reckon that
they are completely free from sin. People with a more accurate and
serious understanding would not dare to claim that they are never
affected by unclean thoughts.[39] Grace does not immediately drive
out sin, as we have seen; neither do our sins drive out grace, at
least as long as we are in this life.[40]

Grace does not immediately eliminate sin; but it does progressively allow us to recognise it for what it is: a foreign body from
which, in principle, the soul can be disengaged.[41] Even if we remain

largely helpless, we can begin to *want* to love the Lord, to want to believe in him and to want to pray.⁴² And the resulting struggle is the proof that we are indeed alive.⁴³

Macarius reckons that many people have far too superficial a view of the extent of our problem. They acquire a few external virtues and think that the job is done. But the inner virtues are at least as important.⁴⁴ We must not be misled by appearances: people whose outward behaviour is quite virtuous may in fact be in a much worse position than people who are entangled in various manifest sins, but are inwardly humble, trusting and courageous. These latter are much closer to healing than the former.⁴⁵ In fact one major reason for stressing the extreme goodness which is required of us is to prevent conceit and complacency. Nothing less than 'unspeakable perfection' will do.⁴⁶ Macarius stresses that this is a realistic goal to set ourselves; we must not make do with imperfect virtue, on the grounds that anything more is impossible.⁴⁷ On the other hand, we shall rapidly discover that perfection is not attainable by our own efforts. It is a recurrent theme in Macarius that it is only God who can actually free us completely from all sinfulness.⁴⁸

We have to force ourselves to the utmost of our ability to practise the virtues, but our own efforts will not bring us success.⁴⁹ We cannot deliver ourselves from the tension between the two 'spirits' at work in us; what we can and must do is refrain from cultivating both these spirits. We must resolutely identify ourselves only with the good,⁵⁰ and we must go on doing this however much our thoughts and even our actions are still controlled by sin.⁵¹ If we persevere in this inner struggle, then the Lord will himself 'avenge us against our enemies' and give us the 'great healing'. Therefore the most important aspect of our struggle is precisely that we should pray persistently and passionately, like the widow woman in the parable who pestered the unjust judge until she got what she wanted.⁵² After all, even a helpless invalid can at least clamour for the doctor.⁵³

It is on the subject of our need to have recourse to grace that Macarius waxes most lyrical, and a host of passages could be cited, of which only a few are in fact given here.

Let no one claim, 'I cannot love the only true good or think or trust in the only good, because I am enslaved and bound by sin.' It is certainly not in your power to be able to accomplish perfectly the works of life or to rescue yourself by your own strength or to free yourself from indwelling sin, because God has assigned that to himself. He alone condemned sin, he alone takes away the sin of the world, he himself has promised to free those who love him and trust in him from their enslavement to the passions of sin, and it is those whom he sets free who are free indeed. What you can do, though, is think and trust and love the Lord and seek him; you can do that and you can also refuse to cooperate with indwelling sin and to share its delights; only be an occasion of life to yourself by seeking the Lord, by thinking of him and loving and waiting for him, and he will provide the power and the deliverance.[54]

O how inexpressible is the love and compassion and mercy of the Lord! He makes himself like a bird, so that the wandering soul can take refuge under his wings. The lifegiving Word says, 'How often have I desired to gather you as a bird gathers her brood under her wings, and you refused.' See, he has stretched out his wings and is waiting for the soul to come and rest under his wings.[55]

Let us throw ourselves with unhesitating faith into praying to the Lord to give us the promised Spirit, who gives life to the soul. If a beggar is so shameless for the sake of material bread, knocking at the door and begging and only pushing his way further in if he is not given anything and begging even more shamelessly for bread or clothes or shoes, for his bodily comfort, refusing to go away until he has got something, even if people try to chase him away, how much more we, who seek to receive the true, heavenly bread to strengthen our souls, and heavenly garments of light and the spiritual shoes of the Spirit, for the comfort of our immortal soul, how ceaselessly, how tirelessly, with what faith and love we ought to persevere, always knocking on God's heavenly door. . . . Let us come to him who is the spiritual door and knock, so that he will open to us. Let us beseech him who is the bread of life and say to him, 'Give me the bread of life, Lord, that I may live, for I am perishing, fearfully constrained by the famine of wickedness. Give me a coat of the light of salvation with which to cover the shame of my soul, because, being naked and unclothed with the power of your Spirit, I am shamefully disgraced and disfigured by passions.' And if he says to you, 'You had a coat, what have you done with it?' answer him, 'I fell among thieves and they stripped me and left me half dead.'[56]

Christ is the 'tower of strength' to which we must flee.[57] He will speedily deliver us, as he promised; and if we ask why he sometimes seems to be so slow about it, Macarius assures us that he has not delayed: our very ability to go on struggling and praying is already a very great grace.[58]

Our whole experience of being oppressed by sin should be viewed as a genuine way of taking up our cross daily and sharing in the sufferings of Christ. With considerable audacity, Macarius even suggests that our 'persecution' by the powers of evil (including our own proneness to sin) is as good as martyrdom.[59] Our moral sufferings therefore provide an expression of love for Christ, which Macarius describes in terms which anticipate medieval devotion to the passion. If we love Christ, we should love to suffer with him.[60] We should be like Mary at the foot of the cross, love and compassion making us suffer even more than he does. We should keep our minds the whole time on the thought of how much he suffered for us, and be bound to him and suffer with him in everything. And if we do this, then the 'stone will be rolled away' and we shall see him, that is to say, the 'veil of sin' will be taken away and we shall, in part, see his face and find repose in him.[61]

If we continue faithful, we can look forward to a double reward: here on earth, we can hope for full deliverance and complete sanctification by the Holy Spirit, and hereafter we shall become heirs of eternal life.[62]

Macarius is explicit that the blessings of the Spirit are given to us in this life,[63] and on occasion he even suggests that we need to reach perfect sanctification in this life.[64] But this cannot be taken at its face value. This world is not the place of perfect repose, it is the place of tears and struggle, in which the consolation of the Spirit is only part of the picture.[65] Grace sometimes works in us so powerfully that for a time we may be completely free from every fault and even from every temptation; but then the intensity of grace is relaxed, and we find that sin is still there. Macarius reckons that he has never met anyone who is perfectly free.[66]

It seems rather that there is a process of sanctification which begins in baptism and, in principle, goes on indefinitely throughout our lives, breaking the power of sin and of our passions bit by bit. The Paraclete whom we await as the promised liberator from all uncleanness is the Paraclete whom we have already received in baptism.[67] The goal is perfect liberation, so that we can perfectly obey all the commandments,[68] but it is a big mistake for us to imagine that we have arrived there.[69] People may go for years full of joy and grace, thinking that concupiscence is extinct, only to discover that after all they are still as vulnerable to sin as ever.[70] The experienced believer learns neither to lose heart when things are going badly nor to become complacent when things are going well; he knows that neither situation is going to last.[71]

The transformation being worked in us by grace consists essentially in the development of love of God in our hearts, and the true lover of Christ has to make progress in both of the ways in which Christ shows himself to us, in his sufferings and in his glory.[72] If sometimes we seem to rise above all difficulties, it is because love occupies our attention so completely that we have no time left for the trivia of wickedness.[73] But love, if it is genuine, far from making us content, goads us on to desire ever more. It is the Pharisee, not the christian, who wants nothing more than he already has.[74]

In view of his strong awareness of human helplessness, it is not surprising that Macarius should ascribe a supremely important role to prayer, as did the Messalians.

> We prosper in those affairs in which we call upon him (Christ), and we come to grief in those affairs in which we forget him. We ought not to do anything or say anything or engage in any battle or suffer any disturbance at things without crying to him. . . . You want to achieve some work? Pray to him. You want to speak? Remember him. You want to be rescued from evils? Call upon the Lord. Is sin ruining you? He is the Lamb who takes away the sins of the world. Is somebody scaring you? He is a tower of strength against the enemy.[75]

Prayer is the most important task of all, and Macarius, like the Messalians, thinks that all encouragement should be given to those who wish to devote themselves to it as a full-time occupation.[76] But he adds various qualifications, which do not seem to be characteristic of Messalianism. He does not suppose that everybody ought to devote himself to full-time prayer; different people have different functions in the community.[77] And the most important thing of all is that they should see each other as complementary, because they do in fact benefit from each other. The person who does nothing but pray should never look down on the manual worker, wondering censoriously, 'Why is he not praying?'; conversely the worker should not despise the person who is praying as if he were simply a parasite.[78] If the pray-er despises anybody else, his praying becomes diabolical.[79]

And full-time praying should never be regarded as an easy option. Since prayer is the most important task, it is natural that those who particularly devote themselves to it should find themselves engaged in a greater struggle and in harder work than anyone else.[80] Macarius' notion of prayer is an energetic one. He certainly accepts that people may have dramatic visionary experiences from time to time, but he is anxious to put such phenomena in a proper perspective. While they last, they are very consoling and can truly be regarded as a gift from God, giving such an intensity of love that sin, for the moment, is entirely removed. But Macarius tells us of someone he knew who was given a grace like this, and it resulted in him becoming quite useless. All he could do was 'lie in a corner, high and intoxicated'. Macarius intimates that he would prefer people to be less 'high' and more concerned with fraternal charity. And there is another danger too: people can be deceived by the very abundance of grace which they enjoy into thinking that sin is entirely defeated in them, when it is in fact not so.[81]

Whatever flights of spiritual experience may be enjoyed, then, Macarius insistently brings us back to the essential kernel of his christian message: if we understand clearly the objective set before us by divine revelation, we shall discover how impossible it is for us to attain to it; we shall therefore be obliged to recognise our need of redemption. And it is on that basis that we can truly appreciate what Christ means for us: he is, precisely, our Redeemer.

Bibliography and Abbreviations

Editions used, abbreviations

B   ed. Heinz Berthold, *Makarios/Symeon: Reden und Briefe*. Berlin 1973 (references are given to the vol., page and line nos. of this edn).

C   ed. Erich Klostermann and Heinz Berthold, *Neue Homilien des Makarius/Symeon*. Berlin 1961; ed. Vincent Desprez, *Pseudo-Macaire: Oeuvres Spirituelles, I* (SC 275). Paris 1980 (references are given to the no. of the homily and the paragraph, common to both edns, and also to the subsections, as numbered in the SC edn).

E   ed. Werner Strothmann, *Schriften des Makarios/Symeon unter dem Namen des Ephraem*. Wiesbaden 1981 (references are to the homily and paragraph nos.).

GL   (*Great Letter* or *Epistula Magna*) in Werner Jaeger, *Two Rediscovered Works of Ancient Christian Literature: Gregory of Nyssa and Macarius.* Leiden 1965 (references are to the page and line nos. of this edn).

H   ed. Hermann Dörries, Erich Klostermann and Matthias Kroeger, *Die 50 geistlichen Homilien des Makarios*. Berlin 1964 (references are to the homily and paragraph nos.).

H 51 G. L. Marriott, *Macarii Anecdota*. Cambridge (Mass.) 1918 (references are to the homily and paragraph nos.).

Translations

A. J. Mason, *Fifty Spiritual Homilies*. London 1921.
There is a French tr. in the SC edn of C.

Notes

[1]On Macarius' influence in general, see the detailed account in Vincent Desprez, 'Pseudo-Macaire (Syméon)', *Dictionnaire de Spiritualité* X (Paris 1980), 39–41. John Wesley's diary, 30 July 1736; John Wesley, *A Christian Library* I (London 1819), pp. 69–131.

[2]The main collections have now been edited; the corpus is discussed in detail in the introductions to B and the SC edn of C. So far little work has been done to fuse the different texts into a single edition.

56   WAYS OF IMPERFECTION

³See Vincent Desprez, *Pseudo-Macaire: Oeuvres Spirituelles* I (Sources Chrétiennes no. 275. Paris 1980), pp. 37–46, for an informative and balanced assessment of the evidence and previous scholarly discussions. Andrew Louth claims bluntly that the Macarian homilies 'are the product of . . . the Messalians' (*The Origins of the Christian Mystical Tradition* [Oxford 1981], p. 114).
⁴Cf. above, ch. 4 n 57.
⁵Hermann Dörries, *Die Theologie des Makarios/Symeon* (Göttingen 1978), pp. 12–13.
⁶Desprez, op. cit., pp. 32–56; for the Syrian influence, cf. also G. Quispel, *Makarius, das Thomasevangelium und das Lied von der Perle.* Leiden 1967.
⁷H 15:41–2; C I 3:3 (Since Macarius repeats himself a lot, I only give a few references in the notes here to establish the interpretation I am offering; in most cases it would be possible to list many more references.)
⁸H 15:41.
⁹C I 1:3; H 3:4–5 (of which there is a divergent text in E 5:4–5).
¹⁰C XII 1:1; H 15:14–15; B II, p. 74:2–4.
¹¹B II, p. 19:8–33 (H 15:13–15).
¹²C III 1:1.
¹³C I 3:3.
¹⁴H 2:2–3.
¹⁵H 15:30; B I, p. 122:16–17.
¹⁶E 2:9.
¹⁷Hebr. 3:14.
¹⁸B II, pp. 74–5; cf. GL, p. 236 (Macarius uses the Cappadocians' image of the 'talent') and B I, p. 18:6–20 (birth contains an 'image of perfection').
¹⁹C XII 2:1–2.
²⁰C XII 1:4.
²¹B II, pp. 164:19–165:2.
²²B II, pp. 167:23–168:7.
²³H 5:6.
²⁴H 27:8.
²⁵C I 3:4.
²⁶H 19:6.
²⁷GL, p. 261:9–21.
²⁸H 16:7.
²⁹H 15:49.
³⁰C XVIII 1:2.
³¹GL, p. 233:10–18. On the diverse ways in which God instructs us, cf. B II, pp. 51:27–52:15. We also learn much from Satan's war against us: H 51:2.
³²H 11:3.
³³B I, p. 25:24–6.
³⁴H 24:3; B I, p. 81:9–12.
³⁵B II, p. 74:22. The idea that it is the gift of the Spirit which grows was unacceptable in 'orthodox' circles; it is interesting to contrast GL 236:3 with *De Instituto Christiano* 44:26 (ed. Werner Jaeger, *Gregorii Nysseni Opera Ascetica.* Leiden 1952; the ascription to Gregory of Nyssa is disputed: see, for instance, Jean Gribomont, *Epektasis*, pp. 623–4. For the priority of GL,

see Reinhart Staats, *Gregor von Nyssa und die Messalianer*. Berlin 1968): GL refers ambiguously to 'growth', but *De Instituto* specifies that it is *the person who receives the gift* who grows. Cf. Dörries, op. cit., pp. 426–7.

[36]Cf. GL 276:13–277:11.
[37]H 11:14, 17:6, GL, p. 247:3.
[38]E 6:13.
[39]B I, p. 180:9–12.
[40]E 6:12; B II, p..20:24–8.
[41]GL 235:12–14; C XVIII 1:2, H 15:49, 16:1; B II, p. 192:12–13. (It is the devil who wants us to think that sin is natural to us.)
[42]B II, p. 190:4–5.
[43]H 11:14.
[44]GL, pp. 241ff, 289:9–19; H 3:4.
[45]C VII 7:2–3.
[46]GL, pp. 253:23–256:3.
[47]GL, p. 291ff.
[48]H 3:4.
[49]H 19.
[50]GL, pp. 245–6.
[51]C XXVI 3.
[52]C VIII 3:5; H 1:12, 4:27; GL, p. 247:9–13; E 3:3–4.
[53]H 46:2; C XXVI 3:2,
[54]C XXVI 3:1.
[55]B I, p. 40:21–6.
[56]C XVI 7–8.
[57]E 2:9.
[58]B I, p. 15:29–31.
[59]B II, pp. 164:16–18, 168:15–169:10 (E 1:17–19).
[60]B II, p. 172:4–5.
[61]C III 1.
[62]E 1:26 (slightly divergent text in B II, p. 171:14–15).
[63]E 6:11.
[64]H 44:9. In general, though, perfection is for Macarius strictly a 'Zielbegriff' (Dörries, op. cit., p. 39); Macarius accepts the Pauline redefinition of perfection as an unceasing reaching out to what lies ahead, and that has to continue 'until our last breath' (GL, p. 285:5–18). All God actually *requires* of us is our good will (C XXVI 3:4).
[65]C X 3:3.
[66]B I, pp. 50–3. Macarius' account of himself is awe-inspiring, as Mason noted.
[67]B I, pp. 198:19–20, 226:31–227; II, p. 74:13. Although Macarius usually refers to complete sanctification, he mentions growth in sanctification in B II, p. 62:15 and partial sanctification in B II, p. 136:2.
[68]B I, p. 17:11–12.
[69]H 10:3; C I 3:4; GL, pp. 254:26–255:5; E 6:21.
[70]H 17:6.
[71]C X 1:2.
[72]C III 3:2.
[73]C VII 5.

[74]H 10:1; C I 3:4.
[75]B II, p. 54:9–17.
[76]GL, pp. 270–2.
[77]GL, p. 280:11–15.
[78]H 3:1–3 (E 5:1–3).
[79]GL, p. 273:11–18.
[80]GL, p. 272:12–14; cf. Dörries, op. cit., p. 267.
[81]B I, pp. 50–3.

6

Augustine and Western Controversies about Grace and Baptism

The development of the church's understanding of grace and baptism in the west was rather different from that in the east, largely because of the imposing figure of Augustine, whose views dominated Latin christianity for centuries. Once he had himself outgrown the drastically simplistic solution proposed by Manichaeism to the tangled problems of life in this world,[1] he devoted a considerable amount of his time and energy to combating other simplistic beliefs. One thing at least he learned from the Platonists, that nothing in this world is totally pure and limpid. It came to be a basic premiss in his thought that saints and sinners are mixed up in the church, and that even in the individual there is no clear demarcation between the saint and the sinner.

Towards the end of the fourth century Augustine became involved in a savage dispute with the Donatists, and one of the essential issues in the controversy was baptism. The Donatists baptised their converts, even if they had already been baptised as catholics; the catholics did not rebaptise their converts.

The Donatist position was traditional in Africa. Tertullian had argued that the baptism of heretics and schismatics was worthless. Unfortunately we do not possess the full statement of his position, which he only alludes to in the surviving *De Baptismo*,[2] but at least one of his concerns appears to be the need to safeguard the decisiveness of baptism. Christians practise only a single 'washing', unlike the Jews, because after baptism christians should not need any further cleansing; their baptism is not 'a plaything for sinners'. It is the church which has received the message of salvation; what goes on outside the church is clearly nothing to do with it, and so there cannot be a real, effective baptism there. Therefore heretical baptism is no baptism at all. Therefore, whatever rites converts to the church may have undergone elsewhere, their entry into the church is by way of the decisive, once and for all, cleansing of baptism.

The need to baptise converts from heresy and schism was maintained energetically by Cyprian, with the solid backing of the

African episcopate. Although the argument turns largely on the impossibility of an unworthy minister bestowing grace on anyone, the underlying presupposition is that the church is a 'closed garden': the church is the place of salvation, and outside the church there is no salvation. There is a clear boundary between them, which must not be blurred.[3]

Cyprian was an authority to whom the Donatists could and did appeal. They denied absolutely that grace could be imparted by an unworthy minister, and, as their manifesto at the public debate held in Carthage in 411 made clear, they regarded it as essential to maintain a sharp division between the church and the realm of darkness.[4]

Augustine sets himself stalwartly against the Donatist vision of the church as an assembly of the elect, manifestly separate from the corrupt mass of humanity. In his view, their position is totally incompatible with our Lord's parable about the wheat and the tares (Matthew 13:24–30). The wheat and the tares are to be allowed to grow together until the end of time. It is not even lawful for us, here and now, to presume to be able to distinguish between them, because people who are now wicked may well turn out to be among the elect, and vice versa.[5]

This necessarily entails a much less demanding understanding of the consequences of baptism. In Augustine's view the church contains people who are not yet spiritual, but they are 'protected' by baptism, so long as they are making some progress, even if they never succeed in becoming spiritual in this life.[6]

It is not particularly difficult for Augustine, then, to acknowledge that there can be a valid baptism outside the church. He is not impressed by the Donatists' anxiety about the quality of the baptiser, because in his view, whoever the human minister of the sacrament may be, and whatever condition he is in, the true baptiser is always Christ himself.[7] As far as baptism itself is concerned, it makes no difference at all what the subjective condition of any of the participants may be, though from the point of view of the salvation of the person being baptised it does make a crucial difference.[8] Outside the church baptism will not do anyone any good; it cannot impart the all-important gift of charity, which is the *proprium donum* of the catholic church.[9]

Augustine thus posits a radical separation between the objective fact of baptism and its subjective conditions and consequences in the baptised. And this involves at the same time a radical separation between the sacrament in itself and the working of the Holy Spirit or grace.[10] As a result, it is, as Augustine himself says, difficult to say quite what baptism, in itself, achieves. The 'good thief' was not baptised (though Augustine presumes that the will for baptism was present in him), but was saved;[11] others are baptised, but because they are not genuinely converted they are not saved. On the other hand, babies who are not capable of conversion are certainly not baptised in vain. It is all very mysterious.[12]

Augustine may be content to leave the relationship between the sacrament and grace mysterious, but there is one thing he is quite clear about: baptism belongs intrinsically to the catholic church, even when it is administered outside the church. Therefore all the baptised, whatever the circumstances of their baptism, are to be regarded as wearing the badge of Christ's army; if they are not in the church, they are to be viewed as 'deserters'.[13]

It is only a short step from there to saying that heretics and schismatics ought to be brought back into the church by coercion, if need be, and it is well known that Augustine became less and less scrupulous about the use of force against heretics. 'This is not the time to put questions to people who are not found in the church; they should either be put right and converted, or otherwise they should not complain if they are disciplined.' And if it is suggested that this is contrary to the freedom of choice involved in conversion, Augustine replies that people are encouraged to change their attitude quite freely by the threat of punishment.[14] The Lord's own parable (Luke 14:23) provides authority for compelling people to come in; once they are in, they will find reason to rejoice that they have come in. The Lord can turn unwilling guests into willing guests.[15]

The logic of Augustine's position seems to be something like this. The workings of grace are such that we cannot chart them, but at least being in the church and being baptised constitute a beginning. They do not guarantee salvation, but there is no salvation without them.[16] What happens afterwards is up to God.

At the opposite extreme from the Donatists we find another group of people who were apparently maintaining that absolutely anybody ought to be admitted to baptism, with no ethical restrictions whatsoever. They claimed that it was the wrong way round to give moral instruction before baptism; it should be given after baptism, and if people ignored it and continued in their immoral ways, at least they would be saved because of their faith, even if only by way of a gruesome purgatory.[17] This position, like that of the Donatists, though in a different way, is presumably a relic of an original strong doctrine of baptismal transformation: moral teaching should be given after baptism because it is the grace of baptism which makes moral achievement possible.[18]

This kind of doctrine was not acceptable to Augustine. His view of the church was certainly much less exclusive than that of the Donatists, but he was not prepared to allow the church to become so all-embracing that it would effectively be little more than the Roman empire at prayer. The mixture of good and bad people in the church must not be allowed to become so extreme that the discipline of the christian life would collapse entirely.[19] And this does not mean that he is trying to anticipate the Judgment, as he accused the Donatists of doing: 'We are not trying to root out the tares before their time, but we refuse to imitate the devil and sow extra tares.'[20] In normal cases candidates for baptism should be given moral instruction first, because salvation is not promised to faith alone without works. The baptised must live in a way which fits their baptism.[21] And this does not invalidate the Pauline principle of justification 'without works', because the 'works' are not an anterior condition required before justification, they are required as a conse-quence of justification.[22]

Augustine was not the only one who was unhappy with the preachers of justification by faith alone regardless of morals. They were also attacked in no uncertain terms by the British ascetic, Pelagius, in his *De Malis Doctoribus*.

Pelagius was even less reconciled to the worldliness of the church after the conversion of the empire than the Donatists were. He complains about a wholesale collapse of christian morality[23] and his message is deliberately aimed at those who are prepared to do something at least about the quality of their own lives, not at those who are fatalistic about it all.[24] He vigorously denounces the cruelties which were a routine part of the administration of Roman justice, even in the hands of christian officials,[25] and he is categorical in his condemnation of the unequal distribution of wealth and in his denial that wealth can, except in very unusual circumstances, be regarded as a gift from God, since, in his view, wealth is almost without exception simply the product of human injustice.[26]

Conversion ought to be immediately apparent in a radical change of life and attitudes; the difference between the works of believers and those of unbelievers should be as obvious as the difference between God and the devil. There can be absolutely no compromise between christian values and expectations and those of the world.[27] The church is supposed to be immaculate here and now.[28] *All* christians are supposed to keep *all* the commandments.[29] No allowances are to be made for individual circumstances.[30]

Pelagius is unsympathetic to people who plead that they *cannot* keep all the commandments; in his view, this can only mean that they *do not want* to keep them, because it is difficult and troublesome to break ourselves of our habits.[31] He accordingly undergirds his message with a demonstration that it is within our natural powers to avoid sin entirely; this is shown by the moral achievements of the pagan philosophers and even more by the righteous men of the

Old Testament.[32] Pelagius certainly left himself wide open to the charge that his doctrine made justification possible quite independently of Christ.[33] Strictly speaking he apparently did believe that it was possible to be righteous before becoming a disciple of Christ, so that what is new in Christ is the call to a perfection beyond mere righteousness.[34] Christian progress, in his view, is not progress towards righteousness, but progress from righteousness to perfection.[35]

In actual fact, Pelagius recognises that most of us had lost the freedom which we originally had; but he denies that this comes from any inherited taint. The overpowering tyranny of sin which people find 'in their members' comes from an original abuse of freedom, hardened into unbreakable habit.[35a] But everything is changed by our baptism.

> You should understand that through baptism you have been crucified with Christ, in being made a member of his Body. He affixed his guiltless body there, so that you would suspend your guilty body from vices. . . . 'That the body of sin might be destroyed, so that we should no longer be slaves to sin.' That is, so that all vices might be destroyed, because any individual vice is a member of sin, and all together they are the body of sin. Christ was not partially fixed to the cross, but totally. . . . 'Anyone who has died is justified from sin.' That is, separated from sin, because a dead person does not sin at all. So, 'anyone who is born from God does not sin'; someone who is crucified will hardly be able to sin, when all his limbs are gripped by pain.[36]

We are saved by grace in as much as we who were sinners were given righteousness in baptism.[37] But that means that sin is now over and done with. In his commentaries on the epistles of St Paul Pelagius points out over and over again that Paul refers to sin as being *in the past*,[38] and when Paul refers to the tension between flesh and spirit, between the law in the mind and the law in the flesh, Pelagius is confident that he cannot be referring to his own present condition.[39]

If we go on sinning, that shows that we are not under the domain of grace at all,[40] and the regime of grace is even more demanding than that of the Old Law.[41] Since Christ does not command the impossible, total obedience to his commandments must be both possible and obligatory[42] – and Pelagius likes to draw our attention to the places where grace is referred to in the New Testament as 'law'.[43] In baptism we received the 'power to overcome': our past sins are destroyed, and Christ has shown us by his teaching and by his example how we ought to live in the future.[44] What more do we want? If we really believed in God, we should never sin, either because the thought of all that he has done for us would fill us with such love that we could not bring ourselves to sin against him, or at least because we should be deterred by fear of the punishment he threatens sinners with. If we sin, it shows we do not really believe what he tells us.[45] Christians ought to live as if they *could not* sin.[46]

Pelagius knows that actually most christians do sometimes sin[47] and, in spite of his reputation for sinlessness,[48] he admits to being a sinner himself.[49] But he allows no room in his vision of the christian life for the real difficulties which most of us experience. In spite of everything, one of his associates, Caelestius, managed to maintain that it is easy to redirect our wills towards the good.[50] And Pelagius himself was extremely irritated by Augustine's account of the difficulties of his conversion in book X of the *Confessions*.[51]

But it was precisely the difficulties which impressed Augustine. His own conversion had been slow and tortuous. He knew from experience how difficult it is to come to any knowledge of the truth, and could sympathise with the difficulties of others.[52] Even inside the catholic church it is hard enough to hold an absolutely correct faith, believing nothing contrary to the truth, and Augustine seems to take it for granted that many christians in fact have some very inadequate ideas.[53] And discovering the truth is only the first problem. Augustine knew from his own experience how the will can dither and contradict itself and resist even when, in principle, the mind has assented to truth.[54]

As we have seen, Augustine abandoned the idea that baptism should normally involve a sudden, drastic change in us.[55] And he does not know quite what to put in its place; he can only admit that it is difficult to say just what baptism does. But the one thing he is absolutely sure of is that we are totally dependent on grace throughout the whole long process of our salvation.

He does not deny the Pelagian contention that sinlessness is possible, so long as it is understood that sinlessness would only be possible as a gift from God. But he does deny that there is any case of sinlessness on record, apart from Christ and his Mother.[56] And if the gift of sinlessness has not otherwise been given, this can only be because God, for his own inscrutable reasons, willed it to be so.[57] The people Pelagius alleged as examples of sinlessness are not anything of the kind; they can be called 'righteous', but this does not mean that they did not commit frequent slight sins.[58]

In Augustine's view the whole discussion of whether or not sinlessness is possible is rather beside the point. He does not care where or when we reach perfect righteousness; for him the only essential point is that wherever or whenever we reach it, we can only be made perfect by the grace of Jesus Christ.[59] But in fact there can be no question of perfection in this life, because perfection must result from perfect love of God, and we shall only love God perfectly when we see him perfectly.[60] Until then we are subject to the grim compulsion of sin, which lasts 'until our sickness is entirely healed and we receive such freedom that we shall be freely and happily constrained to live well and sin no more, just as we cannot abandon our desire to live happily'.[61] In this life, we shall always be defective to some extent.[62] No one can escape from the need to pray, 'Forgive us our trespasses'.[63]

Against Pelagius, Augustine argues that St Paul's remarks on the tension between flesh and spirit, between the two laws which we find in us, are addressed to the baptised, and cannot be regarded as characteristic only of our unredeemed past. 'He is not recalling the past, he is witnessing what is present.'[64] By the gift of the Spirit we do truly delight inwardly in God's law, but the other law 'in our members' can still not just oppose us but actually constrain us, until 'all that is old in us is changed and passes into the newness which increases in our inner man day by day'.[65] This is why it is important to recognise that not all sins are committed with self-assurance and pride; many are committed by people who weep and groan as they sin.[66] In our attempts to perform good deeds too we are liable to be overcome by a certain weariness induced by the seeming futility of what we do.[67]

Pelagius' concern is essentially to get people to do the right thing, and he is not much interested in their motives. Augustine, by contrast, is sceptical of the value of our deeds unless they are properly motivated. People who are merely cowed into being good by fear of punishment are not really virtuous at all, because they would prefer to sin, if only they could get away with it.[68] In Augustine's view, the only proper function of laws and threatened sanctions is to make us seek refuge in grace.[69] Essentially the law of God *is* love.[70] Without love, good deeds are worthless.[71] And since it is only God who inspires this love in us, the difference between the law of works and the law of grace can be summed up by saying that in the law of works God says to us, 'Do what I command you,' but in the law of faith we say to God, 'Give what you command.' So Augustine concludes that it is better 'to know who it is from whom you hope to receive what you have not got than to attribute to yourself what you have got.'[72]

In this life our righteousness is a process rather than an achievement.[73] We are not dealing with whatever powers unfallen men and women might have possessed, but with the man whom the robbers left half-dead by the wayside. Even if he is now safely in the inn, he is still only convalescent.[74]

The essential thing to remember, though, is that, however wounded we still are, we are in the hands of the doctor. The whole process, from beginning to end, is due to God's grace. It is he who makes us into believers.[75] It is he who creates a good will in us.[76] Even if we cannot yet make our good will very effective, it is God's grace which makes it possible for us to delight inwardly in his law; it is only this divine delight which can oust the base delights of concupiscence and stop us enjoying sin.[77] This initial conversion makes us pray for more help. One of the things Augustine finds objectionable in Pelagius' doctrine is that he leaves no room for this kind of praying for help.[78] As God increases our good will, it becomes a strong will, a fuller love, which allows us to move on from mere velleity to an effective will which enables us actually to do the good we desire.[79] In this way we truly merit eternal life, but our merits are entirely due to God's gift, even though our own will is involved. 'In crowning our merits, God is crowning his own gifts.'[80]

If this insistence on grace seems to endanger our free will, Augustine has no fears. It is precisely by giving us love that God changes our will into a good will, and what could be more free than pursuing what we love? *Trahit sua quemque voluptas*, as Augustine quotes Vergil as saying. And he is confident that anyone who is in love, or in any state of desire, will see what he means.[81] The whole law is summed up in the two precepts of love, which make no sense at all unless we are free, because love which is not freely given is not love at all. But it is precisely from God that love comes.[82]

Exactly as Macarius did, then, Augustine sees the process of our salvation as being the process whereby grace forms love in our wills. Like Macarius, he appreciates that the actual story of our christian development is slow and immensely unstraightforward. But the Pelagian controversy has forced Augustine to a much clearer awareness than any of the Greek fathers had of the absolute priority of God's grace. At every stage it is God who makes the first move. And, in the last analysis, the whole mysterious and seemingly precarious process is rooted in the sheer determination of God to save those whom he wants to save, for no other reason than that he wants to save them.[83]

Pelagius objected to the idea that God's favours might be given 'at random',[84] which is fine for those who are confident of their own powers. But for the ordinary, muddled and weak-willed, believer, it is far more consoling to believe that God does simply and unaccountably have mercy on whom he will have mercy. Augustine has no explanation of why God chooses those whom he chooses. He simply chooses them. It is his affair.[85]

There are many differences between Macarius and Augustine. Macarius supposed that christianity involved a drastic renunciation of the world,[86] while Augustine seems to have become more and more reconciled to the ordinary, rather worldly, christians who tried to be christians without abandoning their responsibilities to society. Augustine had all kinds of speculative interests and talents, of which Macarius was largely innocent. But in spite of the differences, their doctrines of grace are remarkably convergent. If Macarius' orthodoxy has been called into question because of his supposed involvement with Messalianism, it is worth suggesting that, judged by the standards of western orthodoxy, which were so heavily influenced by Augustine, Macarius appears to be considerably more orthodox than any of the orthodox opponents of Messalianism.

Abbreviations

Bapt.	De Baptismo
Civ. Dei	De Civitate Dei
Conf.	Confessions
DP	De Dono Perseverantiae
Ep. Ioh.	Tractatus in Epistolam Ioannis ad Parthos
Ev. Ioh.	Tractatus in Ioannis Evangelium
GLA	De Gratia et Libero Arbitrio
NG	De Natura et Gratia
PJH	De Perfectione Iustitiae Hominis
PS	De Praedestinatione Sanctorum
SL	De Spiritu et Littera

These works will be found in standard editions and translations of Augustine.

Notes

[1]On Manichaeism and Augustine's Manichaean period, see the magnificent ch. 5 of Peter Brown, *Augustine of Hippo*. London 1967.
[2]Tertullian, *Bapt.* 15.
[3]Cf. W. H. C. Frend, *The Donatist Church* (Oxford 1952), pp. 135–9. It is in the context of this controversy that Cyprian enunciates his famous statement that 'there is no salvation outside the church' (*Ep.* 73:21). Cf. also his *De Unitate* 11.
[4]PL 11:1408–14. Cf. Petilian's *Epistola ad Presbyteros* (Frend, op. cit., pp. 253–4).
[5]PL 38:298; *Civ. Dei* I 35.
[6]*Bapt.* I 15:24.
[7]*Ev. Ioh.* V–VI.
[8]*Bapt.* III 14:19, IV 10:16.
[9]*Ev. Ioh.* VI 13–14; *Bapt.* III 16:21.
[10]*Bapt.* III 16:21, VII 18:37.
[11]Augustine allows for 'baptism of desire' only in the case of explicit

faith, but some medieval writers envisaged the possibility of the salvation of unbelievers on the basis of their fidelity to the natural law (e.g. Langland, *Piers Plowman* B XII 277–90; cf. also W. A. Pantin, *The English Church in the Fourteenth Century* [Cambridge 1955], p. 131; J. I. Catto, ed., *History of the University of Oxford*, vol. I [Oxford 1984], p. 120). In the sixteenth century the issue was hotly debated in the wake of the discovery of the Americas. Cf. Francisco de Vitoria, *De eo ad quod tenetur homo cum primum venit ad usum rationis*, ed. with a useful introduction in Teofilo Urdanoz, ed., *Obras de Francisco de Vitoria* (Madrid 1960), pp. 1292–1375; for Domingo de Soto, see Karl Josef Becker, *Die Rechtfertigungslehre nach Domingo de Soto* (Rome 1967), pp. 42–52, 296–8, 388–90. The possibility of salvation for those who are unbelievers through no fault of their own is officially taught by the Second Vatican Council, *Lumen Gentium* 16.

[12]*Bapt.* IV 22:29–23:30.

[13]*Bapt.* I 3:4–4:5, 15:23, III 19:25, IV 10:16, VI 28:54.

[14]PL 43:317–18. It is in this connection that Augustine proposes his very dubious principle, 'Love and do what you like' (*Ep. Ioh.* 7:8), as if motive justified everything and *any* behaviour, however savage, could be treated as a legitimate manifestation of love. Cf. Herbert McCabe's comments on 'love is all you need' in *Law, Love and Language* (London 1968), ch. 1. On Augustine's attitude to coercive discipline, see Brown, op. cit., ch. 21.

[15]PL 43:722–3.

[16]No salvation outside the church: *Bapt.* IV 17:24, quoting Cyprian. No salvation without baptism: NG 8:9 (no one, not even an infant born in a place where there is no possibility of its being baptised, can be saved without baptism. If this seems hard, Augustine can only reply that it is very kind of God to save anyone at all: ibid. 5:5).

[17]PL 40:197–8.

[18]It may well have been the primitive practice in some circles to give moral instruction after baptism: cf. *Didascalia*, ed. cit., p. 147. And this would certainly be the logical implication of the belief that the candidate's ears must be opened before he can hear the Lord's word, and this 'opening' is associated with baptism in *Odes of Solomon* 15:4 and Ambrose, *De Sacramentis* I 1:2.

[19]PL 40:199.

[20]PL 40:218.

[21]PL 40:227.

[22]PL 40:211.

[23]PLS 1:1434–5.

[24]PLS 1:1507.

[25]PLS 1:1386.

[26]PLS 1:1389–90, 1406.

[27]PLS 1:1139, 1299, 1303, 1403.

[28]PLS 1:1304.

[29]PLS 1:1306, 1387.

[30]PLS 1:1297, 1377.

[31]PLS 1:1421–2, 1459–60.

[32]PL 30:16, 18, 19ff.

[33]Augustine, NG 2:2.

34PLS 1:1394–5.
35PLS 1:1401–2.
35aPLS 1:1143–4.
36PLS 1:1139.
37PLS 1:1137.
38E.g. PLS 1:1135, 1140.
39PLS 1:1145, 1539, 1542–3.
40PLS 1:1140.
41PLS 1:1431, 1441.
42PLS 1:1376, 1461; PL 30:16.
43E.g. PLS 1:1145, 1286, 1413, 1431, 1441.
44PLS 1:1137, 1140, 1180, 1304.
45PLS 1:1291, 1294, 1424.
46PLS 1:1138.
47PLS 1:1460.
48PLS 1:1458.
49PLS 1:1419–21, 1458.
50Augustine, PJH 6:12.
51Augustine, DP 20:53.
52PL 42:174.
53*Bapt.* III 14:19.
54Cf. *Conf.* VIII 8–9:19–21.
55Brown, op. cit., pp. 368–9, brings out well that it is Augustine who is the innovator in this matter, and that he himself had earlier been much closer to the older, more dramatic, belief. For the development of Augustine's thought, see J. Patout Burns, *The Development of Augustine's Doctrine of Operative Grace.* Paris 1980.
56SL 2:2–4; NG 36:42.
57SL 5:7.
58NG 38:45.
59NG 68:82.
60SL 36:64; PJH 3:8.
61PJH 4:9.
62NG 38:45.
63PJH 7:16.
64NG 53:61, 55:65; PJH 6:12.
65SL 14:26.
66NG 29:33.
67PJH 8:18.
68SL 8:13, 14:26.
69SL 9:15–10:16.
70SL 17:29.
71GLA 18:37.
72SL 13:22.
73PJH 8:18.
74NG 43:50.
75SL 33–4; GLA 5:10; PS 8:16.
76GLA 15:31, 16:32.
77SL 3:5–4:6, 16:28, 29:51.

[78]SL 13:22; NG 18:20; GLA 14:28.
[79]GLA 15:31, 16:32.
[80]GLA 6:15; PL 33:880.
[81]*Ev. Ioh.* 26:3–4; the quotation is from Vergil, *Eclogues* 2:65.
[82]GLA 18:37.
[83]DP 7:14, 8:19 etc.
[84]PLS 1:1150.
[85]PS 6:11, 8:16 etc.
[86]C VII 1:3.

7

Monastic Rules in the West

St Augustine, as we have seen, came increasingly to rely on external constraints and discipline, and this can be connected with his increasing awareness of the frailty and the unfathomable complexity of the human heart. Our hearts contain an abyss of weakness of which we may be quite unaware ourselves, but which is not hidden from God,[1] who is more intimately present in us than we are ourselves.[2] We cannot control our own hearts or thoughts, and so the mystery of ourselves is something we cannot really do very much about; we must leave it to God, who 'works in us both to will and to do'.[3]

In the development of monasticism, particularly in the west, we can see a similar conviction at work, and a similar increase in the reliance on external discipline.

At first, it seems, people could become monks in the Egyptian desert without putting themselves under any kind of supervision. Two young strangers came to see Macarius of Egypt one day, wanting to be monks; he showed them how to build a cell and how to weave baskets, and then left them to get on with it. They never came back to him for advice, nor did they go to anyone else. Eventually Macarius' curiosity got the better of him and he went to pay them a visit, and found that they were both doing admirably. There is not the slightest hint that they *ought* to have been subject to the guidance of some more mature monk.[4] It is the discipline of 'staying in your cell' which forms the monk, even without any great feats of asceticism.[5]

But, as Poemen pointed out, it is possible to spend a hundred years in your cell without ever learning anything.[6] And so, alongside the other typical desert virtues of humility and discernment, we find obedience to a spiritual father coming to the fore and even being acclaimed as the greatest virtue of all.[7]

At the same time there was a growing pressure upon people to practise a more impersonal form of obedience, obedience to monastic norms. This was in part simply an inevitable consequence of the fact that successive generations left behind them a deposit of practical wisdom; for instance norms for fasting came to be part of the monastic tradition.[8] But norms like this, which served to temper people's immoderate enthusiasm for austerity, were joined by much less innocent norms, so that it came to be much harder for anyone to give realistic advice to the weaker brethren, as such advice would almost inevitably be insufficiently 'monastic'.[9] Eventually the monastic life as a whole comes to be seen as governed by 'proper procedure'.[10]

In the west 'proper procedure' wins an almost total victory. Cassian re-interprets the traditional monastic virtue of discernment (*diakrisis*) to mean almost the opposite of what it meant originally. Far from being the virtue which enables an individual to respond creatively and accurately to the various unpredictable circumstances in which he finds himself, for Cassian it consists essentially in not trusting your own judgment.[11] It means following the advice of the brethren and the rules of the elders (*instituta maiorum*).[12] And both these recommended norms are well on the way to becoming coterminous with 'custom' or established practice.[13] The mood of Cassian's monasticism is very similar to the intellectual mood of his contemporary, Vincent of Lérins, expressed in his famous canon of orthodoxy, requiring us to hold fast to 'what has been believed everywhere, always and by everybody'.[14] A largely mythical sense of the weight and coherence of 'tradition' has ousted the need for, and indeed any toleration of, individual responsibility and originality.

It is not surprising that the next stage in the development of western monasticism was the codification of monastic tradition in the form of Rules, and from the early sixth century onwards western monasticism is unthinkable without monastic Rules. From the eighth century onwards monks can simply be referred to as 'regulars' (*regulares*), people living by a Rule.[15]

Of the early western Rules one of the most striking is the Rule of the Master, which is of considerable historical importance too, as it is a major source of the Rule of St Benedict.[16] The exact circumstances of its composition are not known, nor is it known who the 'Master' is, but it was probably written early in the sixth century somewhere near Rome.[17]

The Master is unflinchingly confident that his words are the words of God. Each section of his Rule takes the form of a question followed by 'the Lord's answer through the Master', and he accordingly consigns to Hell anyone who does not obey the Rule.[18] But he has little confidence in anyone else's judgment, leaving almost nothing to the discretion of the individual monk or even to that of the abbot.[19] In principle, as a glance at the list of chapters reveals, the Rule is meant to tell everybody exactly what they are supposed to be doing at any hour of the day or night in any circumstances.

The monks are subjected to continual supervision to make sure that they cannot commit any faults unobserved; each group of ten monks is 'guarded' by two 'provosts', and the reason why so few monks have two people in charge of them is that if, for some reason, the group has occasion to split up, both parties can still be supervised. It is only with great circumspection that any monk can be sent off on his own without anyone to watch him.[20] Even guests are to be spied upon by day and by night to make sure that they do not steal anything, and at night they are to be locked up.[21] A very curt chapter encourages the monks to be kind to those who are sick, but this is preceded by a much longer chapter requiring that anyone who claims to be sick must be subjected to a variety of tests to ensure that he really is sick; he is, for a start, to be given so little to eat that unless he is actually ill he will be driven from his bed by sheer hunger.[22] To make sure that the monks listen to the reading of the Rule in the refectory, the abbot is to stop the reading every now and then and ask people without warning what has just been read.[23]

A certain amount of abbatial snooping is occasionally found in earlier monastic literature,[24] and it was generally expected that the ruler of a cenobium would wield a more positive discipline than would be suitable among hermits,[25] but even so the Master seems to be an unusually untrusting pedagogue. He would never be in the position of, say, abba Agathon who, we are told, once had two disciples living with him and who plainly did not know anything about how they regulated their lives until 'one day' (casually enough) he asked them; and even then he contented himself with a brief comment on what they told him.[26]

The grounds for the Master's reluctance to allow his monks any freedom of initiative and for his insistence on continual supervision can be found in his profoundly negative view of the human will. He very nearly identifies free will with the will of the flesh, and sees its main function in practice as being to deliver us over to the devil.[27] Salvation is accordingly seen primarily in terms of the denial of our own will, so that we walk 'by someone else's judgment and commandment'.[28] Where Cassian sees the monk as one who has come out from under the law to live under the grace of the gospel,[29] the Master regards the monastic life as precisely the way to escape from a diabolical freedom into a state of subjection to the law.[30] Precisely because of the constraints of the cenobitic life the Master can more or less identify it as being the 'narrow way' which leads to salvation, as against the 'broad way' of those who live without such constraints.[31] The novice is faced with a very simple choice: either he must 'establish himself with God' by making monastic profession or he must 'return forthwith to the devil' by returning to the world.[32]

The Master's doctrine clearly has some connection with the older monastic belief that 'the human will is a bronze wall between us and God',[33] but the older tradition does not seem to be attacking free will as such, but only self-will and stubbornness in insisting on our own desires. This kind of self-will is contrasted with the proper christian attitude of disburdening ourselves of our cares[34] and with obedience to our own conscience.[35] As we should expect, there is a more pervasive emphasis on obedience and on not following one's own will in cenobitic circles, but the reason given for this in the *Logos Asketikos* associated with St Basil is that the unity and coherence of the monastic community will be endangered if the monks simply do what they individually want to do.[36]

The Master does not seem to be unduly concerned to foster any sense of personal responsibility among his monks, nor does he appear to expect that their motives will mature very far. The monks are to hand over to the abbot complete responsibility even for their souls; at the judgment it is he who will have to answer for whatever they have done, whether good or bad, provided they have always been totally obedient to him.[37]

Fear of punishment, whether temporal or eternal, is an ever-present motive in the Rule, and the Master interestingly differs from Cassian in his expectation of how the monks may grow beyond this fear. At the culmination of the 'steps of humility' Cassian says that charity will cast out fear, so that 'all that you used to observe out of fear you will begin to keep naturally, as it were, without difficulty, not with a view to escaping punishment, but from love of the good in itself and from delight in the virtues'.[38] The Master takes over this passage, with its reference to charity casting out fear, but he significantly makes two alterations: he expands 'naturally' into 'naturally, from force of habit' (*ex consuetudine*) and in place of 'love of the good in itself' he says, 'from love of good custom in itself' (*amore ipsius consuetudinis bonae*).[39] Acclimatisation to the routines of monastic discipline seems to have taken the place of love of the good. There is, I think, only one place in which the Master speaks of people wanting to live in the monastery out of love of God, and it is suggestive that he immediately goes on to qualify this in terms precisely of 'discipline and the norms of holy living'.[40]

The degree of the Master's scepticism and even cynicism about his monks' motivation becomes clear in the directives he gives about the appointment of a new abbot. It is the dying abbot who appoints his successor and, in the meantime, he is not to appoint any officials in the monastery who might appear to be heirs apparent; and the reason for this is that he wants all the monks to compete with one another in good deeds and in humility, in the hope of becoming the next abbot.[41] It would be difficult to imagine a more bizarre way of promoting humility than by this frank appeal to ambition!

If the monastery is to be 'a school of the Lord's service',[42] it is clearly important to ensure that the 'master' (one is tempted to say 'headmaster') who is in charge of it[43] is someone who can be relied upon to maintain the necessary discipline. Pachomius evidently thought that his monks had the right to choose their own superior,[44] but the author of the Rule of the Master is not prepared to take this risk; as we have seen, the new abbot is appointed by the old abbot on his deathbed, and the monks are to accept him as having been appointed by God himself.[45]

St Benedict, in his Rule, reverts to the practice of electing abbots, but he too is patently worried that the monks may elect the wrong man, someone who will 'consent to their faults', and so he introduces various complications into the electoral procedure. If the vote is not unanimous, it is not necessarily the majority vote which carries the day; even 'a small part of the community' is to prevail, if they are voting *saniore consilio* (with sounder judgment). And even a unanimous vote can be overthrown, if need be, by the intervention of the bishop or neighbouring abbots or indeed anyone else in the vicinity.[46] Thereafter it remains constant in western monasticism to devise some way or another of ensuring that a majority vote will not succeed in producing an unsuitable superior;[47] the Dominicans in the thirteenth century appear to be the first to abandon this precaution in favour of a straightforward election in which the candidate who secures more than half the votes straight away becomes Master of the Order.[48]

In other ways too Benedict mitigates, but does not abandon, the Master's attitude of suspicion towards his monks. He makes much less provision than the Master does for keeping the brethren under supervision, but he requires the abbot to search the monks' beds frequently to make sure they are not accumulating any private property,[49] and he also directs that one or two senior monks are to be appointed to go round the monastery at the times when the monks are supposed to be reading to make sure that they are not wasting their time or chatting to each other.[50] On the basis of this latter regulation, later monasticism developed official monastery spies (the *circatores*) of a most sinister kind.[51]

Benedict is far more modest as a legislator than the Master was, and his Rule is far more humane and flexible; but it still seems to presuppose that the monks need to be scared into behaving themselves,[52] though Benedict is more optimistic than the Master was about their motivation changing from fear to love. He quotes Cassian's 'steps of humility' more or less in the form given by the Master, but he re-introduces 'love of Christ' as well as 'good custom'

into the final stage.[53] Benedict reproduces the Master's critique of
freelance monks who do not live under a Rule and an abbot, but
he seems genuinely appreciative of those who eventually progress
from the cenobitic life to a life of solitude. He regards his Rule as
no more than a Rule for beginners; it is not meant to be a sufficient
guide for the whole of a monk's life.[54]

The Rule of St Benedict did not immediately oust all other Rules;
it was only gradually that it came to be *the* Rule for western monks,
and its eventual ascendancy was brought about to some extent as
a result of a deliberate campaign, initially launched by Charlemagne, to standardise monastic life. This meant that there was a
greater emphasis on uniformity than was perhaps intended by St
Benedict. It is typical of the monastic reform undertaken by St
Benedict of Aniane, Charlemagne's chief collaborator in this matter,
to find a list of directives beginning with this chapter:

> First of all there is to be no variety among the men of this
> profession [i.e. among monks] in anything, except where this is
> prevented by some real impossibility.[55]

And this call to uniformity is at the same time a call to greater
strictness of observance, which is intended both to discipline the
more tepid monks and to restrain the imprudent enthusiasm of
others, as well as fostering unity of heart. And it is recognised that
the Rule itself does not provide enough detail to secure this kind of
uniformity, so more elaborate legislation is provided to cover the
monks' life and observances more thoroughly.[56]

Essentially the same programme is adopted a little later on in
England in the late tenth century, as we learn from the proemium
to the *Regularis Concordia*.[57]

As a result of this insistence on the Rule of St Benedict as the
one Rule which all monks should follow, an insistence which was
not at first wholly in accordance with the instincts of the monks
themselves,[58] the Rule came to be seen no longer as a guide for
beginners, but as a sufficient basis for a whole christian life. The
eleventh-century *Liber Tramitis* from Farfa is a good example of the
attitude inspired by the Cluniac reform. In the prologue the author
presents the reform as calling monks back to the pristine observances laid down by the fathers and especially St Benedict, which
will provide the antidote to the current decline in christian standards. The model of Cluny is to be followed exactly and minutely,
and it is faithful observance of the resulting customary which will
lead to eternal bliss. Sincere fidelity to the monastic life, as codified
in this way, will make the monk 'lovable to God and attractive to
other people' and will win him the revelation of 'the secrets of

heaven'; but anyone who abandons proper monastic observance will be abandoned by God.[59]

At the origins of the Cistercian reform of Benedictine monachism at the very end of the eleventh century we find an even more emphatic desire to return to strict and primitive observance.

[The founders of Cîteaux] while they were still at Molesme, very often used to talk to each other, under the inspiration of God's grace, about the way in which the Rule of St Benedict, the father of monks, was being violated. They used to complain sadly about this, seeing that they and all the other monks had solemnly promised to keep this Rule, but were in fact doing nothing of the kind, thereby knowingly incurring a charge of perjury. Because of this, on the authority of the papal legate, they sought refuge in this wilderness, so that they could fulfil their profession by observing the holy Rule.[60]

The earliest Cistercian legislation is primarily concerned with the implementation of this programme of strict observance. Later on they had to make decisions about the relationship between Cîteaux and other Cistercian monasteries, and their laws make it clear what their essential concern is. The mother house makes no material claims on any other monasteries, but it does retain the right to supervise their regular observance, 'so that if – God forbid! – they try to deviate even a little from our holy purpose and from the observance of our holy Rule, they may be able to return to rightness of life by means of our concern'. There is also to be complete uniformity in the interpretation of the Rule, so that all Cistercian monasteries will agree exactly in their observances with those followed at Cîteaux.[61]

That this carefully and thoroughly regulated way of life was envisaged as a protection against human frailty is shown by the Cistercians' reaction to the various less structured forms of religious life being espoused by an increasing number of people in the twelfth century. St Bernard seems to see little but dangers in any form of solitary life; people adopt the eremitical life thinking they will attain to greater spiritual heights, but in fact they only become lax and tepid.[62] Throughout the twelfth century it seems to have been the Cistercians who were most opposed to new 'apostolic' movements,[63] and it was almost certainly Cistercians who intimidated a group of hermits at Oigny, making them abandon their 'dangerous' way of life and put themselves under a rule and an abbot.[64] In the thirteenth century we find some Cistercians expressing anxiety about St Dominic's practice of sending his young men out to preach.[65]

The Cistercians had a profound influence not only on monastic reform but also on reformed congregations of canons. It is a Cistercian ethos which we find, for instance, in the constitutions of the Praemonstratensians; it is admirably expressed in the prologue which the Praemonstratensians added at some stage in the twelfth century, which explains that the reason for the existence of the Book of Customs is to ensure that everyone knows exactly what he is supposed to be doing. Meticulous fidelity even to the smallest details will facilitate uniformity of observance which in turn will foster and express unity of heart and soul in the Lord.[66]

The danger with this emphasis on uniform and strict observance is obviously that religious life could degenerate into mere, hollow formalism, and it is not surprising that the charge of 'Pharisaism' was levelled against the Cistercians in the thirteenth century.[67] But we must not forget that the monastic routine was regarded as embodying, precisely, the christian life, and there is nothing obviously wrong in supposing that by *behaving* like christians we gradually *become* new creatures in Christ. We rejoin here the eminently sane Augustinian principle that human minds and wills are far too erratic to provide a dependable basis for the christian life; it is on the objective fact of the church that we must build, leaving it to the grace of God to perfect people's inner conversion.

And there are certain manifest advantages to be gained from the regulated life of a monastic community. Already Cassian had pointed out that the 'constraints' of cenobitic life relieve the individual of practical worries and responsibilities and from the random interference of other people, so that there is much less to prevent inner peace and tranquillity.[68] It is on this basis that St Bernard claims that there is nothing to prevent monks from 'tasting and seeing that the Lord is good'.[69] A willing acceptance of monastic discipline actually engenders 'freedom of spirit'.[70]

According to the Augustinian tradition, inherited by the monks, freedom is not something we have by right from the outset, it is something which grows in us gradually as we are freed from the tyranny of the old Adam, until, in heaven, we reach the 'blessed constraint' of not being able to sin, which is perfect freedom.[71] And the discipline of monastic observance is a radical way of denying power to our fallen instincts. The pessimistic view of monastic life as largely a way of keeping people out of mischief can be subsumed into a much more positive view of monastic life as providing space within which the new creature in Christ can come to maturity. If the cell is a tomb, it is also a womb.[72]

Precisely because the unity of the monastery is vested in the externals of monastic life, there is no pressure on the monks to be inwardly uniform.[73] The monks, like Augustine, having secured the objective minimum, can allow people to develop inwardly in their own time and in their own way. The observances which, at first, are simply an external constraint on the beginner, become delightful to him as he becomes accustomed to them – the Rule of the Master had already said as much – but they continue to shape the external life of the more mature monk, even though they now serve a very different purpose from a subjective point of view.[74]

The common observances provide an objective point of reference, which allows the monks to relax with themselves and with each other; the monastic life as a whole, undisturbed by individual quirks, becomes both a unique 'school of charity' and a continual drama of charity. The love of God and the love of neighbour are inextricably entwined in the life of inner unity of heart and outward uniformity of observance, so that the monastery can be described as 'not an earthly paradise, but a heavenly one'.[75]

Bibliography and Abbreviations

Carta Caritatis, ed. Canisius Noschitzka, *Analecta Sacri Ordinis Cisterciensis* 6 (1950), pp. 16–22.

CCM   *Corpus Consuetudinum Monasticarum*, ed. K. Hallinger. Siegburg 1963ff.

Parvum Exordium, ed. Noschitzka, art. cit., pp. 6–16.

Regularis Concordia, ed. Thomas Symons. London 1953.

RM   *Rule of the Master*, ed. Adalbert de Vogüé (SC 105–7). Paris 1964–5; English tr. Luke Eberle (Cistercian Studies Series 6). Kalamazoo 1977.

RSB   *Rule of St Benedict*, text and tr. ed. Timothy Fry. Collegeville 1981

Notes

[1]PL 36:473.
[2]*Conf.* III 6:11.
[3]*De Dono Persev.* 13:33.
[4]AP Macarius Aeg. 33.
[5]AP Moses 6, Arsenius 11, Paphnutius 5.
[6]AP Poemen 96.
[7]AP Pambo 3, Rufus 2.
[8]AP Poemen 31.
[9]Cf. AP Poemen 22.
[10]Cf. AP Herakleios (notice the use of the word ἀκολουθία).
[11]*Conf.* 2:10. Basil goes even further: if a religious raises any questions about the superior's way of running things, he is falling into the 'passion of discernment' (πάθος τῆς διακρίσεως) (*Reg. Fus.* 48).
[12]Cassian, *Conf.* 2:5.
[13]Cf. Philip Rousseau, *Ascetics, Authority and the Church* (Oxford 1978), pp. 189–98 (though Rousseau exaggerates the novelty of the 'need for

consultation', which is already present in Athanasius, *Life of Anthony* 16, for instance).

[14]Vincent of Lérins, *Commonitorium* 2:3.

[15]Cf. Du Cange, *Glossarium Mediae et Infimae Latinitatis* s.v. *Regulares* III.

[16]There has been much debate about the relationship between RM and RSB, but the priority of RM is now generally conceded; cf. Timothy Fry, ed., *The Rule of St Benedict* (Collegeville 1981), pp. 79–83.

[17]Adalbert de Vogüé, ed., *La Règle du Maître*, Sources Chrétiennes no. 105 (Paris 1964), I, pp. 221–33.

[18]RM Pr 21.

[19]Cf. Brian Davies, 'The Rule of the Master and Christian Practice', *Downside Review* 97 (1978), p. 36.

[20]RM 11.

[21]RM 79:1–22.

[22]RM 69–70.

[23]RM 24:34–7.

[24]E.g. Theodoret, *Hist. Rel.* 5:3, 10:4.

[25]Cf. AP Isaac of Cellia 2.

[26]AP Agathon 20.

[27]RM Thp 6, 24–34; 7:43; 74; 90:51, 90–1. He only once refers to 'good free will', in RM 44:18.

[28]RM 7:47–52; notice the Master's use of Psalm 43 in RM 90:33–45.

[29]Cassian, *Conf.* 21:7.

[30]RM Th 19–23.

[31]RM 7:22–50.

[32]RM 88:6.

[33]Cf. AP Poemen 54.

[34]Cf. AP Sisoes 43.

[35]Cf. Esaias 11:102.

[36]PG 31:881–8. On the authorship, see Jean Gribomont in P. J. Fedwick, *Basil of Caesarea, Christian, Humanist, Ascetic* (Toronto 1981), I, pp. 42–3.

[37]RM 7:53–6. Contrast the attitude of Pachomius' successor, Theodore, *Catechesis* 3 (Corpus Scriptorum Christianorum Orientalium 160, p. 45:23–6).

[38]Cassian, *Inst.* 4:39,3.

[39]RM 10:87–90.

[40]RM 83:3.

[41]RM 92.

[42]RM Ths 45.

[43]The abbot is to be both father and schoolmaster (*magister*): RM 2:24.

[44]First Greek *Life of Pachomius* 114, and cf. ibid., 117.

[45]RM 92:73–93:5.

[46]RSB 64:1–6.

[47]Cf. K. Hallinger, 'Reg. Ben. 64 und die Wahlgewohnheiten des 6–12 Jh.', in the Festschrift for R. Hanslik, *Wiener Studien*, Beiheft 8 (Vienna/Cologne 1977), pp. 109–30; A. H. Thomas, *De oudste Constituties van de Dominicanen* (Louvain 1965), pp. 208–16.

[48]Dominican Primitive Constitutions II 11 (Thomas, op. cit., pp. 348–9). Cf. Simon Tugwell, 'Dominican Risks', *Dominican Ashram* 2 (1983), pp.

182–4 (there is a 'not' missed out before 'surprising' in the last line of p. 182, and a whole line is missed out on p. 183, but without totally ruining the sense).

⁴⁹RSB 55:16.

⁵⁰RSB 48:17–18.

⁵¹For early examples of this official, cf. CCM I, pp. 103–4; *Regularis Concordia*, ed. cit., p. 56, with n 3. There is a singularly full and alarming account of the *circator* at St Victor (E. Martène, *De antiquis Ecclesiae Ritibus* (Bassani 1788), III, pp. 276–7).

⁵²Cf. Brian Davies, 'The Rule of Saint Benedict and Christian Practice', *Theology* 84 (1981), pp. 21–9.

⁵³RSB 7:69.

⁵⁴RSB 73, and cf. 1:3 on becoming a hermit after training in the cenobium.

⁵⁵CCM I, p. 341.

⁵⁶CCM I, pp. 312–13.

⁵⁷Ed. cit., pp. 1–9.

⁵⁸Cf. Jean Leclercq, 'Le Monachisme du Haut Moyen-Age', in *Théologie de la Vie Monastique* (Paris 1961), p. 439.

⁵⁹CCM X, pp. 4–5.

⁶⁰*Parvum Exordium* 3. On the problem of early Cistercian sources, see David Knowles, *Great Historical Enterprises* (London 1963), pp. 199–222.

⁶¹*Carta Caritatis* 1–2.

⁶²Bernard, *Serm. in Circumcisione* 3:6ff; *Super Cantica* 64:4. Cf. Jean Leclercq, 'L'érémitisme et les Cisterciens', in *L'Eremitismo in Occidente nei secoli XI e XII* (Miscellanea del Centro di Studi Medievali IV. Milan 1965), pp. 573–6. The letter cited is 541 in *Sancti Bernardi Opera* VIII. Rome 1977.

⁶³Cf. H. Grundmann, *Religiöse Bewegungen im Mittelalter* (Darmstadt 1970), pp. 174–5.

⁶⁴Pl. F. Lefèvre and A. H. Thomas, ed., *Le Coutumier de l'Abbaye d'Oigny en Bourgogne* (Louvain 1976), pp. viii, 43.

⁶⁵MOPH XXII, p. 10. For other similar reactions to the Dominicans, cf. Simon Tugwell, *Early Dominicans* (New York 1982), pp. 135, 137. Cf. Jacques de Vitry's comments on the Franciscans: R. B. C. Huygens, ed., *Lettres de Jacques de Vitry* (Leiden 1960), pp. 131–2.

⁶⁶See Simon Tugwell, op. cit., pp. 456–7, for a translation of this text, with the parallel Dominican text; for some comments suggesting that, though the Dominicans adopted the text, they were not really in sympathy with it, see ibid., pp. 21–2.

⁶⁷MOPH XXII, p. 10; Hugh of St Cher, *Postillae in Bibliam* (Venice 1703), VI 239.

⁶⁸Cassian, *Conf.* 19:3, 5–6.

⁶⁹Bernard, *De Diversis* 9:4.

⁷⁰Bernard, *In Ascensione* 3:6.

⁷¹Cf. Bernard, *De Gratia et Libero Arbitrio*, especially ch. 4 and 7.

⁷²William of St Thierry refers to the cell as a 'womb' in *Golden Epistle* 34.

⁷³Bernard, *De Diversis* 42:4.

⁷⁴William of St Thierry, op. cit., 45, 97 and cf. ibid., 187–90.

[75]William of St Thierry, op. cit., 75; id., *De Natura et Dignitate Amoris* 9:25.

8

Two Spiritual Fathers in the East: Barsanuphius and John

While monastic spirituality was becoming more disciplinarian and rigid in the west, two very remarkable monks were helping to keep alive in the east the traditions of a more fluid and flexible monastic ethos. In the first half of the sixth century – the half-century which witnessed the composition of the Rule of the Master and the Rule of St Benedict – two recluses who lived at Thavatha, a few miles south of Gaza, were much in demand as spiritual fathers and advisers, Barsanuphius and John, known respectively as 'The Great Old Man' and 'The Other Old Man'. Some eight hundred and fifty letters survive from them to all sorts of different correspondents, giving us a unique picture of the way in which spiritual fatherhood could operate during this period.

We have already seen in an earlier chapter how the emphasis on humility, which came to be typical of Egyptian monasticism, made it difficult for people to accept the role of teacher. Barsanuphius and John resolve the problem in a rather unexpected way, by claiming the authority of God himself for their words. Over and over again throughout the collection we find claims like this: 'I write all these things not from my own will, but at the bidding of the Holy Spirit.'[1] Divine inspiration even extends to Barsanuphius' secretary, who is assured by him that the Holy Spirit will prevent him from making so much as the slightest mistake in writing down what the Old Man has told him to write, even if he is given a thousand words at a time.[2] In one letter Barsanuphius claims that one of his correspondents will find 'the whole of the Old and New Testaments' in his series of letters, so that he will not need any other books at all; meditating on the letters will be as good as meditating on scripture.[3] But it is clear that the claimed inspiration does not simply reside in the fact that the Old Man is passing on scriptural doctrine; he expressly claims verbal inspiration for his own writing.[4]

The claim to inspiration allows the spiritual father to disclaim any personal competence. 'I did not say anything of myself; I prayed and then said whatever God gave me confidence to say. It is not because I am capable of anything myself that this answer was given through me; there was a need and God opened the ass's mouth.'[5] Barsanuphius can present himself as a good-for-nothing wretch, who cannot even rule himself, and who can only be regarded as moved by pride if he presumes to give advice to anyone else; yet, fool that he is, charity obliges him to respond to those who seek his advice – and this charity is God's doing. This is why he overreaches himself and gives advice which he is not qualified to give.[6] He does not wish to be anyone's teacher.[7]

If it is charity which constrains someone to give advice to others, in spite of his unworthiness, it is faith that makes it possible to do so without undue anxiety. A layman who had been asked to become a monk and the superior of the monastery at the same time was reassured by John that he need not be afraid to undertake such a responsibility:

> Say to them, 'Since the Lord Jesus Christ is looking after you, who said, "I will not leave you orphans, I will come to you", pay attention to yourselves in all humility and love for God'. . . . Tell them not to hide their thoughts (*logismoi*) from you . . . and if any of them reveals his thought to you, say in your own thought, 'Lord, if there is anything which will help the salvation of his soul, grant that I may say it to him, and that I may speak your word, not my own.' And then say whatever comes to you, telling yourself, 'This is not my word, for it is written "If anyone speaks, let it be as oracles of God that he speaks." '[8]

In another letter we see John trying to combine humility about himself and confidence in his own advice. His correspondent had already received advice from Barsanuphius, so John tells him to follow it, because Barsanuphius' words come from experience and from the Holy Spirit. 'I too have said some nonsense or other to you, but it did not come from practical experience or the Spirit. . . . Even so my conscience bears witness that I did not wish to lead you astray at all in anything, and for this reason I believe that neither my words nor my advice are harmful to you.'[9]

The quality of the reply given by a spiritual father does not depend on the competence or holiness of the father, but on the condition of the person seeking advice.[10] The reason why it is essential for people to consult the elders is not necessarily that the elders are in themselves wiser or holier, but because it is a gesture of humility, which will win God's blessing on people's undertakings.[11]

It is not from a position of superiority that the fathers address their correspondents, but from a position of profound identification. 'I write to you as to my own soul,' writes Barsanuphius to one of his clients.[12] With marvellous tact and gentleness he writes to a sick, worried old monk:

All that God requires of you is thanksgiving, patience and prayer for the forgiveness of your sins. But now see how proud I am! Mocked by the demons, I seem to think that I possess a Godlike charity! I have so far lost control of myself to say to you, 'I will carry half of your burden now, and for the future, God can help us again.' I speak madly. I know I am weak and powerless and devoid of any good deed. But my shamelessness does not let me despair. I have a master who is kind and merciful and loving towards us, and he reaches out his hand to sinners until their last breath.

The old monk evidently does not appreciate the delicacy of Barsanuphius' offer, so Barsanuphius writes to him again:

God knows how I hold myself to be dust and ashes, a mere nothing. If I say things which are beyond me and beyond my power, it is because I am stirred by the love of Christ. . . . You did not understand why I said to you that I am carrying half of your burden. I was making you my colleague. I did not say, 'I will carry a third', leaving you to carry more than me. And I said what I did to banish self-love too; I did not say I would carry two thirds, making myself out to be stronger than you. That would have been vainglory. And I did not say, 'I will carry the whole thing', because that belongs to the perfect, who have become Christ's brothers, who laid down his life for us. . . . What is more, if I had spoken otherwise than I did, I should have banished you from the spiritual work. I am not vain enough to ascribe the whole thing to myself, nor was I too mean to allow you some part in it. If we are brothers, let us divide our Father's substance equally. . . . But if you want to put the whole burden on to me, out of obedience I shall receive it.[13]

The spiritual father, driven by charity to involve himself in the spiritual struggles of other people and encouraged by faith to take such a risk, even though he feels himself to be at least as much a sinner as anyone else, is very far indeed from being a professional 'spiritual expert', who can tell people exactly what is going on. Precisely because they depend on the inspiration of the Holy Spirit, their interventions in other people's lives are characterised by exactly the randomness which Hermas believed to be the mark of the true prophet; unlike those whom Hermas stigmatised as false prophets, they have no wisdom 'on tap'.

According to Barsanuphius, some people keep running after the old men, hoping no doubt for words of wisdom, and they receive nothing; meanwhile someone else, who has made no move to approach a spiritual father, finds that the fathers have been sent to him by God.[14] Answers have to be given when God sees fit, not precisely when the questioner wants them.[15] And the answers will not always be of the kind that the questioner wanted. The spiritual father may give advice when a precept was asked for, or he may give a precept when advice was asked for; sometimes he may speak without being asked at all.[16]

The spiritual father represents both the immediacy and the elusiveness of God's providence in our various situations. This is why, according to John, it is right to consult only one father on any one matter (which, of course, does not mean that one may not consult other fathers on other matters). To ask for a second opinion from someone else is tantamount to lack of faith in God. On the other hand, it is quite proper to ask the same question more than once of the same father. The reason given for this is most revealing: it may well be that, because of some development in the situation, God wishes to say something different the second time, and if the second response came from a different father, it would look as if the saints were not in agreement, which would cause scandal, whereas if it comes from the same father, it is quite clear that God has, for reasons of his own which may or may not be apparent, changed his advice.[17]

The spiritual father's words must be accorded immense authority, since they are viewed as coming from God; but they are at the same time to be treated as words addressed to a particular situation. If the situation changes, they are no longer binding. If it is not possible to have recourse to the father, John advises one of his correspondents to pray, 'God of my father, do not let me go astray from your will or from the answer given me through your servant, but assure me of what I ought to do'; then he should do whatever he feels confident to do, trusting in the inspiration of the Holy Spirit.[18]

It is the role of the spiritual father precisely to preserve the flexibility that is needed, if we are to be 'led by the Spirit'. This is the antidote to the human tendency to want to fix things 'once and for all'.

Do not give yourself any absolute regulations, because it will only lead you into conflicts and anxieties; instead, probe what is at hand at each moment, in the fear of God and not in any contentious spirit, doing your best to be free from anger. . . . Give yourself no regulations. Be obedient and humble, and demand an account of yourself each day. The prophet indicated this day by day principle with the words, 'I said, now I have begun', and

so did Moses when he said, 'Now, O Israel'. So you too should
hold fast to the 'now'.[19]

Holding to the 'now' is the way to be faithful to the continual
novelty of God's deeds; failing to do so goes with lack of faith and
hardness of heart, and leads to seeking guarantees, just as the
Pharisees asked for a sign.[20]

To bring people back to the 'now', the spiritual father often has
to confront people with the plain truth of what is going on, showing
up their high dramas as little more than fantasy. 'If you see someone
going up to heaven by his own will, grab his leg and pull him down
again.'[21] As we browse through the letters of Barsanuphius and
John we find the two Old Men defusing one drama after another
with relentless common sense.

For instance, on one occasion some of the monks were afraid that
they were going to be subjected to hostile government action, so
they wondered whether they ought to hide their possessions and
flee. In response to their enquiries, Barsanuphius just reminded
them that everything is in the hands of God. Not satisfied with this,
they asked him, 'Why does it say, "If they drive you out of this
city, flee to the next"?' He calmly replied, 'We have not yet been
driven out.'[22]

Planning for a future which may never come to pass goes with
wanting to know exactly what is going to happen in the future
(which is not our business). One man wrote to Barsanuphius, 'I
have heard that if anyone has a dream three times, it is a true
dream. Is that so, father?' The Old Man tartly replied, 'It is not
so and you ought not to put any faith in such a dream; he who
appears to deceive you once can do it again three times or any
number of times. So do not be taken in. Pay attention to yourself.'[23]

The delicacy of Barsanúphius' touch can be seen in a curious
exchange of letters with a pious layman whose servant had been
bitten by a dog; the layman wanted to know whether the boy was
going to die or not. The Old Man adroitly evades the question in
the sense in which it was intended and answers a far more important
question that had not been asked: 'There is nothing wrong with
him; do not be afraid. Just take note of what it says, "A sparrow
does not fall into a snare without your Father who is in heaven."'
The layman takes this to mean that the Old Man is promising him
that his servant will not die, so when the boy does die, he is highly
perplexed and writes to ask whether he is really dead. Back comes
a very curt answer (only one word in the Greek): 'He's dead.' The
layman then asks why Barsanuphius had said that there was
nothing wrong with him. The Old Man replies that death comes
from God, not from dog-bites, and so there is nothing wrong with

being dead.[24] The ordinary concern for the fate of someone close to us is taken up by the Old Man to provide an occasion for a basic reminder of what our faith is all about; we may not believe that everything will be resolved here and now in the way we want, but we must believe that God knows what he is doing in running this world.

Our own frailty can be a real source of anxiety to us, making us want to know exactly whether we have or have not consented to a wrong desire and encouraging us to seek some kind of assurance that we are not going to consent to such desires in the future. One man wrote to ask what he should do about his unclean thoughts, of which he was afraid. The answer was, 'Say to God: Lord, forgive me if I have conceived of anything which is against your will, whether knowingly or not, for mercy belongs to you for ever. Amen.'[25] It is not, after all, necessary to know whether we are guilty or not, nor to know that we shall not become guilty in the future. The mercy of God is sufficient, and that is what we need to remember.

John has similarly realistic advice about how to deal with our failures. If we find that we have broken a precept that has been laid upon us, the first thing to make sure of is that we do not get into a flap about it. Nor should we fall into despair. This is important, because if we despair and conclude that the precept is impossible, then we shall in fact treat it as annulled and stop trying to keep it. The essential thing is to see the whole business in the proper perspective, and two scriptural texts are adduced to provide this: 'The just man falls seven times a day and gets up again' (Proverbs 24:16) and 'You shall forgive your brother seventy times seven times' (Matthew 18:22). If the just man falls seven times a day, we should not be surprised at our own failures; and if God tells us to forgive each other so extravagantly, how much more readily will he himself forgive. So we must not get anxious or become negligent, but must come back to 'Now, O Israel' and continue to do our best.[26]

It is also unnecessary to waste time wondering what we should do about other people's sins. When some pious layman wrote to Barsanuphius to know how he should react to someone who had offended him, he got a very brisk little letter back: 'Be nice to him.'[27]

The essential simplicity of the christian life runs through the whole correspondence. The message can be seen unfolding in the very first series of letters, addressed to abba John of Beersheba. Abba John is clearly an efficient man, the kind of man who gets put in charge of things, and as such he very easily gets annoyed when things go wrong. He has high expectations of himself and of others and so he generally finds himself and other people disappointing. He is also inclined to worry about things. He worries about the state of the world,[28] he worries about the state of the monastery,[29] and he is constantly worrying about himself. Barsanuphius tries to bring him back to the essential task in hand, which is not to sort everybody and everything out, but to learn how to love God and his neighbours in tranquillity.

The first problem to tackle is John's tendency to lose heart. Barsanuphius assures him that losing heart (akedia) is the root of all evil; correspondingly the root of all good is patience.[30] We must expect to run into all kinds of difficulties in this life, and we must accept them as being the way in which we are brought to the cross of Christ, which is the only way to come to genuine peace.[31] Peace is not won by arranging externals to our own satisfaction, it comes from a continual turning to God, casting our cares upon him. So we should not be pernickety about what goes on outside, but we must be 'accurate in dealing with our thoughts (logismoi)'. Otherwise they will poison us, by making mountains out of molehills (or, in Barsanuphius' own image, making camels out of gnats).[32]

Instead of getting worked up about things, we should thank God at all times. On one occasion John got very angry because some bricks were left out in the rain and got spoiled. Barsanuphius saw that he was going to make a scene with the abbot about it, so he sent the abbot to him with the words, 'Write to Brother John and give him my greetings. He is all set to cause disturbance to others and to be disturbed by others. Say to him: Rejoice in the Lord.'[33]

This was not the kind of remark which John found congenial. His own instinct was to tell people exactly what he thought of them, and if that did not work, he sulked. Letter twelve was written because John had told someone to do something and it had not been done quickly enough to satisfy him, so John duly reprimanded him. The brother was upset at this, so John resolved never to say anything to anybody ever after. A typically petulant attitude ('I'll never talk to him again, ever!'). Barsanuphius writes, 'Tell Brother John, this generation is soft and delicate; you will find it hard to discover a man with a tough heart. But stick to what the apostle says, "Reprove, rebuke, exhort in all patience and teaching."'

In letter thirteen John is warned not to 'enslave' people. Letter twenty-five is prompted by a plan of John's and the abbot's to tighten up the Rule once and for all 'against' (!) the brethren. Barsanuphius comments, 'I have written to you before about patience. And now I say to you: Milk the cow and you will get butter, but if you squeeze the teat in your hand, blood will come out. . . . If a man wants to bend a tree or a vine, he does it in stages. If he forces it all at once, immediately the whole business is ruined.'

Forcing is disastrously wrong in any dealings with oneself or with other people. If we are concerned with other people's progress, we must be quite realistic about it. Barsanuphius says in one of his letters, 'Don't you know what a headache children are to a good teacher?'[34] His own policy is quite clear: 'You know that I have never laid any constraint on anyone, not even on myself.'[35] 'Do not force the will, but sow in hope; our Lord never constrained anyone, but preached the good news and if anyone wanted to, he could listen to it.'[36]

John repeatedly attempts to fix his own religious life, either by making resolves of his own or by asking Barsanuphius to give him a rule. But Barsanuphius always warns him off it. In letter twenty-three, responding to a request for a rule about fasting and psalmody and prayer, he says:

> You are going round and round in too many circles to enter the narrow gate which leads to eternal life. Christ tells you very concisely how to enter. Leave men's rules and listen to him telling you, 'He who endures to the end will be saved.' So if people do not have patience, they will not enter into life. So don't desire a statute. I want you to be under grace, not under law. It says, 'There is no law set for the righteous.' I want you to be with the righteous. Stick to discernment (*diakrisis*) like a helmsman steering his boat in response to the winds.

This insistence on not defining rules for oneself runs through the whole correspondence. John wants to define a clear work for himself to concentrate on, and he proposes to stick to that and not interfere with other people at all. Barsanuphius convicts him of pique and bids him reverse his proposal: he is not to give *himself* orders, but must respond to each situation as it arises; but when it is suitable, he must be prepared to help his brethren.[37]

It is pointless to try to settle everything once and for all, because the inspiration for each situation is given precisely in that situation.[38]

John concedes that a lot of his troubles are his own fault. But even here he finds Barsanuphius opposing him. His apparent humility is shown up as merely a dramatic pose, and Barsanuphius rudely brings him back to the truth. When John says, 'I know, father, that these things happen to me because of my sins and that I am a fool and that all my troubles are my fault,' Barsanuphius says:

> First of all I convict you. You call yourself a sinner and yet you do not believe this, judging from what you do. A man who holds that he is a sinner and the cause of his own troubles does not go round contradicting people and fighting them and getting angry

with them. . . . Pay attention to yourself, brother: this is not the truth.

He is similarly convicted of falsehood in saying that he knows himself to be a fool.[39] Later on, when John has got involved in somebody else's affairs and wishes that he had not, he says to the Old Man, 'Forgive me, I am drunk and do not know what I am doing.' Again the Old Man shows that this is only a pose. He really thinks that he knows perfectly well what he is doing and that everybody else is therefore wrong to disagree with him.[40]

When John clamours for the Old Man to pray for him, to win for him supernatural relief from his temptations, Barsanuphius quietly rebuffs him. He assures him that he does pray for him always, and he must be content with that.[41] There is no need for any high drama about it. And if he finds himself a prey to temptations, then he must cope with them patiently (like anybody else).[42]

Self-dramatisation, of whatever kind, is produced only by anxiety, which results from a failure really to believe in God's providence.[43] Barsanuphius' whole doctrine could be summed up in his formula, 'attending to God in freedom from care'.[44] All our troubles arise because we fail to attend to God, and we cannot attend to God properly unless we take it as axiomatic that he has everything perfectly well in hand. The christian life is not primarily a matter of arranging our circumstances and ourselves into a suitably spiritual pose; it is primarily a matter of resisting the thoughts which confuse and poison our way of seeing things and our reactions to things. It matters relatively little whether we or other people actually *do* the various things that we think ought to be done; it matters enormously what our attitude is to our own and other people's successes and failures.

Bibliography

No complete critical edition exists, though one is in preparation for Sources Chrétiennes. In the meantime the most reliable text is provided by the French translation by Lucien Regnault, Philippe Lemaire and Bernard Outtier, *Barsanuphe et Jean de Gaza: Correspondance*. Solesmes 1972. All references in the notes are given according to this edition.
The only Greek editions available are:
Νικοδήμου Ἁγιορείτου, Βίβλος Βαρσανουφίου καὶ Ἰωάννου. re-ed. Volos 1960.
Derwas Chitty, ed., *Barsanuphius and John: Questions and Answers* (Patrologia Orientalis, XXXI, 3). Paris 1966.

Notes

[1] BJ 13.
[2] BJ 1.
[3] BJ 49.
[4] E.g. in BJ 67 Barsanuphius claims to be reporting words he 'heard' from God.
[5] BJ 808 (the reference to the 'ass's mouth' is to Balaam's ass in Numb. 22:28).
[6] BJ 63–4.
[7] BJ 66.
[8] BJ 577.
[9] BJ 462.
[10] BJ 363.
[11] BJ 693.
[12] BJ 16.
[13] BJ 72–3.
[14] BJ 17.
[15] BJ 35.
[16] BJ 369.
[17] BJ 361, 363.
[18] BJ 364.
[19] BJ 21.
[20] BJ 34.
[21] BJ 693 (citing AP Nau 111).
[22] BJ 786–7.
[23] BJ 418.
[24] BJ 779–81.
[25] BJ 468.
[26] BJ 371.
[27] BJ 679.
[28] BJ 52.
[29] BJ 41.
[30] BJ 13.
[31] BJ 2.
[32] BJ 16.
[33] BJ 16.
[34] BJ 13.
[35] BJ 51.
[36] BJ 35.
[37] BJ 21.
[38] BJ 51.
[39] BJ 17.
[40] BJ 37.
[41] BJ 17.
[42] BJ 18.
[43] BJ 17.
[44] BJ 1.

9

The Christian's 'Spiritual Exercise': Guigo II

Little has been said so far about 'spiritual exercises'. An important step towards a more formal notion of the distinct practices which make up a 'spiritual life' is taken in the twelfth century in a charming and influential little book, the *Ladder of Monks (Scala Claustralium)* by the Carthusian, Guigo II († 1188). He made classic, though he did not entirely originate, a fourfold analysis of what he calls the 'spiritual exercise' (*spiritale exercitium*) of the christian, which consists in reading, meditation, prayer and contemplation.[1]

This fourfold scheme first occurred to Guigo, he tells us, while he was engaged in some manual labour one day, thinking the while 'about a man's spiritual exercise'.[2] The juxtaposition of manual labour and spiritual exercise is certainly deliberate,[3] and serves to demarcate Guigo's topic: he is not concerned with all the ingredients in a christian life, but only with our spiritual practices; he is therefore not going to discuss the manifold outward activities which are proper even for a Carthusian. But it should be noticed that he says 'spiritual exercise', not 'spiritual exercises', emphasising that he is more concerned with our inner life as a whole than with dividing it up into distinct exercises; he does not wish to impose an artificial programme on what is essentially a fluid and continuous process. And the very fact that Guigo's reflections are said to have occurred while he was engaged in manual labour suggests that his inner exercise is not necessarily interrupted by outward occupations. In principle he says that we should want to be *always* engaged in some facet of the spiritual exercise, and any abandonment of it needs to be justified. We may sometimes simply *have* to abandon it (presumably this applies to such things as our need to sleep), and sometimes we shall be obliged to abandon it for the sake of some task which we undertake in order to be useful. Guigo also recognises that human weakness is likely to prevent us from maintaining our exercise the whole time, and this is lamentable; but if we deliberately and wantonly turn our backs on it, that cannot help but be sinful.[4] All of this implies that Guigo thinks of his 'spiritual exercise' as being more all-pervasive than the 'spiritual exercises' for which a specific time is set aside in the Carthusian customary.[5] What he is concerned with is the monk's (or the christian's) interior life as a whole, as something going on during all his waking hours, in as much as whatever he is doing his mind and his will must be engaged in some way or another.

After introducing his four-fold exercise, which, he says, constitutes 'the ladder of monks by which they are raised up from earth to heaven', Guigo proceeds to give a rapid succession of brief definitions of each rung of the ladder:

> Reading is a directing of the mind to a careful looking at the scriptures. Meditation is a studious activity of the mind, probing the knowledge of some hidden truth under the guidance of our own reason. Prayer is a devout turning of the heart to God to get ills removed or to obtain good things. Contemplation is a certain elevation above itself of the mind which is suspended in God, tasting the joys of eternal sweetness. . . . Reading looks for the sweetness of the life of blessedness, meditation locates it, prayer asks for it, contemplation tastes it. Reading, as it were, puts the solid food into our mouths, meditation chews it and breaks it down, prayer obtains the flavour of it and contemplation is the very sweetness which makes us glad and refreshes us.[6]

The first two rungs, reading (*lectio*) and meditation (*meditatio*), are in themselves quite secular occupations, common to saint and sinner, believer and pagan.[7] Guigo does not seem to believe that monastic or christian reading and thinking have any special quality which distinguishes them intrinsically from anybody else's reading and thinking. They are straightforward applications of the mind to the universal problem of how we are to attain to happiness. We read books because we are interested in what they may have to tell us, and we think about what we read because we want to understand it. The christian reads the bible because he is interested in what God has to tell us, but the nature of the activity of reading is not changed just because the book in question is the Word of God.

At first sight there appears to be a slight discrepancy between Guigo's theoretical account of meditation and his illustration of how it works. The strictly rational definition he gives does not prepare us for the enthusiastic way in which he weaves all kinds of scriptural texts together in his demonstration of what meditation is like. The specimen text he adopts is from Matthew 5:8, 'Blessed are the pure in heart, for they shall see God.' The meditation on this text consists chiefly in relating it to other texts, and Guigo juxtaposes and interweaves these texts with considerable dexterity and with little respect for context. He even adapts the wording of scripture, when it suits him.

Meditation begins to consider how glorious and delightful it would be to see the long-desired face of the Lord, beautiful in form before all the sons of men, no longer abject and vile, no longer having the appearance with which his mother clothed him, but robed in the garment of immortality and crowned with the diadem with which his Father crowned him on the day of his resurrection and glory, the day which the Lord has made.[8]

This single sentence is constructed out of Psalm 44:3, Isaiah 53:2, Ecclesiasticus 6:32, Canticle 3:11 and Psalm 117:24, but the verse from the Canticle is used in rather a cavalier way. The Canticle says, 'Go out and see king Solomon in the diadem with which his mother has clothed him on the day of his wedding', but Guigo has detached the reference to his mother, turning it into an allusion to the dingy garment of the Incarnation, which can then be contrasted with the robe of immortality supplied by Christ's *Father* on the day of his resurrection.

This very free use of scripture is typical of medieval monastic meditations, and it is worth bearing in mind that 'meditations' are a favoured literary genre, not all that different from monastic sermons. In fact, the whole procedure is well summed up in a phrase which the thirteenth-century Dominican, Humbert of Romans, uses of preaching: 'all proper preaching is woven (*texitur*) out of words of scripture'.[9] Traditional monastic meditation is, from one point of view, an art-form as well as a spiritual exercise.

This kind of meditation is plainly not the kind of rigorous intellectual exercise which Guigo's definition might have led us to expect; yet in its own way it is quite scientific. If we allow that the whole bible is God's book, then it must be quite proper and reasonable for us to try to understand the significance of one part of it by referring to other parts of it. That is, after all, how we try to understand other books. And that is essentially what Guigo is recommending. His way of using the bible was already being challenged in the twelfth century by much more exact methods of exegesis,[10] but, granted his premisses, the emotional excitement and the hectic combining of different scriptural texts can quite legitimately be regarded as part and parcel of a genuinely rational undertaking.

Reading and meditation lay the foundation for the rest of the spiritual exercise, and they are indispensable. Without reading, meditation has no protection against error, and it is as a result of reading and meditation that we are moved to pray. Meditation both indicates what we need to pray for and fires our will so that we shall pray with real eagerness.[11]

The result of meditating on Guigo's chosen text is that the soul

conceives a passionate desire for the purity of heart which meditation has shown to be so delightful in its consequences; and it is, in
fact, the vision of God rather than purity of heart which focuses the
soul's desire, so that the resulting prayer is essentially a prayer for
God to reveal himself:

> I sought your face, O Lord, your face, O Lord, have I sought, I
> have long meditated in my heart and in my meditation a fire
> grew and a desire to know you more. While you break the bread
> of sacred scripture for me, you have come to be known to me in
> the breaking of bread, and the more I know you, the more I long
> to know you, no longer in the husk of the letter, but in sensed
> experience (*in sensu experientiae*).[12]

While the soul is calling for the Lord like this, he

> does not wait until it has finished speaking, but interrupts the
> flow of its prayer in mid-course and hastens to present himself
> and come to meet the yearning soul, bathed with the dew of
> heavenly sweetness, drenched in the finest perfumes. He streng-
> thens the wearied soul, refreshes it in its hunger, fertilises its
> aridity, makes it forget earthly things, marvellously bringing it to
> life by mortifying it in forgetfulness of itself and making it sober
> by inebriating it.[13]

This divine interruption is the *effectus contemplationis*, and it is a pity
that both the French and English translations render this 'the effects
of contemplation', which suggests that Guigo is talking about effects
produced by contemplation. What he means is that contemplation
itself is the 'effect'. Previous chapters are entitled 'the job (*officium*)
of reading', 'the job of meditation', 'the job of prayer'; contemplation
has no 'job', because it is our goal, not a means to an end, and it
is an 'effect' in that it is a consequence of what has gone before.
This does not mean that contemplation can be produced to order;
in Guigo's view it depends on God's good pleasure, it is a 'grace',
which God gives as and when he likes.[14] It is, speaking more strictly,
only a 'quasi-effect of prayer',[15] but it is unlikely to be given to
anyone who has not passed through the three preceding stages. God
may occasionally 'take the bull by the horns' and as it were force
some people to desire him even when they did not want to, by
giving himself to them without waiting to be asked. But this is not
normal and we should not presume on its happening; if we aspire
to contemplation, we should 'do what belongs to us, namely to read
and meditate on the law of God, and pray to him that he will help
our weakness'.[16]

What Guigo understands by 'contemplation' is made clear in
chapter eight:

Lord, how shall we discover when you are doing this, what is the signal of your coming? Is it sighs and tears which proclaim and attest consolation and happiness? If so, this is a strange contradiction and an unheard of symbolism.

Yet sure enough it is tears and sighs which are the evidence of the 'coming of grace':

> My soul, in these tears recognise your spouse, embrace him whom you desire. . . . These are the wondrous gifts and comforts which your spouse has brought you, groans and tears. . . . O Lord Jesus, if these tears which are stirred by the thought (*memoria*) of you and desire for you are so sweet, how sweet will be the joy which will be won with the clear vision of you?

It is plain that there is no sharp break between the thought of and yearning for Christ which characterise prayer and the tears and groans which attest the 'coming of grace' in contemplation. What is distinctive of contemplation is the degree of absorption in the desire for God, which, for the time being, makes the soul oblivious of all carnal impulses.[17] There is no indication that any real seeing or vision is involved, or that Guigo is thinking of raptures and ecstasies such as later mystical writers allude to. In contemplation the soul can say, 'I feel the grace of God (*ecce sentio gratiam Dei*)'.[18] And this is attended by that quality so beloved of late medieval spiritual writers and so vexatious to English translators, *dulcedo* or *suavitas*, 'sweetness'.[19] This feeling of grace is, according to Guigo, an answer to prayer,[20] but all the same the sweetness which it produces is still only a sweetness of desire, as the text quoted above shows; so the answer to the prayer for contemplation is itself scarcely other than a more intense and more delightful prayer – and there can be little doubt that this convergence is one factor in the development of the later terminology, according to which contemplation is actually *called* 'prayer'.

The experience which Guigo calls 'contemplation' is one which the Cistercian fathers also advert to in their comments on the visits of the Beloved in the Canticle.[21] And William of St Thierry shows us how it is possible for the sudden intensification of desire to be identified as 'contemplation':

> Since we cannot see God's face and live, that is, since we cannot in this life grasp the full knowledge of him, God entrusts to anyone who loves him a certain image of knowledge of him which he places in his lover's feeling, an image which does not consist of any vain fantasy, but of a certain pious affection.

In this way it is quite precisely accurate, or so William claims, to say that love *is* our understanding of God. And it is on the basis of this 'image of knowledge' which is love, that we approach God in prayer, and it is by way of this image that we contemplate God.[22]

Ultimately this doctrine derives from a very sophisticated argument of St Augustine's, based on the statement in 1 John 4:8 that 'God is love', from which it seems to follow that 'anyone who has love, sees God'.[23] In a somewhat debased and oversimplified form, Augustine's doctrine passed to the middle ages through St Gregory, who taught that 'anyone who wholeheartedly desires God, already possesses him whom he loves, for no one would be able to love God, if he did not possess him whom he loves'.[24]

Guigo is thus within a recognisable western tradition in identifying an intense feeling of love as a feeling of the presence of God. It can be regarded as a special 'grace', inasmuch as such sensations cannot be produced at will. They come and go, like the Bridegroom in the Canticle. Guigo, however, is careful to clarify exactly in what sense we can talk about the 'coming and going' of the Lord. He withdraws himself in one sense, namely by withdrawing the 'sweetness of contemplation'; but he remains present in us 'with regard to guiding us, with regard to grace and with regard to union'.[25] Strictly speaking, then, there is no change in our supernatural status, nor are we objectively more united with Christ, when we receive a gift of contemplation. In fact contemplation does not bestow any kind of status at all, since it is necessarily a transient experience. The only difference is that sometimes we 'feel' grace, and at other times, more usually in fact, grace is 'hidden'.[26]

In chapter ten Guigo explains why it is good for us that grace should be hidden. If we had the feeling of grace the whole time, we might become conceited and despise other people, and we might come to take grace for granted, ascribing the consolation that we feel to nature and not to grace. Guigo quotes the proverb 'Familiarity breeds contempt' in this connection. The Beloved withdraws himself to make us desire him more eagerly, so that we shall receive him the more thankfully when he does come to visit us. And there is the further danger that 'if this consolation never failed . . . we might perhaps think that we had here an abiding city and be less earnest in seeking the future kingdom'. So the Bridegroom comes and goes 'to stop us confusing our exile with our homeland'.

He allows us a little taste of how sweet he is, and then withdraws himself before we have fully perceived him, and in this way he flies over us with outstretched wings, encouraging us to fly; it is as if he were saying, 'Now you have had a small taste of how good and sweet I am, but if you want to be completely filled with this sweetness, run after me in the fragrance of my perfumes, hold your hearts on high, where I am, seated at the right hand of the Father. There you will see me, not in a glass darkly, but face to face and your heart will be filled with joy and no one will take your joy from you.'

After taking us up to the heights in this way, Guigo recapitulates the whole scheme:

Reading is, as it were, the foundation and comes first; it supplies material and then refers us to meditation. Meditation earnestly enquires what we should seek, and, as it were, digs out and finds the treasure and shows it to us, but, since it cannot obtain anything by itself, it refers us on to prayer. Prayer raises itself up with all its might towards God and asks for the desired treasure, the sweetness of contemplation. This, when it comes, rewards the labour of the preceding three. . . . Reading without meditation is arid, meditation without reading is erroneous; prayer without meditation is tepid, meditation without prayer is fruitless. Prayer with devotion wins contemplation, but the attainment of contemplation without prayer is rare or miraculous.[27]

Ideally we should spend all our time on one or other of the four rungs of Guigo's ladder. Since it is impossible to live permanently on the highest one, after we have enjoyed an interlude of contemplation we must descend gently, 'lingering now on one rung, now on another, as we are moved by our own free will, according to the dictates of time and place, since, it seems to me, one is the nearer to God the further one is from the first rung'.[28]

This last remark is rather surprising and seems to contradict the freedom which Guigo gives us to opt for whichever rung we like. It is probable that Guigo is torn between his recognition of the value traditionally ascribed in western monasticism to reading and meditation and his awareness that, in themselves, they are not intrinsically spiritual activities at all. We shall return to this problem in the next chapter. But Guigo's essential point is clear. These four rungs constitute what is really only a single 'spiritual exercise', within which we move around freely, except that we cannot choose when we are going to ascend to the highest rung, contemplation.

There also seems to be a slight awkwardness at the end of chapter twelve, when Guigo allocates the four rungs to four different groups of people: 'the first stage belongs to beginners, the second to proficients, the third to the devout and the fourth to the blessed'. This clearly cannot be taken at its face value, as at least a foretaste of blessedness is apparently offered to some people here on earth. And Guigo's illustration of his 'exercise' shows that we move from reading, through meditation, to prayer at a single sitting. The whole tenor of his book makes it impossible to suppose that he can mean anything more than that it is typical of beginners to be primarily engaged in reading, and of proficients to be primarily engaged in meditating on texts with which they are already familiar; the 'devout' will be those who can move themselves to prayer without needing to spend much or any time on reading or meditating. But this does not mean that any of them will be totally debarred from the other rungs of the ladder.

The popularity of the *Ladder of Monks* in the middle ages is shown by the number of manuscripts which survive and by the various adaptations which were made of it.[29] It is, indeed, a very charming book and its doctrine is pleasing and sensible. However, it represents a very fragile synthesis, poised precariously over the changes in temperament and understanding which were to bring about a revolution in christian piety. Its coherence depends in large measure upon the text chosen to illustrate the method, which allows Guigo surreptitiously to lead us from meditation to contemplation by inviting us to meditate on a text which promises the vision of God. He beguiles the reader into not asking what would happen if we were to take a different text, which might lead us to pray for a very different kind of boon, which would destroy the ladder.

To see both the strengths and the weaknesses of Guigo's exposition, we need to situate his four rungs in a rather broader historical context, and this we shall do in the following chapters.

Bibliography and Abbreviations for Chapters 9 to 11

Editions used, Abbreviations

Aelred, *De Institutione Inclusarum*, ed. Charles Dumont (SC 76). Paris 1961.

Ancrene Riwle — references are given according to Morton's pagination, which is indicated in most edns; there is a modern English version by M. B. Salu. London 1955.

Eckhart, DW — ed. Josef Quint, *Die Deutschen Werke*. Stuttgart (in progress); two vols of a projected complete English tr. of the German works have been published by M. O'C. Walshe. London 1979, 1981.

Guigo, SC — *Scala Claustralium*, ed. Edmund Colledge and James Walsh (SC 163). Paris 1970; English tr. by the same eds, *The Ladder of Monks*. London and Oxford 1978.

Hugh of Balma — the critical edn is still awaited; there is a convenient text in A. C. Peltier, ed., *Omnia Opera S. Bonaventurae*, VIII (Paris 1866), pp. 2–53. References are given to this edn.

Hugh of St Victor   I have used the edn in PL 175–7, except for *De Meditatione*, ed. Roger Baron, *Hugues de Saint-Victor: Six Opuscules Spirituels* (SC 155). Paris 1969.

Ps. Bonaventure, *Meditationes de Passione Christi*, ed. M. Jordan Stallings. Washington, D.C. 1965; *Meditationes Vitae Christi*: in Peltier, ed. cit., XII (Paris 1868), pp. 510–630.

Rolle, *English Writings*, ed. H. E. Allen. Oxford 1931.

Savonarola, *Operette Spirituali*, ed. Mario Ferrara in the Edizione Nazionale. Rome (in progress).

William of St Thierry, *Expos. Cant.*, ed. J. M. Déchanet (SC 82). Paris 1962; *Golden Epistle*, ed. Jean Déchanet (SC 223). Paris 1975. There are English translations of both works in the Cistercian Fathers series, following the paragraph numbering of the SC texts.

Notes

[1]The same four elements are found in reverse order in Guigo I, *Meditationes*, ed. J. Wilmart (Paris 1936), no. 390, and in a different order in the Carthusian customary drawn up by Guigo I (PL 153:757–8); they are found with the addition of a fifth ingredient, *operatio*, in Hugh of St Victor, *Didascalicon* V 9, *De Meditatione* 2:1. It is likely that Hugh is in fact one of Guigo's sources. There is another list, with 'compunction' added between 'prayer' and 'contemplation' in a twelfth-century Benedictine sermon cited by Jean Leclercq as anonymous (*Revue Mabillon* 33 [1943], pp. 71–2), but listed as a sermon by William of Flavigny in J. B. Schneyer, *Repertorium der lateinischen Sermones des Mittelalters* II (Münster 1970), p. 458 (no. 15). After Guigo, see Bonaventure, *De Triplici Via*, Prologue; Rolle, *Emendatio Vite* 12; Hilton, *Scale of Perfection* I 15; *Cloud of Unknowing* 35; Domenico Cavalca, *Frutti della Lingua* 24; Savonarola, *Expositio Orationis Dominicae* (the whole treatise is structured on Guigo's fourfold scheme), *Lettere* (ed. R. Ridolfi. Florence 1933), pp. 22, 39. Other texts are cited in J. Leclercq, *Études sur le Vocabulaire Monastique* (Rome 1961), p. 138[45,46]; *Mediaeval Studies* 37 (1975), p. 92. And it may be due to the influence of Guigo that St Thomas, though he cites Hugh of Victor, in fact only lists Guigo's four rungs in IV *Sent.* d.15 q.4 a.1.

[2]SC 2.

[3]It is found in the Carthusian customary (PL 153:699–700); cf. also, for example, Peter of Cluny (PL 189:128–9) and William of St Thierry, *Golden Epistle* 85. All three texts, however, have the plural, *exercitia spiritualia*.

[4]SC 14–15.

[5]PL 153:699–700.

[6]SC 2–3.

[7]SC 5.

[8]Ibid.

[9]J. J. Berthier, ed., *Humberti de Romanis Opera de Vita Regulari* (repr. Turin 1956), II, p. 375. English tr. in Simon Tugwell, *Early Dominicans*, p. 185.

[10]Cf. Beryl Smalley, *The Study of the Bible in the Middle Ages* (Oxford 1952), ch. 3.

[11]SC 12–14.

[12]SC 6.

[13]SC 7.

[14]SC 10.

[15]SC 13.

[16]SC 14.

[17]SC 7.

[18]SC 14. *Sentire* is difficult to translate without being misleading; it means 'perceive with the senses' rather than 'respond emotionally' to something. The 'feeling' of grace refers to a kind of direct 'sensing', as distinct from merely believing that grace is present.

[19]SC 12 (*contemplationis suavitas*), 13 (*contemplationis dulcedo*); but the idea is all-pervasive.

[20]SC 13–14.

[21]E.g. Bernard, *Super Cant.* 57; William of St Thierry, *Expos. Cant.* II 181ff.

[22]William of St Thierry, op. cit., 20–2. The germ of this is found in Gregory, PL 76:1207A, which is quoted by Bernard, *De Diversis* 29.

[23]Augustine, *Ep Ioh.* 9:10; on the subtleties of his doctrine, cf. Paul Agaësse, ed., *Saint Augustin: Commentaire de la Première Épître de S. Jean* (SC 75) (Paris 1961), pp. 47–53.

[24]Gregory, PL 76:1220C.

[25]SC 9.

[26]Notice the title of SC 9.

[27]SC 12, 14.

[28]SC 14.

[29]On the MSS and adaptations, see Colledge and Walsh's SC edn, pp. 10–14, 45–52.

10

The Ladder Dismantled: The Lower Rungs

Guigo's fourfold scheme is, to some extent, derived from an earlier, simpler scheme, involving only reading and prayer. These are frequently presented as the two essential constituent elements in our relationship with God. As Augustine said, 'When you read, God is speaking to you; when you pray, you are speaking to God.'[1] Similar sentiments are expressed by Ambrose and Jerome.[2] Augustine's words were duly culled by the great Spanish encyclopedist, St Isidore of Seville († 636),[3] and through him they became a commonplace in the middle ages.[4] Leclercq cites a considerable number of medieval monastic texts which juxtapose reading and prayer in much the same way.[5] And the tradition goes back to the Desert Fathers. Although there are not many references to reading in most of the Egyptian monastic texts,[6] we find St Anthony's life immediately after his conversion summed up by Athanasius in terms of manual labour, prayer and reading,[7] and there is an identical triad in Cassian.[8]

In general prayer and reading seem to be recognised as two practices which do not need to be subordinated to one another in either direction, since each one has its own, distinct value. When someone asked the thirteenth century Dominican, Jordan of Saxony, whether it was better to spend one's time in prayers or in studying the bible, he gave the classic response, 'Which is better, to drink the whole time or to eat the whole time? Surely it is best for them to take their turn, and so it is in the other case too.'[9]

Nevertheless there is a significant difference in the way in which these two practices enter into monastic legislation. Reading is inserted into the timetable, as something that the monks are obliged to do at set times.[10] But, apart from the celebration of the divine office, no time was originally prescribed for prayer. Instead we find statements about *how* the monks are to pray – not in the sense that there are any 'methods of prayer', of course, but the monks are reminded of the importance of concentration and reverence. And to facilitate this, they are bidden to pray briefly, although St Benedict allows that when a monk is praying alone he can extend his prayer if he is inspired to do so by God's grace.[11] He also allows monks to go to the oratory to pray when they want to, provided they behave themselves properly.[12]

The recommendation that prayer should be brief is taken from Cassian, who says that prayer should be frequent and brief.[13] St Augustine also passes on the same tradition, and it became proverbial and lasted well into the middle ages.[14]

It is clear that reading is regarded as much more of an 'observance' than prayer. Reading, in the nature of the case, needs to be reasonably protracted if it is to be useful, and so times for it can be legislated for; but prayer is normally not protracted and has to be left much more to the discretion of the individual, or indeed to the vagaries of grace.

This is why reading, on its own, sometimes appears to be the essential spiritual practice of the monastic life. The Pachomian tradition laid great emphasis on reading and memorising the bible; even during their manual labour the monks were expected to be reciting scriptural texts that they had learned.[15] In the Rule of the Master someone is to read to the monks while they do their manual labour, if there are enough of them working together to justify it; otherwise they too are encouraged to recite psalms or other passages of scripture.[16]

One story among many may be cited to illustrate the extraordinary devotion to reading which early monasticism fostered. St Lioba, who was a relation and close friend of St Boniface in the eighth century,

> applied herself with such diligence to the pursuit of reading that, unless she was giving time to prayer or restoring her frail body with food or sleep, the sacred page never fell from her hands. . . . It was the custom for the bible to be read beside her bed even when she was sleeping at night or at noon. This task the younger girls gladly took it in turns to perform, and, wondrous to relate, they could not omit a single word or even a syllable without being immediately corrected by her, even though she was asleep.[17]

This is reminiscent of the account Jerome gives of Origen's way of life:

> Ambrose mentions that he never took food in Origen's presence without there being reading, nor ever go to sleep without one of the brethren reciting the sacred text. This was his practice by day and by night, so that reading followed prayer and prayer followed reading.[18]

This is not just a product of Graeco-Roman culture. Vööbus draws attention to the tradition of study among the Syrian monks,[19] and quotes a fine text from St Ephrem: 'He who hammers upon books will cleanse his heart from rust.'[20] Chrysostom similarly tells us that the hermits near Antioch were 'nailed to their books'.[21] It is very probable that the insistence on reading and study is a very primitive christian tradition derived from contemporary Judaism. Hillel is quoted as saying, 'He who does not study deserves to die,'[22] and one of the rules at Qumran is that 'the community shall keep vigil together for a third of every night of the year, to read in the scriptures, to study the Law and to bless (God) together'.[23]

The importance of reading was still recognised in at least some monastic circles in the twelfth century. In response to what was apparently a rather reductionist exposition of religious life by an Augustinian, St Aelred of Rielvaux expresses 'amazement' that reading is not even mentioned, and goes on to list it as (by implication) part of the essential substance of religious life.[24] And Guigo I describes the solitary life as 'attending to books, and especially recognised, religious books'.[25]

Early in the thirteenth century there is a striking text in the *Ancrene Riwle*: 'Often, dear sisters, you should pray less for to read more. Reading is good petition. Reading teacheth how and what to pray, and asking then gets it. Amid the reading when the heart liketh cometh up a devotion that is worth many petitions.'[26]

'Meditation' (*meditatio*) was originally entirely parasitic upon reading, and it is important to be clear what it means. The Latin *meditatio*, like the Greek *meleté*, essentially means 'rehearsal'[27] and both words were used in the bible to translate a Hebrew root, *hāgāh*, meaning 'recite', so that initially 'meditation' can be envisaged as something audible, something done with the tongue and the mouth, as in Psalms 34:28 and 36:30. Thus in the *Sayings of the Desert Fathers* we are told that some brothers 'heard' one of the monks 'meditating' (*meletountos*) a text from scripture,[28] and the Rule of Pachomius says that the monks, while they are walking or working, should either 'meditate' scriptural texts or keep silent.[29] Similarly in the Rule of the Master the monks are told to be absolutely silent when they go out of the oratory, 'not even "meditating" psalms' – 'meditating' being clearly equivalent to 'repeating'.[30]

This usage, probably thanks to the Latin psalter, survives into the middle ages, though it is vulnerable to corruption in the manuscripts. In the late thirteenth-century *Nine Ways of Prayer of St Dominic* we are told that Dominic sometimes 'stood as if he were reading very reverently and devoutly before God, and then he seemed to be "meditating" the words of God in his mouth and as it were sweetly reciting them to himself'.[31] Even in the fourteenth century what may be the correct text of Suso in one place tells us that the thought of the passion should be 'in your heart by memory, in your mouth by devout rumination and in your deeds by affectionate imitation'.[32]

Suso uses the word 'rumination' rather than 'meditation', and this is a very ancient association, going back to the allegorical interpretation of the food laws in the Old Testament concerning ruminants. Philo, for instance, links 'ruminating' with 'meditation', the aim being to imprint the words of the sacred text on our memories.[33] The same connection is made by Barnabas.[34] There is no essential difference between this 'rehearsal' of texts and reading. As J. A. Burrow says, 'The old way of reading, known in the monasteries as *rumination*, was a slow and noisy process – an audible "chewing over" of the precious words of the text.'[35]

In some places the emphasis shifts rather more on to the actual memorising of the sacred text. St Ambrose asserts that the purpose of 'meditating' the words is to remember them,[36] and Isidore says, 'What we do not know, we learn by reading; and we retain what we have learned by "meditations".'[37] The few references to 'meditation' in the Rule of St Benedict have to be taken as referring to 'memorising',[38] and this is undeniably so in the early ninth-century legislation.[39] This is why Smaragdus can simply slip in 'meditation' as part of 'reading'.[40]

'Meditation' in the sense of 'thinking about something' is found at least as early as Cassiodorus († c. 580), though in him it goes side by side with other meanings,[41] but even when the other meanings have largely been ousted, the link with reading is only gradually broken. Richard Rolle, for instance, in the fourteenth century, defines the 'lower part of the contemplative life' as consisting in 'meditation of holy writing, that is, God's words, and in other good thoughts and sweet that men has of the grace of God about the love of Jesu Christ'.[42] The more technical Latin term seems still to be associated with the meditation on scripture, and for other kinds of 'good thoughts' Rolle uses the ordinary vernacular term.

But the emphasis is definitely shifting. Whereas earlier 'meditation' was parasitic upon 'reading', the roles come to be reversed, so that it is the meditation which is important and reading begins to be downgraded, if not entirely abandoned. In the text quoted above from the *Ancrene Riwle* prayer seems to be played down in favour of devotion, but far more normally it is reading which falls victim to devotion.[43] St Bonaventure mentions all four rungs of Guigo's ladder in his *De Triplici Via*, but in order to fit them into a tripartite scheme he has to subsume reading under meditation[44] and it is not surprising that some later manuscripts omit reading entirely; and at the end of the fifteenth century it was probably from one such defective manuscript that Garcia Jiménez de Cisneros derived his list of the exercises which should be practised every day, 'meditation, prayer and contemplation'.[45]

Reading eventually resurfaced, but only in the very debased form of 'spiritual reading', as an exercise in its own right, consisting in the reading of 'spiritual books', designed on the whole to tell people how to be pious, rather than to enlighten their minds with truth.[46] It is not surprising that Tanquerey, in his magisterial exposition of the spirituality that prevailed from the time of the Counter-Reformation onwards, regards spiritual reading as a form of spiritual direction, having nothing directly to do with meditation.[47]

One of the reasons for the relative downfall of the old tradition of reading as the essential discipline of the spiritual life was the combination of more rigorous canons of exegesis with a more frankly speculative notion of *meditatio*. The wide-ranging intellectual interests of someone like Hugh of St Victor needed to break loose from a text which could no longer be interpreted in sublime disregard for its obvious meaning.

Meditation takes its beginning from reading, but it is not bound by any of the rules or precepts of reading. It delights to run about in some suitable space, where it can direct its gaze freely towards the contemplation of truth, embracing now these causes of things and now those, and then at other times probing all the depths of things, leaving nothing doubtful or obscure. So the beginning of doctrine is in reading, but its fulfilment is in meditation.[48]

Elsewhere Hugh in fact recognises that some kinds of meditation do not start from reading at all. In his *De Meditatione* he mentions three sorts of meditation, one concerned with reflecting on creatures, one concerned with the bible and one concerned with morals; it is only the second of these which 'arises from reading'.[49]

Hugh was happy to be an intellectual, but the battle between learning and piety was already engaged, and this meant that not only was reading falling into disfavour, so was meditation, understood as a serious intellectual activity. Neither reading nor meditation features in St Francis' Rule. Where the old monastic Rules prescribe manual labour and reading as the remedies for idleness,[50] St Francis prescribes work and prayer.[51] And he only permits St Anthony to 'read theology to the brethren' on condition that he does not quench their 'application to prayer and spirit of devotion'.[52] St Thomas has to respond to the suggestion that 'meditation and contemplation' are inimical to devotion,[53] and Suso can speak scathingly of people who know things 'merely by meditation'.[54]

Guigo seems to be straddling several different worlds. His practice of *meditatio* is clearly dependent on the old 'chewing over' of the bible, but his definition of it presupposes the newer, more overtly intellectual, usage. He is too traditional to jettison reading, but he supposes it to be 'arid' without meditation; he reckons that a spiritual life not based on a continual return to the Word of God will probably go astray, yet he sees reading and meditation as secular activities, admitted to the 'spiritual exercise' only on sufferance, and needing to be turned into devotion by prayer.

Devotion, understood in a predominantly affective sense, is in fact well on the way to becoming the most highly regarded spiritual value. St Aelred analyses love of God into a mere pair of elements: interior affection and external works (*affectus mentis et effectus operis*). The latter consists in the practice of the virtues, the former 'in the sweetness of spiritual taste'. Reading, interestingly enough, is classified as part of the 'ordered pattern of life' in which the practice of the virtues is enshrined, whereas meditation is given the function of nurturing affection.

The sort of meditation which Aelred has in mind is evidently quite different from the intellectual speculation which so enchanted Hugh of St Victor. He recommends three kinds of meditation: meditation on things past, on the present wretchedness of the human condition, and on the Last Things. The first consists of a series of highly imaginative meditations on scenes from the gospel.

> Go with the blessed Mary into her chamber and read with her the books in which the childbirth of the Virgin and the coming of Christ are foretold. There await the coming of the angel, so that you will see him entering, hear his greeting and, filled with wonder and amazement, greet your sweetest Lady with the angel, saying, 'Hail, full of grace. . . .'

We are told to 'run and join in the joys' of the Visitation and prostrate ourselves at the feet of Mary and Elizabeth. Then we follow the virgin mother to Bethlehem and go into her lodgings with her and make ourselves useful to her while she gives birth. So it goes on until the Resurrection.[55]

We find here, at least in germ, a kind of meditation which became enormously successful. The aim of the exercise was to stir intense emotions by way of a vivid imagining usually of the passion, but sometimes of other scenes from the gospel. An English adaptation of the very popular *Meditations* ascribed to St Bonaventure explains clearly what it is all about:

> Whoso desires to find comfort and ghostly gladness in the Passion and in the cross of our Lord Jesu, him needs with a busy thought for to dwell in it and all other business forget and set at nought. And soothly I trow fully that whoso would busy him with all his heart and all his mind and bethink him of this glorious Passion and all the circumstance thereof [i.e. all the details], it should bring him and change him into a new state of living. For he that insearches it with deep thought and with all his heart lastingly

he shall find full many things therein stirring him to new compassion, new love, new ghostly comfort, and so shall he be brought into a new ghostly sweetness. . . . I trow that a man behoved to raise up all the sharpness of his mind and open wide the inner eye of his soul into beholding of this blessed Passion . . . and that he make himself present in his thought as if he saw fully with his bodily eye all the things that befell about the cross and the glorious Passion of our Lord Jesu.[56]

One of the most energetic practitioners of this kind of piety was Margery Kempe. Almost anything was enough to set her off. On one occasion she tells us how she was overwhelmed by the sight of a pietà:

Through the beholding of that pietà her mind was all wholly occupied in the Passion of our Lord Jesu Christ and in the compassion of our Lady, St Mary, by which she was compelled to cry full loud and weep full sore, as though she should have died. Then came to her the lady's priest saying, 'Damsel, Jesu is dead long since.' When her crying was ceased, she said to the priest, 'Sir, his death is as fresh to me as he had died this same day, and so me thinketh it ought to be to you and to all christian people.'[57]

When she was in Rome one time, the sight of women carrying their babies made her 'roar and weep as though she had seen Christ in his childhood', and any good-looking man made her burst into tears as if she had seen 'him that was both God and man'.[58] It is presumably this kind of blurring of the distinctions between everyday sensible realities and spiritual realities which makes the author of the *Cloud of Unknowing* protest against 'fantasy' which, he says, is 'nought else but a bodily conceit of a ghostly thing or else a ghostly conceit of a bodily thing'.[59]

This kind of meditation escaped largely from the control of the biblical text. The author of the pseudo-Bonaventure *Meditations* explicitly mentions that some of the details are presented on the authority of Franciscan visionaries.[60] It is worth bearing in mind that one of the prominent Franciscan spirituals, Olivi, got into trouble for substituting a visionary account of the Passion for that in the New Testament.[61]

The most startling feature of this kind of meditation is the extent to which the meditator is not only imaginatively present to the various scenes from the life of Christ, but actually becomes a participant in them. Margery Kempe appears to be involved in the life of the Holy Family over several generations. She assists at the birth of our Lady, and then looks after her for twelve years. She usurps

Gabriel's role, so that it is she who tells Mary, 'Lady, you shall be the mother of God.' She acts as midwife at the birth of John the Baptist. She books the hotel rooms when Mary and Joseph go to Bethlehem and again when they go to Egypt. When Jesus is born, she goes round begging clothes and blankets for him. She thoroughly enjoys the visit of the Magi, having, typically, a nice cry the while.[62] She is, of course, present at the crucifixion and, when it is all over, she takes our Lady home and puts her to bed. 'Then she made for our Lady a good caudle [a nice cup of tea, as it might be] and brought it to her to comfort her.'[63]

The details of the passion story have little to do with the gospels; they are in fact taken from the pseudo-Bonaventuran meditations and Margery is only doing what pseudo-Bonaventure tells her to do in looking after our Lady and making sure she has something to eat.[64]

After this kind of maundering, it is with considerable relief that we welcome the forces of law and order in the sixteenth century, who subjected imaginative meditation to the disipline of a much more formal 'method'. St Ignatius insists that meditations on the gospel must be properly grounded in the authentic story as narrated in the bible[65] and, even if the emphasis is still on the desired affective response, Ignatius recognises that the application of the will and affections must be preceded by an application of the understanding to the matter in hand.[66] And the whole exercise is subordinated to a very practical concern to discover the will of God and to accomplish it promptly and diligently.[67] And it should be noted that Ignatius resisted the tendency to confine 'devotion' to specifically devotional exercises. He was more interested in encouraging people to find God in all their activities, and he considered this preferable to long meditations.[68] People should find as much devotion in *any* work of charity and obedience as they do in meditation.[69] And students, who will probably not feel as much devotion as they would like, must recognise that their study, if undertaken for the right motives, is in itself a very good devotion.[70] Jesuits engaged in the academic life are in fact told not to engage in *largas meditaciones*, which will interfere with their work.[71] And, more generally, Ignatius is not happy with people who get so carried away by their meditations that they do not give enough time to eating, sleeping and relaxing.[72]

It is a pity that Ignatius never seems to have suspected that there had once been a much more intimate connection between study and meditation; he takes a predominantly devotionalist understanding of meditation as his starting point. But he is evidently determined to put such meditation firmly into its proper place in the context of the christian life as a whole.

Bibliography and Abbreviations

See above, p. 100.

Notes

[1]PL 37:1086.

[2]PL 16:50A; Jerome, *Ep.* 22:25.

[3]PL 83:679.

[4]See, for instance, Smaragdus (PL 102:597); Peraldus, *Summa de Virtutibus* Oratio 3; Thomas Hibernicus, *Manipulus Florum* Oratio 2.

[5]Jean Leclercq, *Études sur le Vocabulaire Monastique du Moyen Age* (Rome 1961), pp. 131–4.

[6]Cf. the strictures in A. J. Festugière, *Les Moines d'Orient*, I: *Culture ou Sainteté*. Paris 1961.

[7]Athanasius, *Life of Anthony* 3.

[8]Cassian, *Inst.* II 5:2, adapted from Eusebius, *Hist. Eccl.* 2;17, based on Philo, *Vit. Cont.* 3. Notice that 'manual labour' is Cassian's own addition.

[9]MOPH I, p. 146.

[10]E.g. RM 50; RSB 48.

[11]RM 48; RSB 20. It is only later on that monastic customaries begin to prescribe a short time of private prayer for the monks, usually after matins; the earliest such prescription known to me is in the eighth-century *Memoriale qualiter* (CCM I, p. 260:1–3). On the later history of this practice, cf. Paul Philippe, 'L'Oraison Dominicaine au XIIIᵉ siècle', *La Vie Spirituelle, Supplément* 4 (1948), pp. 424–54, where further references to monastic and canonical texts are given.

[12]RSB 52.

[13]Cassian, *Conf.* 9:36; *Inst.* II 10:3.

[14]Augustine, PL 33:501, quoted by St Thomas, *Summa Theol.* IIᵃIIᵃᵉ q.83, a.14. For the medieval proverb, 'Short prayer pierces heaven', see *Cloud of Unknowing*, ch. 37; Langland, *Piers Plowman* A 11:303a, C 12:296a; Hans Walther, *Lateinische Sprichwörter und Sentenzen des Mittelalters* VII (Göttingen 1982), no. 313. The proverb is used amusingly by the tempter in the Macro play, *Mankind*, 558. Cf. also Savonarola, *Operette Spirituali* I, p. 52; Francisco de Osuna, *Third Spiritual Alphabet*, Tr. 21, ch. 3; St John of the Cross, *Living Flame* 1:33.

[15]Amand Boon, ed., *Pachomiana Latina* (Louvain 1932), Pachomii Praecepta 59–60, 139–40; Orsiesii Liber 51.

[16]RM 50:26, 28.

[17]L. d'Achery and J. Mabillon, ed., *Acta Sanctorum OSB* III 2 (Paris 1672), p. 252.

[18]Jerome, *Ep.* 43:1.

[19]Arthur Vööbus, *History of Asceticism in the Syrian Orient* II (Louvain 1960), ch. 12.

[20]Ibid., p. 106.

[21]PG 58:646.

[22]*Aboth* 1:13. The translation is taken from Israel Brodie, ed., *The Authorised Daily Prayer Book* (London 1962), p. 253.

[23]Eduard Lohse, ed., *Die Texte aus Qumran* (Munich 1971), IQS 6:7–8 (there is an English tr. of the Qumran texts by G. Vermes, *The Dead Sea Scrolls in English*. Penguin Books 1975). For early christian parallels, see above, ch. 1, p. 6. Barnabas 2:1 (ἐ κζητεῖν τὰ δικαιώματα κυρίου) is exactly equivalent to Qumran's *lidrôsh mishpot*.

[24]*Disputatio contra cuiusdam epistolam*, ed. A. Wilmart, *Revue d'Ascétique et Mystique* 23 (1947), pp. 266–7.

[25]*Letter on the Solitary Life* 4 (*Lettres des premiers Chartreux*, SC 88 [Paris 1962], p. 144).

[26]*Ancrene Riwle* M 286 (Salu, p. 127).

[27]Plato's doctrine that philosophy is a 'rehearsal of death' (μελέτη θανάτου) (*Phaedo* 81a) is taken up in its original sense in Greek and Latin christian texts: e.g. Evagrius, *Prakt.* 52 (parallels cited in the SC edn), Jerome, *Ep.* 60:14. Not surprisingly, though, the phrase is also taken to mean 'meditation on death' in the sense of thinking about death: e.g. Climacus, PG 88:793–7; Ambrose, PL 16:1324B (which exploits the ambiguity).

[28]AP Achillas 5.

[29]*Pachomiana Latina*, Pachomii Praecepta 60; cf. Orsiesii Liber 51–2.

[30]RM 50:26, 43; 68:1–2.

[31]Fifth Way of Prayer. Many of the MSS have *oratione* for *ore*. I hope to publish a critical edition of this text shortly. The translation in my *Early Dominicans*, p. 97, is, I now think, mistaken; I corrected it in *The Canadian Catholic Review* 1 (1983), p. 94.

[32]Suso, *Horologium Sapientiae* I 15. Pius Künzle in his edn (Fribourg, Sw. 1977, p. 502:21) prints *oratione* without mentioning any variant, but several MSS and older printed edns have *ore*, which is supported by the similar passage at p. 509:12–14, in spite of *dinem gebette* in the equivalent German text in the *Little Book of Eternal Wisdom* (K. Bihlmeyer, ed., *Heinrich Seuse: Deutsche Schriften* [repr. Frankfurt am Main 1961], p. 262:5).

[33]Philo, *Spec. Leg.* 4:106ff.

[34]Barnabas 10:11 (parallels cited by Prigent in the SC edn).

[35]J. A. Burrow, *Medieval Writers and their Work* (Oxford 1982), p. 53.

[36]PL 15:1279D.

[37]PL 83:679B.

[38]RSB, ed. cit., pp. 446–7.

[39]CCM I, p. 442.

[40]PL 102:597.

[41]Cassiodorus, *Institutiones* I 3:1, 16:3 (= reflection on something); I Pref. 3, 7 (= re-reading a text with a view to remembering it); II 3:5 (= Plato's rehearsal of death).

[42]Hope Emily Allen, ed., *English Writings of Richard Rolle* (Oxford 1931), p. 118.

[43]Cf. Smalley, op. cit., pp. 282–4.

[44]Bonaventure, *De Triplici Via*, ch. 1.

[45]Cf. the Quaracchi edn, vol. VIII, p. 3⁶; Cipriano Baraut, ed., *G. Jiménez*

de Cisneros: Obras Completas (Montserrat 1965), editor's note to the prologue of the *Exercitatorium Vite Spiritualis*, p. 91[1].

[46]Cf. for example John of Avila, *Epistolario* 1:5.

[47]A. Tanquerey, *The Spiritual Life* (Tournai 1930), §573.

[48]Hugh of St Victor, *Didascalicon* III 11; the 'rules' by which reading is governed are given in III 9.

[49]*De Meditatione*, Prologue.

[50]RM 50; RSB 48:1.

[51]*Regula non Bullata* 7:10–12.

[52]*Letter to St Anthony.*

[53]*Summa Theol.* II^{a}II^{ae} q.82 a.3.

[54]*Horologium Sapientiae* II 1, ed. cit., p. 523:12.

[55]Aelred, *De Inst. Recl.* 29.

[56]C. Horstman, ed., *Richard Rolle of Hampole* (London 1895), I, p. 198.

[57]Sanford Brown Meech, ed., *The Book of Margery Kempe*, Early English Text Society OS 212 (1940), p. 148.

[58]Ibid., p. 86.

[59]*Cloud of Unknowing*, ch. 65.

[60]*Meditationes de Vita Christi*, ch. 7; cf. *Med. de Passione*, ch. 10.

[61]Cf. M. D. Lambert, *Medieval Heresy* (London 1977), p. 197.

[62]*Book of Margery Kempe*, pp. 18–20.

[63]Ibid., pp. 193–5.

[64]*Med. de Passione*, ch. 11.

[65]Ignatius, *Spiritual Exercises*, 2nd Annotation, §2.

[66]Ibid., §50.

[67]Ibid., §§1, 91.

[68]Cf. Jacques Lewis, *Le Gouvernement Spirituel selon St Ignace de Loyola* (Montreal 1961), p. 114; José Calveras, *Manresa* 28 (1956), pp. 155–61.

[69]Letter to Urbano Fernandes, 1 June 1551.

[70]Letter to Bartolomé Hernández, 21 July 1554.

[71]Letter to Miguel Ochoa, 9 June 1550; to Antonio Brandao, 1 June 1551; cf. Miguel Nicolau, *Manresa* 28 (1956), pp. 94–5.

[72]Letter to Teresa Redajell, 11 September 1536.

11

The Ladder Dismantled: The Higher Rungs

Guigo would have us climb from meditation to prayer and then, if we are lucky, to contemplation; it is implicit throughout that meditation only really becomes spiritual in so far as it debouches into prayer, that prayer is essentially prayer for the vision of God, and that therefore contemplation is properly the result of prayer, both in the sense that it is properly prayer which leads to contemplation and in the sense that it is contemplation which properly crowns prayer. If this seems to us perfectly straightforward, it is largely because of the success of Guigo's presentation.

The artificiality and restrictiveness of Guigo's scheme can be seen by a comparison with Guigo's likely source, Hugh of St Victor. Hugh's scheme contains five ingredients: reading, meditation, prayer, practice (*operatio*) and contemplation. The first four items are things in which the life of the christian is 'exercised', but the fifth is not so much an 'exercise' as the 'fruit' of the other four. Reading belongs to beginners (in itself it is only a beginning, without much value if it does not lead to any kind of understanding)[1] and contemplation belongs to the perfect, but there is no simple hierarchical relationship between the other three elements.

Meditation can be seen as an end in itself,[2] or it can be seen as an indispensable preliminary to prayer (on the grounds that prayer arises from the twin considerations of our own wretchedness and the mercy of God),[3] or it can be seen as leading to christian moral behaviour.[4] It is not sharply distinguished from 'contemplation', but when he wants to Hugh can suggest an ad hoc distinction between them, making 'meditation' refer to the mind's struggle to discover the truth and 'contemplation' refer to the mind's lively penetration of a truth already discovered.[5] The contemplation of truth fires the mind with love, but it is in itself an intellectual occupation, restoring in us the 'eye of contemplation' which Adam had before the fall, by which he was always 'present to his Creator', 'always attending to his Creator in his reason'.[6]

If prayer is subordinated to anything in Hugh's scheme, it is to practice (*operatio*). Meditation shows us what we ought to do, but since it is God who must enable us to do it, we need to turn to him in prayer to ask for the necessary grace. And if anything is the essential precondition for contemplation, it is, once again, practice, because contemplation is the reward for a whole christian life.[7]

Guigo no doubt omitted practice (*operatio*) because he did not regard it as part of his 'spiritual exercise', but the omission evidently bothered the medieval English adapter of Guigo, who added a whole section to remedy it.[8] The main consequence of the omission, and it does not seem to be entirely unintentional on Guigo's part, is to tighten up the sequence, meditation-prayer-contemplation, considerably reducing the scope of the first two and linking contemplation much more immediately with prayer than in Hugh's scheme. Meditation is directly subordinated to prayer, and not to anything else, and prayer is no longer essentially seen as pervading a whole christian life, but rather as directed immediately to contemplation. Contemplation similarly is no longer seen as a reward for a whole christian life, any more than it is seen as the fulfilment of the intellectual life, it is a gift given directly in response to prayer and is indeed little more than a spontaneous intensification of prayer.

The presuppositions which make Guigo's scheme plausible become much clearer once we realise that prayer, like meditation, was undergoing a process of redefinition. It was losing its original, diffuse, meaning (petition) and being drawn into the much narrower perspective of devotionalism.

There is nothing intrinsically difficult about regarding meditation as leading to prayer. This is a facet of meditation which Hugh of St Victor recognises, as we have seen, and St Bernard makes a similar point: 'Meditation teaches us what is lacking, prayer obtains it for us. . . . By meditation we recognise the dangers which beset us and by prayer, at the gift of our Lord Jesus Christ, we escape them.'[9] And the traditional ruminating on the Word of God inevitably included a ruminating on texts which were in fact prayers, such as the psalms. Jordan of Saxony tells us about something that happened one day while he was 'praying' one of the psalms 'with a certain attentiveness of mind' and 'ruminating' one of the verses.[10] Conversely, monastic meditations were always liable to burst into prayer, so that, for instance, Anselm could entitle his book 'Prayers or Meditations'.[11] Sometimes a more formal movement is indicated from 'meditation' to 'petition', as in the meditations of Stephen of Sawley.[12]

Something rather different happens, however, when both 'meditation' and 'prayer' converge on the burgeoning interest in affectivity and sweetness. Hugh of St Victor is once again an important witness. In his *De Modo Orandi* he tackles a question which was evidently worrying some of his contemporaries: 'What is the use of saying words in prayer in which we find ourselves asking nothing from God? It is mockery rather than prayer and provokes God to anger, to come before him as if to ask for something and then suddenly start reciting other things which have nothing to do with the matter in hand.' The problem arises because of the traditional understanding of the word 'prayer', and Hugh's response shows how that understanding can be lost.

> In prayer which is made to God narration [i.e. explicitating what we want] is not necessary, except in as much as we relate things in order to understand our own petition better so that, prompted by our own words, we may consider what we are asking for and, by this consideration of our own petition, be stirred to pray with greater devotion. . . . There is no way to make God more ready to grant a request than for the mind of the person praying to turn to him with affections filled with devotion (*toto devotionis affectu*). So whatever a person says in prayer is not pointless, provided that it can appropriately be used either to stir the affections of the person praying to love of God, or better still to show that they are already so stirred. . . . The sheer devotion of the heart would be enough, as far as God is concerned, except in as much as the forming of a prayer in words kindles a greater devotion in the mind of the person praying.

In Hugh's view, 'supplication' suffices, which he defines as a 'humble and devout praying without specifying any petition', and the purest kind of prayer is 'when the mind is so much on fire from an abundance of devotion that when it turns to God to ask for something, it actually forgets its petition because of the greatness of its love of him'.[13]

The tendency to collapse prayer into desire for God is already apparent in St Gregory,[14] and it is much more pronounced in William of St Thierry. He sees prayer less as a matter of asking for something from God, than as a matter of offering something to God. He allocates the word 'postulation' to petitionary prayer, which he regards as an 'animal' kind of prayer, proper to those with no understanding of spiritual things. Spiritual people may sometimes make petitions, but even in them it is 'animal' prayer; petition is really characteristic of people who do not know how they ought to pray, who desire something other than God and seek 'neither feeling nor affection towards God'. Prayer proper is defined as 'the affection of someone cleaving to God, and a kind of intimate and pious talking to him, and the stability of the enlightened mind remaining to enjoy God as long as it may'.[15]

William, as we should expect, retains the traditional monastic discipline of reading and manual labour,[16] but the spiritual exercise in which he is most interested can be designated more or less indifferently prayer, meditation or contemplation.[17] Whichever word is used, what William wishes to recommend is the ascent to God by way of love, which is, as we have seen, the 'image' of knowledge which is the closest we can come in this life to knowing God.

The shift in the meaning of the word 'prayer' emerges very clearly from a comparison of two closely related texts. St Thomas Aquinas offers us a magisterial exposition of the traditional sense of prayer, showing exactly what the theological significance of petition is, and how it can be said that prayer, precisely as petition, is a genuinely religious act, involving a very real worship of God.[18] In the course of his treatise, he discusses the question whether it is necessary for us to be fully attentive while we are praying, and to clarify the question he identifies three different functions of prayer: its proper function is precisely to seek some gift from God, and for this all that is needed is a sincere intention to pray, and our prayer will not be invalidated if our minds wander. Prayer may also be envisaged as a good work, like any other, and for this too intention is sufficient. But there is also the possibility that we shall obtain immediate spiritual refreshment as a result of praying, and this does depend on the degree of our attentiveness to what we are doing.[19] Savonarola, in the fifteenth century, follows this teaching of St Thomas very closely indeed, so closely that any deviation, however slight, can certainly be regarded as deliberate. And there is one small, but vastly significant, difference between Savonarola's exposition and that of St Thomas; Savonarola does not say that 'impetration' (obtaining something from God by petition) is the proper effect of prayer. In his view, the immediate spiritual relish which we may expect to feel if we concentrate on our prayer is far more important.[20]

There is a similarly illuminating comparison to be made between St Teresa's doctrine and that of her medieval precursors. It had been more or less a commonplace to say that all prayer, if it is prayer at all, is 'mental prayer', without seeing any essential distinction between mental prayer and vocal prayer. If there is no involvement of the mind at all, then there is no human act at all, and so there cannot be any genuine prayer.[21] St Teresa agrees that there is no essential difference between mental and vocal prayer, and she agrees that all prayer worthy of the name is mental prayer, but she interprets this to mean that unless we are properly recollected in our prayer we are not praying.[22] In this, she aligns herself with Savonarola rather than with St Thomas.

This shift from the conviction that prayer needs to be *deliberate* to the belief that it needs to be *recollected* is part and parcel of the increasing convergence of prayer and meditation to the point at which they both mean more or less the same thing, namely a stirring of the heart towards God, which is meant to be affectively as intense as possible and will, it is hoped, result in an even more intense enjoyment of God.

This convergence of 'prayer' and 'meditation' carries 'contemplation' along with it. There never had been any very rigorous distinction between 'meditation' and 'contemplation', although various ad hoc distinctions could be suggested when it suited anyone's purpose. Like Hugh of St Victor, St Bernard, in slightly different terminology, proposes a distinction between 'consideration' and 'contemplation', but he is honest enough to point out that the two terms are generally used interchangeably. And they are both clearly intellectual terms for Bernard.[23]

Guigo introduces a much sharper distinction, by leaving 'meditation' in what is already becoming the rather depreciated category of 'merely' intellectual occupations, while appropriating 'contemplation' to designate an intensely affective experience, a usage which was made possible, as we have seen, by the Augustinian tradition which recognised a kind of knowledge of God precisely in the feeling of love, but which Guigo adopts without comment, as if there was no problem at all about using the word in this seemingly quite unintellectual way. A distinction not unlike Guigo's eventually succeeds in establishing itself, but it is an arbitrary and rather artificial distinction.

'Contemplate' is in itself, of course, a perfectly harmless word, meaning to 'look at' something, either with the eyes or with the mind. 'Contemplative' words acquired their more aristocratic connotations from a philosophical tradition deriving ultimately from Aristotle.[24] After a rather shaky start[25] they found their way into christian language, but the philosophical background did not prevent christians from using them in a variety of different ways.

In a text which is close to philosophical usage, Augustine maintains that contemplativity and activity are both facets of the pursuit of wisdom, the latter being concerned with shaping our morals, while the former is concerned with 'examining the causes of nature and the purest truth'.[26] In a rather earlier work he had made a similar distinction between 'active virtue' and 'contemplative virtue', both regarded as belonging essentially to everybody's christian life; the 'contemplative virtue' consists in faith and attentiveness to the teaching of Christ.[27] It could quite properly be translated as 'intellectual virtue', but it is evidently not some exalted mountaintop beyond the reach of the average christian.

St Gregory offers a classic account of the difference between the 'active' and 'contemplative' lives, but it is deceptive in its appearance of simplicity: the active life consists in works of charity, the contemplative life 'is to hold on to the love of God and of neighbour with all one's mind, but to rest from external activity, to cling solely to desire of our Creator, so that the soul no longer desires to do anything, but only to trample down all cares and yearn passionately to see the face of its Maker'.[28] It is not all clear that Gregory actually believes the contemplative life, as defined like this, to be a good thing. In the sense that any christian hopes ultimately for the beatific vision, all christians aspire to the contemplative life, but here and now it is wrong to withdraw entirely from all activity, and may in some cases even be seriously sinful.[29]

In the text quoted above, Gregory seems to make out the contemplative life to be essentially affective, but elsewhere he makes it clear that contemplation is about the *knowledge* of God, and for this very reason it can be dangerous. Love is the 'mind's crane' which lifts it up to seek knowledge of God, and without this love, combined with a healthy fear, the attempt to know God will result only in 'the mistake of wrong understanding', and this is also what will happen if we try to go beyond the limits of our own intellectual capacity. The contemplative and active lives are like our two eyes, and if the former is going to lead us astray then we should, as the Lord commanded, pluck it out and cast it from us and enter safely into eternal life solely on the strength of the active life.[30]

Gregory's warning became part of the medieval tradition,[31] and there are cautionary tales to support it. For instance, the Dominican *Lives of the Brethren* contains a story of someone who lost his belief in God because of 'too much contemplation'.[32]

A rigorously intellectualist interpretation of the 'contemplative life' is offered by St Thomas, along Aristotelian lines. He applies the phrase to a life in which speculative interests prevail over practical interests, though he recognises that this can never be more than a matter of degree, as a purely intellectual life is not possible in this world.[33] In line with this Thomistic usage, some later Dominicans unhesitatingly apply the word 'contemplative' to natural scientists.[34] St Thomas quite realistically admits that the contemplative, as such, is less fervent in his love of God than someone engaged in a more active life, but, like Gregory, he insists that a christian contemplative life must be motivated by love of God and cannot help but lead to an enjoyment of God in so far as it achieves its objective.[35]

In view of all this, it is not surprising that 'contemplative' can sometimes be used in a pejorative sense to mean 'merely theoretical'.[36] Less radically, Hugh of Balma relegates it to an inferior role in his account of the spiritual life in this world, though he describes our heavenly bliss as being the 'contemplation' of God 'face to face'.[37] But otherwise 'contemplation' is used to refer to the speculative activity of the mind which belongs to the 'illuminative way', which has to be abandoned if we are to advance to the 'unitive way', in which the intellect is not involved at all.[38] Rachel, as usual, is taken to symbolise the 'contemplative life', but she is far surpassed in Hugh's scheme by Mary, who represents the 'way of love', which is 'more noble than any meditation or intellectual struggle designated by Rachel'.[39] The highest state attainable in this life is one in which the soul rises to God affectively without any previous or concomitant activity of the intellect.[40]

For very different reasons Meister Eckhart also reduces the status of contemplation. In one sermon he lists four ingredients which are involved in the perfection of charity, and Leah and Rachel, symbolising the active and contemplative lives, merely feature as two such ingredients, together with 'detachment' or 'apartness' (abegescheidenheit) and an 'upclimbing spirit' (ûfklimmende geist). But all four elements fade into insignificance beside the real goal of the christian life:

What would it help me, that Mary should be full of grace, unless I too am full of grace? And what would it help me that the Father should give birth to his Son, unless I too give birth to him? Therefore God gives birth to his Son in a perfect soul . . . so that she can then bring him forth outwardly in all her works.[4]

It is the whole range of works, springing spontaneously from the fertile presence of Christ in the soul, which constitutes perfection.[42] Contemplation does not seem to be a very important notion to Eckhart, as is shown vividly in the way in which he actually suggests that Mary (the contemplative) is inferior in christian maturity to Martha, who has learned how to be a christian in the hard school of life.[43]

On the whole, though, 'contemplation' manages to retain its privileged status, but to do so it has to share in the fate of 'meditation' and abandon its intellectual connotations. James of Milan, a late thirteenth-century Franciscan, in his famous Stimulus Amoris, puts the word to work in an entirely anti-intellectual way. The goal of life in this world is, he says, the 'repose of contemplation'. This is approached by way of three things: compunction and the attempt never to offend God, constant affective union with the Passion of Christ, and the determination to desire nothing but God.[44] Contemplation itself is entirely affective, leading to various kinds of spiritual inebriation, culminating sometimes in 'rapture'.[45] No distinction is made between contemplation and meditation; for instance, when the soul is drunk with contemplation nothing can tear it from its 'continual meditation'.[46]

James, like Gregory, is well aware that intellectual activity can lead us astray, but whereas Gregory sees this as being precisely the hazard to which 'contemplatives' are exposed, James sees 'contemplation' as being the very antithesis of the intellectual life: God is to be praised for making clever people intent on study, 'but he wanted you to rest in contemplation lest you should fall by the wayside, into error, that is; he did not want you to undertake any subtle and inquisitive investigations, so that you might retain your simplicity'.[47]

In the fourteenth century Richard Rolle develops this non-intellectual notion of contemplation. After surveying several definitions of contemplation, he rejects the most intellectual ones, approves of two which are purely affective, and then offers his own view that 'contemplation is exultation in the love of God, taken up into the mind with the sweetness of angelic praise'.[48] The 'angelic praise' to which he alludes refers to his own experience of hearing angels' song, which, together with the experience of heat (so graphically described at the beginning of the *Fire of Love*) and sweetness, Rolle regards as constituting the highest attainable love of God.[49]

What is novel in Rolle's doctrine is that he identifies exactly the point at which someone becomes a contemplative: it is when they have the experience of the 'opening of the gates of heaven' so that they can see in, with the result that thereafter they are 'ravished in love'.[50]

Rolle's sharp demarcation between those who are and those who are not contemplatives has no immediate influence. At the very end of the fifteenth century García Jiménez de Cisneros regards the highest contemplation as consisting in an 'inflaming of love' by which the soul raises itself on high 'without any speculative thought of God', but he does not make any radical distinction between these 'true contemplatives' and 'beginners in contemplation' who still need to think.[51]

Osuna, famous for his doctrine of 'thinking nothing',[52] rather surprisingly makes no attempt to claim the word 'contemplation' for his recommended exercise of recollection, though its practitioners are called 'contemplatives'; *contemplar* is used to refer to speculative theology, which he regards as vastly inferior to his own 'mystical theology'.[53]

St Ignatius makes no systematic distinction between meditation and contemplation, but it is interesting to note a comment made on him by Nadal: 'He felt and contemplated the presence of God and the emotion of spiritual things (*rerum spiritualium affectum*) in all things, in all his actions and words, he was a contemplative in action, which he used to explain like this: God is to be found in all things.'[54] It is typical of Ignatius to want to overcome the dichotomy between action and contemplation, and it is also typical of him that this should involve a 'feeling' of the presence of God.[55]

The usage which eventually prevailed, for better or for worse, was established by the two famous Carmelites, St Teresa of Avila and St John of the Cross. Both of them posit a sharp distinction between 'meditation' and 'contemplation', the passage from one to the other being marked by an inability on the part of the soul to do anything of its own.[56] This is taken to be the evidence that the soul is progressing into a truly 'supernatural' state.[57]

This very sketchy and incomplete survey, looking both backwards and forwards from Guigo, highlights his position, poised with deceptive tranquillity over the revolution that was brewing. And if it suggests that his particular synthesis is not without an element of arbitrariness, it suggests too that there is nothing fated or definitive about anybody else's deployment of the concepts of piety. The old team, reading and prayer, was perhaps too simple to survive the pressures of more complex, more self-conscious, epochs; but maybe the new team of 'mental prayer' and 'contemplative prayer', forged as it was by the more or less random pressures of differing cultural moods, is far from being sacrosanct. There is, after all, something serious in Guigo's warning that meditation without reading will be erroneous. Scientific exegesis has for centuries deprived us of the easy familiarity with the bible which the old ruminant monks enjoyed. Must it necessarily deprive christian spirituality of its foundations?

Bibliography and Abbreviations

See above, p. 100.

Notes

[1]*Didasc.* III 12.
[2]*Didasc.* III 11.
[3]PL 176:977.
[4]*Didasc.* V 9; cf. III 13.
[5]PL 175;116–17.
[6]PL 176:329, 670–1.
[7]For this whole section, *Didasc.* V 9.
[8]Printed in Phyllis Hodgson, ed., *Deonise Hid Diuinite*, Early English Text Society 231 (1955), p. 102.
[9]Bernard, *Sermon on the Feast of St Andrew* 10. A similar point is made by Peraldus, *Summa de Virtutibus*, Prayer, ch. 4
[10]Jordan of Saxony, *Libellus* 118.
[11]F. S. Schmitt, ed., *Anselmi Opera* III (Edinburgh 1946), pp. 3–4.

[12]André Wilmart, *Auteurs Spirituels et Textes Dévots* (Paris 1971), pp. 339–58.

[13]PL 176:979–83.

[14]PL 75:1107–8

[15]*Expos. Cant.* 14–15, *Golden Epistle* 177–9

[16]*Golden Epistle* 83–4.

[17]Cf. *Golden Epistle* 174, *Expos. Cant.* 22.

[18]*Summa Theol.* II[a]II[ae] q.83 esp. art. 1–3. It is no doubt due to the influence of St Thomas that Luis of Granada can still say in the sixteenth century that 'prayer' basically means 'petition' (*De la Oración y Consideración* III 1), in marked contrast to his friend and mentor, John of Avila (e.g. *Audi filia*, ch. 70). For some general comments on the Dominican tradition on prayer, see Simon Tugwell, 'A Dominican Theology of Prayer', *Dominican Ashram* 1 (1982), pp. 128–44.

[19]*Summa Theol.* II[a]II[ae] q.83 a.13.

[20]Savonarola, *Operette Spirituali* I, pp. 166, 173.

[21]E.g. Humbert of Romans, ed. Berthier, II, p. 92; this is why St Thomas talks of 'adding' vocal prayer, *Summa Theol.* II[a]II[ae] q.83 a.12, and cf. ibid., a.1; Bonaventure, IV *Sent.* d.15 p. 2 art.2 q.3; Savonarola, op. cit., I, pp. 164–5.

[22]St Teresa, *Interior Castle* I 1:7; cf. also Augustine Baker, *Holy Wisdom*, III 1:1.

[23]Bernard, *De Consideratione* II 2:5.

[24]Aristotle, *Eth. Nic.* X 7 appears to be at the source of the philosophical tradition of the supremacy of the contemplative life; from Aristotle it was adopted by the Platonists (cf. Albinus, *Didaskalikos* 2).

[25]'Contemplative' words are used in the bible and the earliest christian writings only in a mundane sense, and at first it is only the christian intellectuals, like Clement of Alexandria, who adopt the more elevated usage of the philosophers. It is only gradually that this usage seeps into more general acceptance. It was the influence of Gregory which established 'contemplative' terminology as part of the stock-in-trade of western monasticism.

[26]Augustine, *Civ. Dei* VIII 4. On the history of the notion of 'contemplative life' in western christendom, see the useful outline by M. Elizabeth Mason, *Active Life and Contemplative life*. Milwaukee 1961.

[27]PL 34:1045–6; cf. also PL 38:925.

[28]PL 76:953.

[29]PL 76:954B; PL 77:19C.

[30]PL 75:761–4.

[31]E.g. Isidore (PL 83:691B); Odo of Canterbury (*Comm. in libros Regum*, ed. Charles de Clercq [Ventimiglia 1980], p. 42); Thomas Hibernicus (*Manipulus Florum*, Contemplatio 20); Cavalca (*Frutti della Lingua* 23).

[32]MOPH I, p. 112.

[33]*Summa Theol.* II[a]II[ae] q.179 a.2.

[34]E.g. Cajetan, comment on *Summa Theol.* II[a]II[ae] q.180 a.4; Tommaso Campanella, *Apologia for Galileo* III 2 ass.4.

[35]*Super Ev. Ioh.* 2487, 2640 (Marietti edn. Turin 1952); *Summa Theol.* II[a]II[ae] q.180 a.1.

[36]Suso at least twice uses the German equivalent, *schoewlich*, in a pejorative sense: Bihlmeyer, ed. cit., pp. 156:31, 339:27.

[37]Hugh of Balma 5b.

[38]Ibid., 42b.

[39]Ibid., 49b–50a.

[40]Ibid., 46b–53b.

[41]DW III, pp. 300–2 (sermon 88 in Walshe).

[42]On this theme in Eckhart, cf. Simon Tugwell, *Reflections on the Beatitudes* (London 1980), p. 36.

[43]DW III, p. 482, (sermon 9 in Walshe).

[44]*Stimulus Amoris* 4.

[45]Ibid., 8–9.

[46]Ibid., 8.

[47]Ibid., 11.

[48]*Emendatio Vitae* 12.

[49]*Incendium Amoris* 14.

[50]*English Writings*, ed. cit., p. 119. This experience was Rolle's own introduction to his form of contemplative life: *Incendium Amoris* 15.

[51]*Exercitatorium* 29, ed. cit., pp. 260–2.

[52]Osuna, op. cit., Tr. 21 ch. 5. This is the one point singled out by John of Avila, *Epist.* 1:5. Osuna's doctrine is attacked by Francisco de Vitoria in his commentary on St Thomas, *Summa Theol.* II^aII^ac q.182 a.4: 'There is a new kind of contemplation which is practised by the monks these days, consisting of meditating on God and the angels. They spend a long time in a state of elevation, thinking nothing. This is, no doubt, very good, but I do not find much about it in scripture and it is, frankly, not what the saints recommend. Genuine contemplation is reading the bible and the study of true wisdom.'

[53]Osuna, op. cit., Tr.6 ch. 2–3.

[54]Nadal, *Epist.* IV 651; cf. Nicolau, *Manresa* 28 (1956), pp. 94–5.

[55]On *sentir* in Ignatius, cf. Jacques Lewis, *Le Gouvernement Spirituel selon St Ignace de Loyola*, pp. 50–3.

[56]Cf. Teresa, *Way of Perfection* 41; John of the Cross, *Dark Night* I 10:1, 5; *Living Flame* 1:9. The Dominicans, it may be noticed, were not happy with this doctrine. Cf. the comments of Juan de Lazcano quoted in Allison Peers, *Studies of the Spanish Mystics* III (London 1960), pp. 89–90, and the row between the Carmelites and the Dominican Pedro de Santa Maria Ulloa (Alvaro Huerga, *Escalaceli* [Madrid 1981], pp. 385–7).

[57]It should be noted that this definition of the 'supernatural' falls foul of the classic catholic criterion of true spiritual effects, as formulated in the controversy with the Montanists: Origen, *Contra Celsum* VII 3; Eusebius, *Hist. Eccl.* V 17, and adopted by St Thomas, *Super Matt.* 849 (in the Marietti edn. Turin 1951). In *Living Flame* 1:9 St John of the Cross is perhaps trying to formulate his doctrine in such a way as to evade this kind of criticism. It is also interesting to contrast a criterion of supernaturalness found in Suso, *Hor. Sap.* II 5, ed. cit., p. 581: what makes a movement of the soul 'supernatural' is that it is meritorious, i.e. rooted in charity and deliberately directed towards God by the will. This is more or less exactly the opposite of the later definition.

12

Francis of Assisi

Few saints in the history of the church have had such an immediate and such a lasting success as Francis of Assisi (1181–1226). His contemporaries were amazed at the rapid expansion of the order which he founded,[1] and even if the figures given in the early chronicles are exaggerated, it was clearly spectacular. His first two followers, Bernard of Quintavalle and Peter of Catani, joined him in 1208, yet by 1222 three, if not five, thousand of them are said to have assembled together for a General Chapter.[2] And in our own time the stream of visitors to Assisi and the flood of books and articles devoted to Francis show that the appeal of the *poverello* has not diminished.

At the same time, however, few saints have been so successfully obscured by the myths which have been allowed or encouraged to grow up around them, and even fewer have been the subject of such diverse and incompatible interpretations as Francis. In the middle ages he was seen as a 'second Christ' and as the 'angel of the sixth seal'.[3] In modern times he has been presented as everything from an embodiment of social protest, if not a deliberate social reformer, to a more or less 'hippy' child of nature.[4]

If we want to understand the real Francis, we must base our study only on the most authentic, early sources,[5] among which we cannot, unfortunately, include the much-loved *Fioretti*, which is a late and tendentious compilation. And obviously the most authoritative source of all is constituted by the genuine writings of Francis himself, excluding, of course, the familiar 'Prayer of St Francis', which is not known even to have existed before the twentieth century and which seems to have become attached to the name of St Francis in 1936 due to a simple misunderstanding.[6]

Francis ('Frenchy')[7] Bernardone was the son of a reasonably prosperous merchant in Assisi, and, if we may trust his biographers, he was a cheerful, popular, self-indulgent youth, who spent money with gay abandon and enjoyed life as a young man about town, but was naturally polite and tried never to be offensive or coarse in anything he said. His parents seem to have worried about his extravagance and lack of commercial seriousness, and they were no

125

doubt also perplexed, as middle-class parents often are, by his style of dress – he apparently anticipated a more recent fashion by sewing patches of old cloth on to expensive clothes.

By temperament he was exuberantly extrovert and self-confident. During a bout of war between Assisi and Perugia he was taken prisoner, but he refused to be depressed. 'Who do you think I am?' he responded to one of his fellow captives, who was complaining about his high spirits, 'I shall still live to be the idol of the whole world!'[8]

Francis' conversion to a more religious way of life was gradual. The first stage was a growing willingness, then eagerness, to give alms to the poor. This does not involve any serious change in his character; he never had been careful with his money. It is simply that his extravagance has now found a new outlet. He is as fond of expensive clothes as ever he was; only he now sometimes gives them away.

As a result of a long sickness and some strange experiences, which his biographers at least interpret as being visions from God, Francis gradually withdraws from his social life. But this does not mean that he stops enjoying himself. The Francis who used to like singing in the streets with his friends is not so terribly changed to become the Francis who makes an enormous racket weeping over the passion of Christ. And the old Francis shows through nearly un-changed in an episode which is both a youthful prank and an act of lavish generosity: one day in Rome he very noisily threw all the money he had into the collection box in St Peter's in Rome, and then went out and swopped clothes with a beggar and started begging in French 'because he liked speaking French, even though he did not speak it well'.

It was probably in 1205 that two events occurred which were to have a decisive effect on Francis' life. The first can be recounted in his own words, composed at the end of his life:

This was how the Lord gave me, brother Francis, a beginning of doing penance: when I was still in my sins, I found it very unpleasant to see lepers. And the Lord himself led me among them and I was kind to them. And when I went away from them, what had seemed unpleasant before was turned into sweetness in my soul and body. And after that I did not wait long, but abandoned the world.[9]

The second event happened in the church of San Damiano: while Francis was praying in there, he heard the crucifix speaking to him, and telling him to repair the Lord's house. It was from this time that Francis' life-long devotion to the passion began, and it was after this experience that Francis began to desire a life of separation from the world.

Francis' first move was to raise all the money he could and present it to the priest of San Damiano; then he settled at San Damiano and devoted himself to rebuilding and refurbishing the church. His father was horrified both at the loss of the money and at the loss of his son, and eventually complained about him to the bishop. Francis happily returned all the money he had to his father and then stripped himself naked and gave back even the clothes he was wearing. 'Up to now,' he said publicly, 'I have called Peter Bernadone my father, but now that I have resolved to serve God, I return to him all the money he was upset over and even all the clothes which I have from his property; from now on I want to say, "Our Father who art in heaven", not "My father Peter Bernadone." '

After that he resumed his life of great austerity and poverty, wandering round doing what he could to repair various dilapidated churches.[10]

Although Francis is described as being 'drunk with love of God' and as 'exulting in the Lord',[11] it is not until 1208 that he finally discovers the path which he is to follow for the rest of his life. On St Matthias' day in that year he went to mass in the church of the Porziuncola, which he had been restoring, and he heard the gospel from Matthew 10 about the apostles being sent out to preach, taking no provisions with them as they went, no staff, no shoes, no bag, and he exclaimed, 'That's what I want! That's what I have been looking for', and immediately he took off his shoes, abandoned his staff and confined himself to a single tunic, and set himself to fulfil the words of the gospel *literally (ad litteram)*.[12]

In this fundamental episode, we can see the two basic elements in Francis' whole vision of the christian life: literal observance of the gospel and that particular kind of poverty which makes you totally dependent on the random generosity of others.

This kind of desire to return to the plain gospel had been characteristic of many of the spontaneous religious movements which had sprung up in the twelfth century and which continued to pullulate in the thirteenth century. All too often they were vitiated by a tendency to appeal to the gospel against the church. But St Francis never envisaged there being any opposition between the gospel and the church. He always insisted on people showing all possible respect to the clergy, however sinful they might be, and he had a high regard for the church's theologians.[13] Within a year or two of his final and decisive 'conversion' he went of his own accord, with his tiny band of followers, to see the pope and to solicit his approval for his way of life.[14] It was probably on the same occasion that he made a solemn promise of obedience to the pope.[15] And this obedience to the pope became a linchpin in the structure of his order: all the friars are to promise obedience to the head of the order, and the head of the order is, in their name, to promise obedience to the pope.[16]

For Francis it was axiomatic that a life of total obedience to the gospel can only be lived within the church, in docility to the institutions of the church. One of his constant concerns was to inculcate respect for the blessed Sacrament,[17] and he insisted on his friars respecting the authority of even the lowliest, most disreputable priest. They were never to engage in any kind of apostolate against the wishes of the local clergy.[18]

St Francis never claimed any kind of evangelical liberty *from* the laws and institutions of the church; what he did claim was an evangelical liberty *within* the church. He resisted all attempts to persuade him to adopt an existing monastic Rule,[19] he rejected all the convenient ways in which most of us dilute the plain teaching of the gospel; he wanted to take the gospel straight, and he dared to believe that it was possible to live simply by the rule of the gospel.[20]

This meant, on the one hand, that Francis did not want his friars to be bound by all the traditional monastic observances. They were to fast, for example, on Fridays and during Lent, in accordance with church law, but for the rest they were to eat whatever food was set before them, in accordance with the gospel rule.[21]

On the other hand, Francis could not allow any tampering with what he regarded as the rule of the gospel. His own Rule was, in his view, nothing other than an expression of the rule of the gospel[22] and, to prevent any blunting of its impact, Francis wanted it to be observed exactly as it stood, without any commentary or interpretation.[23] The Franciscans soon found that things were not quite as simple as this, and Gregory IX had to assure them that they were not obliged by their profession to treat every word of the gospel as a precept,[24] but plainly Francis reckoned that the gospel message was quite clear and straightforward, and that all that was needed was to put it into practice.

A story is told which illustrates how radically Francis interpreted the demands of literal observance of the gospel: when the brother who was doing the cooking wanted to soak the vegetables in hot water overnight in the usual way, Francis forbade it on the grounds that the gospel says, 'Take no thought for the morrow'. Only after they had said matins was the cook permitted to start preparing the vegetables.[25]

On the same evangelical principle, the early friars did not keep anything in stock from one day to the next, but made provision only for one day at a time.[26]

Another principle which the early Franciscans followed literally, in defiance of normal contemporary practice, was the blunt instruction, 'Do not swear' (Matthew 5:34). There is an interesting case in 1225 when some priest wanted to leave the order. He claimed that he had never made profession in the order, but this was denied by the friars. When the case was heard before the pope, the friars refused to give their evidence *on oath*, so, whatever the truth of the matter, their plea was dismissed.[27]

The heart of the gospel, though, in Francis' eyes, is the call to abandon property. In the light of the story of the young man who was told, 'If you would be perfect, go, sell all you have and give to the poor and come, follow me' (Matthew 19:21), Francis identifies the 'perfection of the gospel' with the renunciation of all possessions.[28] Summing up what it means for him to observe the gospel literally, he says, 'I, brother Francis the little one, want to follow the life and poverty of our most high Lord, Jesus Christ.'[29]

In the later Franciscan tradition it is precisely material poverty which is regarded as crucial, and this in turn comes to mean little more than legal poverty; but for Francis himself the essential poverty is seen in the abandonment of rights, in the abandonment of one's own will. In one of his *Admonitions* he is quite explicit: 'Who is it who abandons everything he possesses? It is the person who yields himself totally to obedience in the hands of his superior.'[30]

The fundamental model of poverty is located in the rule which our Lord gave to his disciples when he sent them out to preach. And, as seen by Francis, the essence of this poverty is that we should have no means of shielding ourselves against the slings and arrows of outrageous fortune. Poverty and obedience are inseparable in Francis' vision and they are both pushed as far as they can be pushed. Francis wants his friars to be *minores* precisely in the sense that they are never to be in a position to control things, they are to be at the mercy of whatever happens. Living without property, as Francis explains, means never getting upset by anything that anybody does.[31] Writing to one of the ministers in the order, Francis says that even things which appear to be hindrances to our love of God must be accepted as a 'grace', and that sinners must be accepted with patience and goodwill. 'Do not want anything more from them than what God gives you. Love them like this, and do not want them to be better christians.'[32] In this sense it is quite true to say that 'Francis never wanted to reform anyone or anything'.[33]

The monastic tradition had assumed that the development of a proper spiritual life depended on the monks being protected against disturbances and temptations; but the Franciscans made it their boast that their enclosure was no other than the whole world.[34] If this is God's world, ruled by his providence, we ought not to have to protect ourselves against it. Whatever happens is God's gift to us.

This is the source of Francis' famous love of nature. But we shall misunderstand it entirely if we only look at the obviously attractive features of it. It is easy enough to enjoy the story of Francis taming the wolf of Gubbio[35] or making friends with a cicada,[36] and there is something pleasantly sentimental about his getting a passer-by to purchase for him a solitary lamb that was left in a field full of goats.[37] But Francis' acceptance of all creatures was intended to mean a radical unprotectedness precisely in face of all creatures. So Francis bids his followers not merely to be obedient to all human creatures, but even to be subject (subditi) to wild animals.[38] And subjection does not even stop there. On one occasion Francis' habit caught fire, and he tried to stop his companion putting the fire out, saying to him, 'Dearest brother, do not harm brother fire.' Francis only permitted the fire to be extinguished because the superior insisted on it. And on another occasion the roof caught fire and Francis, instead of helping to quench the flames, left the place, carrying with him an old skin he used as a blanket. Later he came back very contrite for having absconded with something which 'brother fire' wanted.[39]

It is this quality of total resignation to the will even of inanimate things which gives Francis' poverty its special nuance. Originally it seems to have been his intention that his friars should quite literally, like Christ, have nowhere to lay their heads.[40] Within Francis' own lifetime the order began to become more settled and some sites were effectively occupied as rudimentary Franciscan houses. But Francis still insists that such sites must never be regarded as belonging to the friars.[41] The famous Porziuncola, which Francis himself loved so much, was for all practical purposes given to him by the Benedictines, but as a sign that he refused to regard it as his own property he insisted on paying an annual rent to the monks (the rent being a basket of fish).[42] It was written into Francis' Rule that the friars were never to defend their rights to live in any particular place; anyone was welcome to come and turn them out, and while they were living there, all comers were welcome – and the invitation specifically includes burglars.[43]

As an important part of the Franciscan renunciation of rights Francis was increasingly insistent on the friars never handling money.[44] Though later on this developed into an almost magical dread of physical contact with money,[45] the original aim is quite clear. Money gives you rights, it gives you protection, and is therefore incompatible with the state of total exposure to the will of God which Francis wanted to inculcate. The friars were only to have things which they needed for immediate use, and the same applied to money which anybody handled on their behalf.[46]

One very obvious expression of Franciscan poverty was begging, and some later sources suggest that Francis laid a certain emphasis on begging as a gesture of humility,[47] but the Franciscans were not originally mendicant on principle and Francis himself rather stresses the importance of the friars doing casual labour to earn their keep. It is only if they cannot get work or do not get paid that they are to beg 'like other poor people'.[48] And they are not to accept jobs which would put them in any position of authority over other people.[49] Whatever form of life they adopt (and Francis allows for 'pray-ers' and preachers as well as for labourers),[50] the friars are always to be *minores*, always in a position to be exploited by others, never in a position to exploit others.

Francis' essential concern is quite clear. It is not poverty, as such, that he values, it is rather the readiness to be in a position in which it is impossible for you to insist on your own will. The whole point of Franciscan life is a radical conversion away from a life of self-will to a life of submission. Francis sees original sin as consisting precisely in disobedience: eating the forbidden fruit means nothing other than 'appropriating your will to yourself'.[51] The heart of conversion must accordingly be the disappropriation of your own will.

This is why obedience is so important to Francis. Although he continued to regard himself as effectively responsible for his order, even after he had technically resigned, he insisted on promising obedience to the friar whom he had appointed to replace him, and he even asked to be given a personal superior to whom he could be obedient the whole time.[52]

But even this radical obedience is not an autonomous value. The key to the whole enterprise of Francis is the principle of following Christ. Living exactly by the words of the gospel is not, for Francis, to be confused with any slavish adherence to the letter of the law; living by the gospel means following Christ.[53]

Christ came into the world as a servant, not a lord. He was content to be at the mercy even of his enemies. He surrendered himself even to death. Poverty is to be valued because Christ was poor. In the earliest Franciscan sources, Lady Poverty is not Francis' bride, she is Christ's bride and Francis' service of her is dependent on his service of Christ.[54]

Francis' refusal to allow any protection against the slings and arrows derives not just from a general belief in providence, but quite particularly from the example of Christ's unprotectedness. And his acceptance of his cross is the reason why the Franciscan is supposed to be specially glad to be on the receiving end of cruelty and unpleasantness.

On one occasion Francis called brother Leo to him and then dictated to him a definition of true happiness:

> Suppose a messenger comes and tells me that all the Masters in the University of Paris have come to join the order: that is not true happiness. Suppose that all the prelates beyond the Alps, all the archbishops and bishops have come to join the order, suppose that the kings of France and of England have come too: that is not true happiness. Suppose that my brethren have gone to the unbelievers and converted them all to the faith; suppose that I have such grace from God that I heal the sick and work many miracles: I tell you that in all of these true happiness does not reside. So what is true happiness? I am on my way back from Perugia and I arrive here late at night, and it is the muddy time of winter and so cold that there are icicles hanging from the bottom of my tunic, which keep striking my legs so that they are wounded and bleeding. All muddy and cold and covered in ice, I arrive at the door and when I have knocked at the door and shouted for a long time, at last the brother comes and asks, 'Who is it?' I reply, 'It's brother Francis.' He says, 'Go away, this is no time for travelling. You can't come in.' I plead with him, but he repeats, 'Go away; you're an ignorant simpleton. You are certainly not going to come in here with us; we have quite enough people here and they are quite good enough, we do not need you.' Once more I stand at the door, saying 'For the love of God, take me in just for this night.' But he says, 'I won't. Go to the Crutched Friars and ask there.' I tell you, if I have patience and am not upset, this is where true happiness lies, and true virtue and the salvation of my soul.[55]

It is this terrifying text which must govern our understanding of all that Francis says about happiness and submission to all creatures. He is indeed most insistent on happiness, so much so that when he is tormented himself for some reason or another, he tries to keep himself out of the way for fear of scandalising the brethren.[56] But the happiness he preaches is a long way from the simple happiness of a child of nature. It is the rigorously supernatural happiness of those who find all their joy in being identified with the Lord in his passion. The exposure to nature which is a genuine part of Franciscan tradition is not primarily a matter of fresh air and fun, it is most typically a sharing in Christ's exposure to maltreatment and rejection.

Francis was no Romantic, sentimentalising and idealising the raw life of nature; he knew very well what happens to people who strip off the customary ways we have devised of insulating ourselves against the world outside: they get crucified. But it is only on the basis of a readiness to be crucified that redemption can operate.

Although Francis does not seem to have been interested in making any kind of social or political protest, he was clearly interested in building up a new pattern of human relationships. If we are prepared radically to abandon all our attemps to assert ourselves and to protect ourselves, then we can afford to begin being charitable. The following of Christ in his poverty and in his endurance leads to a new way of relating to other people. Francis insists very much that his followers should be a *brotherhood*[57] and he takes steps to ensure that the hierarchy which has to develop within his order does not sabotage the basic brotherhood of all the friars.[58] Francis wanted there to be a real affection, even tenderness between his friars, and this is often expressed in maternal terms.[59] The Rule insists particularly on a warm attention being paid to the sick.[60] And it appears that Francis' dream was realised, at least at first, and that the friars did feel a real affection for one another and a profound joy in each other's company.[61] And Francis himself was so convincing a brother to them all that he was known simply as 'the brother'.[62]

One of the things which impressed Francis' contemporaries was the way in which he and his friars totally ignored the social stratification of the world around them. Anyone who joined Francis simply became one of the brotherhood, whatever his background. Aristocrats and nobodies, scholars and fools, in Francis' eyes they were all the same.[63]

And the friars were not meant to confine their charity to their own circle. As we have seen, an important factor in Francis' own conversion was a change in his attitude to the involuntary poor and especially to lepers, and the early friars made a special point of consorting with lepers and other underprivileged people.[64] Their poverty was evidently meant to be modelled on that of the real poor; if necessary they were to beg 'like other poor people'[65] and poor visitors ought to be able to feel at home among the friars.[66] Just as Christ lived as one of us, so Francis wanted a real involvement of his friars in the lot of the poor.

Francis also believed that God had given him a special task as an ambassador of peace. The greeting which he used with everybody, 'The Lord give you peace', was, he claimed, revealed to him by God,[67] and it was one of his concerns to be a peacemaker wherever he could.[68]

But it would be a mistake to see Francis too much as a 'man with a mission'. He had no formula for social reform; his concern was to follow Christ, and to embody in his own life the methodology of redemption which he learned from Christ, a methodology of total subjection and infinite endurance, and, finally, to call others to follow Christ too. It is no part of his vision of life to have any particular plan of his own; he aims simply to be obedient to whatever God wants of him. This is why his life, from one point of view, is so erratic. One moment he is a preacher, the next moment he is a hermit; one day he is writing Rules for his brethren, another day he is washing his hands of them and wanting someone else to organise them. In a way it was impossible for him to give any clear direction to the order which he had founded, because if, on the one hand, he was quite clear that God had shown him the right way to live,[69] on the other hand it was an essential part of this way of life that he should never attempt to impose his own will on anyone else. His helplessness in face of his own order, as it grew and developed, was only a part, perhaps the most painful part, of his whole policy of radical unprotectedness.[70]

Bibliography and Abbreviations

Editions used
Kajeten Esser, ed., *Opuscula Sancti Patris Francisci Assisiensis*. Grottaferrata 1978.
Th. Desbonnets and others, ed., *François d'Assise: Écrits* (SC 285). Paris 1981.
Sacrum Commercium, ed. the fathers of the Collegio San Bonaventura. Quaracchi 1929.

Recommended translation
R. J. Armstrong and Ignatius Brady, *Francis and Clare: Complete Works.* Classics of Western Spirituality 1982.

Abbreviations
Adm.   Francis' *Admonitions*
1 Cel.   Thomas of Celano, *First Life of Francis* (in *Analecta Franciscana* X).
2 Cel.   Celano, *Second Life of Francis* (ibid.).
RB   *Regula Bullata* (Francis' later Rule).
RNB   *Regula non Bullata* (Francis' earlier Rule).
SL   *Scripta Leonis*, ed. Rosalind Brooke. Oxford 1970.
3 Soc.   *Legenda Trium Sociorum*, ed. Th. Desbonnets. Grottaferrata 1974.
Test.   Francis' *Testament*.

Notes

[1]Cf. Kajetan Esser, *Anfänge und ursprüngliche Zielsetzungen des Ordens der Minderbrüder* (Leiden 1966), pp 45–51.
[2]Jordan of Giano gives 3,000 as the number of friars present (*Chronicle*

16); SL 114 gives 5,000 as do Eccleston, *De Adventu Fratrum Minorum in Angliam*, ed. Andrew G. Little (Paris 1909), p. 40, and Bonaventure, *Legenda Maior* 4:10.

[3]The process of turning Francis into an *alter Christus* begins in the letter which Elias wrote immediately after the saint's death, in connection with Francis' stigmata (*Analecta Franciscana* X, pp 526–7) and eventually reached the point where Francis was acclaimed as a 'new Christ'. On this and on Francis as the apocalyptic 'angel of the sixth seal', see Stanislao da Campagnola, *L'Angelo del sesto sigillo e l'Alter Christus*. Rome 1971; W. C. van Dijk, 'La représentation de St François d'Assise dans les écrits des Spirituels', *Cahiers de Fanjeaux* 10 (1975), pp 214–30.

[4]For social interpretation of Francis, cf. for example, David Flood, 'The Domestication of the Franciscan movement', *Franziskanische Studien* 60 (1978), pp. 311–27; Anton Rotzetter, 'Die Entscheidung des hl. Franz für die Armen', ibid., 64 (1982), pp. 27–53; Michael Goodich, *Vita Perfecta: The Ideal of Sainthood in the Thirteenth Century* (Stuttgart 1982), pp. 211–12. The 'hippy' Francis was exquisitely depicted in Zeffirelli's film, *Brother Sun, Sister Moon*.

[5]There is a useful survey of the older sources in Esser, op. cit., pp. 1–14; Esser himself also considers the *Legenda Trium Sociorum* to be one of the older sources (cf. ibid., p. 254[4]). A good case is made for taking the *Scripta Leonis* seriously in the introduction to Rosalind B. Brooke's excellent edn, Oxford 1970.

[6]Cf. the note by Damien Vorreux in the Sources Chrétiennes volume (no. 285. Paris 1981), *François d'Assise: Écrits*, pp. 403–5.

[7]'Francesco' is apparently a nickname given to Francis by his father, who was away in France when his son was born; his real name was John. Cf. *3 Soc.* 2.

[8]Celano (2 Cel. 4) takes this to be a prophecy of his future renown as a saint, but this is surely wrong. If we discount the pious interpretation, which is not even hinted at in *3 Soc.* 4, there is nothing implausible about the story.

[9]*Test.* 1–3.

[10]The account of Francis' early life is taken essentially from *3 Soc.* 2–20, which has the most complete story; it is complemented by 1 Cel. 1–20.

[11]*3 Soc.* 21–2.

[12]1 Cel. 22.

[13]*Adm.* 26; *Test.* 6–13.

[14]*Test.* 15; 1 Cel. 31–3; *3 Soc.* 46–51.

[15]*3 Soc.* 52. The procedure would have been very similar to that followed when Innocent III gave his approval to Durandus of Huesca and his Poor Catholics in 1208, and to Bernard Prim and his associates in 1210. Both texts are given, for instance, in G. Gonnet, *Enchiridion Fontium Valdensium* (Torre Pellice 1958), pp. 131, 137.

[16]RNB Prol:2–4; RB 1:2–3.

[17]*Adm.* 1; *Letter to the Entire Order* 12–29; *Letter to the Clergy; Letter I to the Custodians* 2–8; *Test.* 10–11.

[18]*Test.* 6–9. The friars are also strictly forbidden to solicit papal documents authorising them to preach: ibid., 25. Francis is evidently repudiating

the faculties given to the Franciscans (as to the Dominicans) by Cardinal Ugolino on the pope's authority (*3 Soc.* 66).

[19]SL 114.

[20]The point is made in Bonaventure, *Legenda Maior* 3:9, that to claim that it is not possible to take the gospel seriously like this is in effect to blaspheme against Christ, the author of the gospel.

[21]RNB 3:11–13, 9:13, 14:3. This was something noted by non-Franciscan observers: e.g. Jacques de Vitry, *Historia Occidentalis*, ed. J. F. Hinnebusch (Fribourg, Switz. 1972), XXXII, p. 160:1–2; Roger of Wendover, *Flores Historiarum* II (Rolls Series 84b. London 1887), pp. 35–6. Fairly or unfairly, it led to the accusation that Franciscans were a bit too keen on their food: cf. Eccleston, ed. cit., p. 31; Hugh of Digne, *Expositio Regulae*, ed. David Flood (Grottaferrata 1979), p. 165: 4ff; Jacques de Vitry, *Sermo Primus ad Fratres Minores*, ed. Hilarius Felder, *Analecta Ordinis Minorum Capuccinorum* 19 (1903), p. 117b.

[22]RNB Prol.:2, 5:17, 22:41; RB 1:1, 12:4; *Test.* 14–15. Cf. Jacques de Vitry, *Hist. Occ.*, ed. cit., p. 159:7–9.

[23]*Test.* 38–9. Cf. SL 113; Angelo Clareno, in H. Boehmer, ed., *Analekten zur Geschichte des Franciscus von Assisi* (Tübingen/Leipzig 1904), p. 87.

[24]*Quo elongati* 39–54, ed. Herbert Grundmann, *Archivum Franciscanum Historicum* 54 (1961), pp. 3–25, 'Die Bulle "Quo Elongati" Papst Gregor IX'.

[25]SL 4.

[26]Ibid., and see Esser, op. cit., pp. 251–2.

[27]Augustus Potthast, *Regesta Pontificum Romanorum* I (Berlin 1874), no. 7373; I. H. Sbaralea, *Bullarium Franciscanum* I (Rome 1759), no. 18.

[28]*Blessing given to brother Bernard.*

[29]*Last Will* 1.

[30]*Adm.* 3:3.

[31]*Adm.* 11:3.

[32]*Letter to a Minister* 2–7.

[33]Esser, op. cit., p. 48[3].

[34]*Sacrum Commercium* 63.

[35]This famous story is first found in a developed form in the *Fioretti* 21, but it is alluded to in a much earlier work, the verse *Legenda* by Henry of Avranches (*Anal. Franc.* X, p. 521).

[36]SL 84.

[37]1 Cel. 77–8.

[38]*Salutation of the Virtues* 17–18.

[39]SL 49–50.

[40]Jacques de Vitry, *Hist. Occ.*, ed. cit., p. 159:24–6; cf. Esser, op. cit., pp. 54–60.

[41]RNB 7:13; RB 6:1.

[42]SL 8.

[43]RNB 7:13–14.

[44]RNB 8; RB 4.

[45]Cf. Lothar Hardick, 'Pecunia et denarii', *Franziskanische Studien* 40 (1958), p. 217. An extreme illustration is found in Thomas of Cantimpré, *De Apibus* II 28:2–3.

[46]RNB 8:3, RB 4:2. In *Quo elongati* 63–76 Gregory IX tried to preserve the principle of the friars never having anything at their own disposal: money handled by the friars' agent must be spent immediately; a 'spiritual friend' can keep something in reserve for them, but it is at his disposal, not theirs.

[47]SL 59–63.

[48]RNB 7:3–8, 9:3; *Test.* 20–2. Cf. *3 Soc.* 41.

[49]RNB 7:1.

[50]RNB 17:5.

[51]*Adm.* 2.

[52]*Test.* 27–8; SL 105–6.

[53]RNB 1:1, 9:1 *Last Will* 1. Cf. Esser, op. cit., pp. 216–29 (pointing out that the earliest sources speak of a 'following' of Christ rather than an 'imitation' of Christ); Sources Chrétiennes edn, pp. 70–1; Duane V. Lapsanski, *Perfectio Evangelica* (Paderborn 1974), pp. 51–9.

[54]*Sacrum Commercium* 16–19; cf. Esser, op. cit., pp. 254–5.

[55]*True and Perfect Joy.*

[56]RNB 7:16; SL 21, 97.

[57]Cf. Esser, op. cit., pp. 265–78.

[58]*Adm.* 4; RNB 5:4–12; RB 10:5–6; *Letter 2 to the Faithful* 42–3.

[59]RNB 9:10–11; RB 6:7–9; *Rule for Hermitages* 1–2; *Letter to Leo* 2. Cf. *3 Soc.* 41; 1 Cel. 98; Jordan of Giano 55.

[60]RNB 10:1–2.

[61]Cf. 1 Cel. 38–9.

[62]Jordan of Giano 17.

[63]Cf. especially *Legenda Monacensis* 54 (*Anal. Franc.* X, p. 709); also 1 Cel. 31; SL 71; 2 Cel. 193.

[64]RNB 8:10, 9:2; 1 Cel. 39.

[65]RNB 7:8.

[66]SL 33.

[67]*Test.* 23.

[68]1 Cel. 23.

[69]*Test.* 14.

[70]Cf. SL 75–7; 2 Cel. 188.

13

Humbert of Romans

St Francis gained papal approval, if only informally, for his project in 1209 or 1210. From 1216 onwards St Dominic obtained increasing papal support for his 'Order of Preachers'.[1]

St Dominic, in his own way, is as significant in the history of christian spirituality as St Francis, and it would not be at all improper to devote a chapter to him at this point. But whereas Francis wanted to be and was a very personal embodiment of the Franciscan ideal,[2] Dominic rather points away from himself. The Franciscans are haunted by the person of their founder, and their early writings are full of anecdotes about him; but the Dominicans seem rather detached from St Dominic and have remarkably little to tell us about him.[3] Francis bequeathed to his followers a model of life and they looked to him as their 'form and exemplar',[4] Dominic left his followers with a job to do and they got on with doing it. Francis probably wanted to be and was certainly taken to be an abiding norm for Franciscan life, and the order developed in an uneasy tension with its founder; Dominic wanted his brethren to make their own decisions about how to do their job, and his order entrusted itself to his prayers and then made new decisions and developed a new understanding of its identity.[5] It is therefore no failure of *pietas* towards St Dominic to devote this chapter not to him, but to the fifth Master of his order, Humbert of Romans (c. 1200–77),[6] who ruled the order at a critical period of its early development and whose writings were recognised for centuries as a classic exposition of Dominican life.

In this chapter we shall be concerned particularly with one work, *On the Formation of Preachers*, in which Humbert shows what it means precisely to be a preacher, to shape a whole christian life round the apostolic calling to be a preacher. Curiously, this work seems to have enjoyed little success during the middle ages, and the order itself preserved almost no memory of it for several centuries and it was rediscovered only at the beginning of the seventeenth century;[7] but in spite of this an exposition of what it means to be a preacher from so authoritative an exponent of the 'Order of Preachers' cannot help but be fraught with significance.

The monastic tradition, as we have seen, had become increasingly concerned with providing a safe milieu in which people could cultivate good habits and escape from the temptations of their own frail humanity. As early as St Jerome it was possible to draw a sharp distinction between active clergy, who took the risk of living in society 'making the salvation of others the way to benefit your own soul', and monks who lived apart from society.[8] 'There are two ways of warding off death: with a shield or with your feet. If you fight defeat is as possible as victory; if I run away, my flight is certainly not a victory, but my reason for fleeing is to make sure that I am not defeated.'[9]

From very early on it was recognised that monastic life was open to the charge of selfishness. St John Chrysostom accused monks of sitting on their mountain-tops gloating over their own purity while other people perished, and exhorted them to come down and get their hands dirty.[10] But monastic propaganda could retort with the plea that, unless you first sort yourself out, you can do no good to others and that, simply by concentrating on your own affairs, you are 'guarding the walls'.[11] In the eleventh century some monks in the west began to undertake more direct apostolic activities and they were opposed on the grounds that, as St Jerome had said, 'it is a monk's business to weep, not to teach'.[12] Their counterclaim was that their ascetic training made it particularly appropriate for them to minister publicly in the church, and this view gained credence in some circles.[13] But either way the same implication was underlined, that the monastery is the safe place in which to be a christian, and it is only after you have matured in the cloister that you can risk coming out again.[14]

The Franciscans, at first, abandoned the cloistered life in its entirety, but it is still a religious *way of life* that Francis was looking for, not a form of apostolate. The Franciscan Rule is entitled, 'The life of the gospel of Jesus Christ',[15] so that, radically different as the content may be, it is still equivalent to the traditional monastic customaries in its intention. Later on in the thirteenth century, when the Franciscans have become to all intents and purposes a clerical and apostolic order, they revive the old argument that they are specially well qualified to do the work of the apostles because of their imitation of the apostolic life.[16]

The Dominicans retain far more than the Franciscans do of the traditional conventual observances, but they are in a different way far more radical in that they redirect their whole life towards the goal of 'being useful' to others. As early as 1220, at the first General Chapter of the order, presided over by Dominic himself, they solemnly wrote it into their constitutions that 'our order is known to have been founded originally for the precise purpose of preaching and the salvation of souls, and all our concern should be primarily and enthusiastically directed to this all-important goal, that we should be able to be useful to the souls of our neighbours'.[17]

The decisive orientation of Dominic's life and work was established in 1206, ten years before the founding of his order, when he was still subprior of the cathedral chapter of Osma in Spain. In that year he and his bishop, Diego, happened to meet the papal legates who had been trying, largely in vain, to counteract the growth of heresy in the south of France. Diego advised them that they would be much more likely to succeed if they adopted a totally different strategy: instead of travelling round with all the pomp and dignity of senior ecclesiastics, they should imitate the manner of the apostles (as, be it noted, the heretics were doing, at least in appearance), going round on foot, without resources, begging their bread from door to door.

Diego and Dominic, like Francis, discover in the instructions given to the apostles the solution to their problem. But whereas Francis' problem is essentially personal to himself, the problem facing Diego and Dominic is an apostolic one. It is the needs of others which persuade them to adopt a new style of life.

It is this resolute focusing on the needs of others which makes the Dominicans such an unusual and difficult order.

Humbert of Romans is as clear as could be desired about the consequences of this Dominican peculiarity. Those who are given the grace to be preachers (a notion to which we shall return) ought, he says, to prefer preaching to *all* the other spiritual practices customarily undertaken by spiritual people. This is spelled out in precise terms: preaching must take precedence over the traditional austerities of monastic life (fasting, rough clothing, vigils and so on), corporal works of mercy, prayers, sacred reading, the mass, hearing confessions, liturgy, including the celebration of sacraments and the Divine Office. And the reason given each time is that preaching is more useful to more people than all these other things.[18]

Humbert gives a fascinating list of factors which sometimes discourage people from preaching. He regards them all as trivial, and some of them are indeed obviously trivial. Some people, for instance, are just too lazy to prepare sermons, or object to the *socius* they have been given (no preacher was allowed to go about without a companion). Some people only want to preach to responsive audiences. Some people are put off because their first attempts to preach go badly; to them Humbert points out that if you want to do *anything* well, you must be prepared to begin by doing it badly.[19]

These are all manifestly inadequate reasons for not preaching. But Humbert describes as equally silly difficulties which might well strike us as rather more serious. There are people who hold back from preaching because they do not feel that they are ready for the job, or because they have not finished their preparation, or because they feel unworthy. Humbert retorts that preaching is too urgent to wait until people feel that they are ready for it. Against the monastic and, to some extent, the Franciscan, instinct to regard preaching as simply the overflow from the preacher's own fulness and maturity,[20] Humbert presents it as being a temptation to want to wait until you are quite sure that you are ready.[21] St Dominic, after all, had sent even his novices and largely untrained young men out to preach, and refused to let them off just because they did not feel qualified to do it; they were to be confident that God himself would speak through them.[22] So to the man who is too humble to go and preach Humbert rudely says that his humility is shown to be false precisely by his refusal to do the job he has been given.[23]

Then there are people who do not want to preach because they prefer a more contemplative, quiet life. Humbert warns them, with a quotation from St Gregory, that they are liable to be held responsible by God for all the good that they might have done if they had come out into the open.[24]

It remains the typical Dominican doctrine to maintain that a life of preaching and teaching is more perfect than a purely contemplative life in this world.[25]

Most shockingly of all, Humbert regards it as a trivial reason for not preaching that some people 'are afraid of the kind of sins which will unavoidably occur in the course of the preacher's active life'.[26] It is not that Humbert wants Dominicans to be careless about occasions of sin,[27] but he is prepared to be realistic in his acceptance of the hazards inseparable from the life of a preacher. After all, the preacher's life is not designed for his own spiritual benefit and convenience, but for the good of others.

In this connection Humbert refers to a sermon of St Bernard's, in which Bernard explains to his monks that they must not be too critical of bishops, because it is only to be expected that, leading the busy lives they do, they will not be as virtuous and self-disciplined and austere as a monk should be. In particular they will be likely to indulge in frivolous amusements and to be rather short-tempered.[28] I presume that this is the kind of thing that Humbert too is thinking of. Anyway, whatever the 'unavoidable sins' are, Humbert evidently takes it for granted that an active preacher is not going to enjoy the untroubled virtue and austerity that he might otherwise have had, and to be put off preaching just because of this shows a complete failure to understand what is involved in being a preacher. Even 'virtue' can be a self-indulgence which has to be mortified in the interests of other people's benefit.

All in all, Humbert makes it quite clear that considerations which would, in another context, be legitimate and important, must be relegated to a much lower place in the preacher's mind. What would elsewhere be regarded as essential concerns of his religious life are not so for him. The preacher must be prepared to risk his own spiritual disadvantage.

However there are some compensating advantages which come his way precisely as a preacher. 'By the merit of their preaching people win many spiritual boons.' First of all Humbert draws our attention to Proverbs 11:25, 'He who makes others drunk will himself be made drunk too; the soul which blesses will be fattened.' Following the standard *Glossa ordinaria* Humbert applies this to preachers. It is precisely because the preacher makes others 'drunk' with the word of God that he himself gets drunk, it is precisely because he brings blessing to others that he himself wins spiritual increase. That is to say, the spiritual advancement and enjoyment of the preacher are consequences of his doing his job. It is not apart from his preaching that he discovers what it is to enjoy God, it is precisely as a preacher.

Secondly the preachers stand to gain 'the washing away of any filth that may be contracted by their active life'. Rather disconcertingly for the modern reader, Humbert cites Job 29:6, 'I washed my feet in butter.' 'God's feet are preachers, and they are not without fault, but they are washed in butter, because the dust they pick up is washed off by the fatness of their good work.' It is taken for granted that preachers have faults, but the remedy is also intrinsic to the preaching. Humbert's position here is interestingly different from that of some other writers. Bonaventure, in his life of St Francis, depicts Francis too as realising that the active life of preaching involves getting your feet dirty; but he does not see the remedy as intrinsic to the job, so he makes Francis withdraw into solitude every now and again to 'wash his feet'.[29] Similarly Jacques de Vitry suggested that the friars who do not go preaching should see it as part of their function to 'wash the preachers' feet' by their prayers.[30] It is only Humbert who sees that the remedy, like the risk, is actually inherent in the activity of preaching itself.

The preacher also stands to gain understanding, precisely because he is a preacher. Again Humbert quotes Job (Job 38:36): 'Who gave the cock understanding?' Just as the cock receives from God the understanding which it needs if it is to crow at the right time, so the preacher can surely presume on God giving him the understanding he needs if he is to 'crow' properly. That is to say, his own growth in knowledge and understanding of God and of the word of God is not a qualification he has to obtain first before he undertakes his mission, it is a gift he is given together with and as a function of his mission.[31]

The preacher also acquires a greater certainty of salvation.

In any work of kindness the Lord usually deals with us in the same way that we deal with one another. 'Forgive and you will be forgiven, give and you will receive gifts in return.' This demonstrates beyond any doubt that the preacher who saves others, even if only as a minister of salvation, will himself be saved. And this is what the Lord says through his prophet: 'If you convert (others, that is), I will convert you.'[32]

In other words, the preacher's business is to convert other people, his own conversion and salvation are God's business.

The preacher also earns a greater reward in heaven because of the charity which makes him work for others as well as for himself.[33]

This last consideration may seem rather mean and mercenary, but it represents an important element in Humbert's mature understanding of Dominican life. In an earlier work, his *Exposition of the rule of St Augustine*, he leaves us with a rather schizophrenic impression of the preacher's life. He suggests various specific reasons why charity is particularly necessary in a preacher, but then complicates the picture by treating the two precepts of charity as two entirely separate considerations. Love of neighbour is patently expressed in preaching, but love of God is connected more with the 'contemplative life' and with the preacher's own personal life, with his concern for his own salvation. Humbert accordingly rebukes people who are too concerned with the 'active life': we ought to be more anxious about our own salvation than about that of others. And 'love of God is necessary to him for his own sake, while love of neighbour is necessary for the neighbour's sake'.[34]

In the *Formation of Preachers* the balance seems to be tilted far more definitely in favour of preaching: the preacher ought to *prefer* preaching to all other spiritual practices. And surely Humbert can allow himself to say this because he has realised that love of God as well as love of neighbour is expressed directly in preaching. This is, after all, what is involved in talking about 'merit'. Humbert has freed himself from the devotionalist model as found already in Guigo, linking 'contemplation' exclusively to the personal 'spiritual exercise' of the individual, and has recaptured the more diffuse link which Hugh of St Victor recognised between *operatio* and contemplation: our final enjoyment of the 'contemplation' of God in the beatific vision depends on a whole christian life in which the crucial factor is that we should *do* whatever God wills.

St Aelred, as we have seen, presents the love of God as consisting in *affectus* and *effectus*, but the emphasis is already on *affectus*; in

Richard Rolle it is only *affectus* which is taken seriously. Nobody
wants to deny that in some way or another an affective element is
involved in our love of God, but it makes a great deal of difference
whether the affective element is regarded as crucial in itself, or
whether it is regarded as attendant upon something else. St Thomas,
like Aelred, can mention 'love in the heart' and 'obedience in practice' together, but the latter is the authentic evidence of the former:
'obedience is the manifest sign of love', and it is by obedience that
we are fitted for the vision of God.[35] Affectivity is not a value in its
own right, but if we do whatever it is that we have to do out of
love, then this will result in our doing it, in varying degrees, with
enjoyment and eagerness, depending on the intensity of our love.
It is love which makes us *want* to undertake the intellectual task of
contemplation,[36] just as it is love which makes people, if necessary,
glad to undergo martyrdom.[37]

In the same way, love makes the preacher enthusiastic in talking
about God and the things of God, and without some such
enthusiasm he is unlikely to have much effect.[38] But, as we have
seen, it is precisely in making others drunk with the word of God
that the preacher himself gets drunk.[39] Love of God does not have
to be seen as operating most typically in the periods in a preacher's
life when he is not engaged in preaching.

This is the significance, in the *Formation of Preachers*, of the section
devoted to a demonstration that preaching is exceptionally pleasing
to God.[40] As such, it is an exceptionally good manifestation of love
of God.

It was generally accepted that love, at least in the sense of charity,
is an elusive thing. St Thomas is in agreement with St Bonaventure
that we can never know for certain that we possess charity, and he
connects this with the psychological impossibility of distinguishing
with certainty between natural and supernatural motivation. The
most we can look for is 'indications' (*signa*) of the presence of
charity.[41] A typical Dominican list of such *signa* is offered by
Peraldus: it is an indication of God's love if we enjoy thinking about
him, if we enjoy being in God's house, if we enjoy talking about
him or with him,[42] if we enjoy listening to his word, if we enjoy
practising generosity for his sake, if we willingly endure hardship
for his sake, if we obey his commandments, if we love what he loves
and hate what is displeasing to him, if we lost interest in worldly
things and finally if we show great respect to God's ministers.[43]
These things are 'indications' of charity only if we do them willingly,
but the emphasis is on *doing* certain things, rather than on any
analysis of the subjective conditions of the person doing them. For
St Thomas too we conjecture that we have charity because we find

ourselves ready to *do* spiritual things and because we *effectively and actually* detest evil.[44]

This is a far cry from the much more introverted broodings of a William of St Thierry, for instance, examining 'all the recesses of my conscience' in order to discover that charity in himself by which God is known. He cannot know whether he really loves God, but 'I am certain by your grace, Lord, that I have a desire to desire you, a love of love of you'.[45]

The direct link between charity and the works of charity is so far taken for granted among the Dominicans that Kilwardby can tell his novices without further ado that they ought specially to rejoice in their Dominican vocation since heavenly rewards are meted out in proportion to what people merit 'by their useful labours'. The Franciscan Pecham is definitely not happy with this, and stolidly reminds us that our reward will be proportionate to our charity, not to our labours.[46] But Kilwardby is surely assuming what Humbert states, namely that the labours undertaken for other people are the evidence of abundant charity.

This does not mean that the preacher can simply forget about all the other demands of the christian life. Humbert says a lot about the moral and ascetic qualities that a preacher needs. But in the *Formation of Preachers* Humbert shows how the vocation to be a preacher provides a single, coherent focus for a whole christian life. It is because one needs, and indeed wants, to say certain things to certain people that one discovers the importance of being a particular kind of person. A bad conscience hinders preaching.[46a] It is therefore precisely because one wants to preach that one will also want to be virtuous. The preacher does not need to be unduly concerned to look out for ways of practising penance and mortific-ation, because the rigours inherent in the life of an itinerant preacher are far more arduous than those of the most austere monks.[47] There is thus no need to impose a double life on the preacher, one consisting of the practices designed to lead to his own perfection, the other consisting of his apostolic work. The life of a preacher can genuinely be seen as subsuming all other facets of a spiritual life.

The early Dominicans did not regard preaching as a part-time job. St Dominic used to preach to everyone he met;[48] on occasion, he would even try to speak to people with whom he did not have a common language.[49] Some of the friars could not bring themselves to sit down to their meal unless they had preached to at least one person during the day.[50] Humbert insists that a preacher's conversation, even when he is not formally preaching, should be edifying to others,[51] and he ought to be able to preach to any conceivable kind of audience at a moment's notice.[52]

When the preacher takes time off, as Humbert advises him to, he should still be preparing himself for further preaching. His reading and meditation should always be in view of preaching, at least indirectly.[53]

All of this perhaps sounds like a programme of rampant activism, but it is not, for the simple reason that the preacher's job is not just a human activity. The preacher does the job of God himself;[54] he is God's 'mouth'[55] and his task is to speak God's word.[56] This is why preaching can be done only by those who have the special grace for it. Humbert mentions people who would appear to have all the necessary qualifications, but who cannot preach, and this is because it is only God who makes people into preachers.[57] Although Humbert does not dwell at length on this notion of the 'grace of preaching', it is clearly vitally important for him, as it was for all the early Dominicans.[58] Preaching is a strictly supernatural task, and so the life of a preacher is a strictly supernatural life. For those who have this 'grace of preaching', preaching is their way of being inserted into the life of grace, it is their way of sharing in the divine life, it is their way of receiving the influence and direction of the Holy Spirit.[59]

There is therefore a real reference to God in all that the preacher does, not just because he talks about God, but because he has constantly to receive his life, as a preacher, from God. So prayer is an integral part of his job, because he has to pray for those to whom he is to preach.[60] It is his business to enter into the grace which God wishes to give to those people.[61] And he must try to be attentive to the particular kind of grace of preaching which God has given him. Humbert is aware that there are different nuances within the grace of preaching, which the individual preacher has to respect.[62]

Being a preacher involves therefore a very intense dependence on God and a continual stance of docility to God. And there is no reason to doubt that it is in doing his job of preaching, in this posture of dependence and docility, that the preacher will discover most intensely what it is for him to be united with God. His own relationship with God is most basically a union with God in God's *act*, in the coming forth of the Word of God.[63]

Humbert is well aware of the sheer hard work involved in being a preacher. A great deal of study and thought is normally required, and there is also the physical and emotional labour involved in traipsing round giving sermons all over the place and then in coping with all the people who want you to give them advice about every subject under the sun and to hear their confessions. And there are plenty of disappointments and misunderstandings too.[64] All of this in itself is just unmitigated slog. But it catches fire precisely in the act of preaching. It is when he is caught up in the incredible self-giving of God to other people that the preacher himself comes alive and finds himself drunk with the joy of the Lord and enlightened in his mind so that he can understand the words of God and the truth of God. The words flow from him ('eloquence' and 'abundance of things to say' are among the benefits which Humbert lists as accruing to the preacher);[65] and they are truly his words, yet he knows that they are not simply his words.

This is the mystery of preaching, and it sheds light on many of the things which Humbert says in his usual dispassionate way. If Humbert does not take seriously the plea of unreadiness made by a reluctant preacher, is it not because he appreciates that no human being ever could be ready to be the bearer of God's word? Anyone who forgets the inevitable disproportion between the word and its bearer and imagines that it is appropriate for him to be a preacher must have lost sight of what preaching really means. This is why Humbert criticises both those who are too coy to preach and those who are too eager to preach.[66] If it is silly to refuse to preach on the grounds that one is not ready for it, it is even sillier to demand the job on the grounds that one is ready for it.

It is only in the light of the high mysteriousness of preaching that we can make any sense of some of the more preposterous claims which Humbert makes for it. Not content with indicating the usefulness of preaching for the human race, he also claims that it is good for the world as a whole.[67] Humbert does not make it very clear how preaching is useful to the world apart from its usefulness to the human race, but it is interesting that he should even want to suggest a cosmic significance for it. In some way, presumably, he appreciated that the whole cosmos depends on the word of God and must therefore benefit from the preaching of that word.

It is not hard to see why Humbert has to recognise that preachers cannot be expected to fit too smoothly into the routine of conventual life.[68] Their tune is called by their vocation as preachers, not by the requirements of community life. Since Humbert's own bias was towards discipline[69] and uniformity,[70] his testimony on this point is particularly impressive.

Humbert directs himself solely to men who have an official preaching position in the church; but what he says about the inner structure of their life can surely be applied, *mutatis mutandis*, to many others whose vocation it is to serve the grace of God for the benefit of other people in an active life. It is not surprising that the Dominican tradition should be insistent on usefulness to other people as an essential element in our love of God. Any pretended 'contemplative life' is falsified at once by the absence of effective love of neighbour: without such love, there can be no 'life' at all, contemplative or any other, because there can be no charity, which is the life of the christian.[71]

Bibliography

Editions used

Constantine of Orvieto, *Legenda of St Dominic*, in MOPH XVI.
Humbert of Romans, ed. J. J. Berthier, *Humberti de Romanis Opera de Vita Regulari*. repr. Turin 1956.
Humbert of Romans, *On the Formation of Preachers* (FP): a critical edn is in preparation; meantime the most important part of the text is available in English tr. in Simon Tugwell, *Early Dominicans*. Classics of Western Spirituality 1982. References are to this translation.
Jordan of Saxony, *Libellus*: a critical edn is in preparation; paragraph nos. are given here in accordance with the edn in MOPH XVI. There is an English tr. by Simon Tugwell, *Jordan of Saxony: On the Beginnings of the Order of Preachers* (Dominican Sources no. 1). Chicago and Dublin 1982.
Primitive Constitutions, ed. in A. H. Thomas, *De oudste Constituties van de Dominicanen*. Louvain 1965.

Notes

[1]MOPH XXV nos. 77, 79, 86 etc.
[2]SL 76.
[3]Cf. Simon Tugwell, ed., *Jordan of Saxony: On the Beginnings of the Order of Preachers*, Dominican Sources no. 1 (Chicago 1982), pp. vii–xiii.
[4]SL 85.
[5]On St Dominic, see M. H. Vicaire, *Dominique et ses Prêcheurs*. Fribourg/Paris 1977: id., *Histoire de St Dominique*. rev. edn Paris 1982. On early Dominican spirituality, see Simon Tugwell, *The Way of the Preacher*. London 1979; id., *Early Dominicans*. New York 1982; id., 'The Dominicans', in the forthcoming *Encyclopedia of World Spirituality*, to be published by Crossroads, New York.
[6]On Humbert, see M. H. Vicaire, 'Humbert de Romans', *Dictionnaire de Spiritualité* VII (Paris 1969), 1108–13; E. T. Brett, *The Life and Works of Humbert of Romans*. University Microfilms 1981; Tugwell, *Early Dominicans*, pp. 31–5, 181–384, containing a translation of the whole of the first part and a selection from the second part of *On the Formation of Preachers* (references in the following notes are to this edn). For some other aspects of Humbert's teaching, see Tugwell, 'Dominican Risks', *Dominican Ashram* 2 (1983), pp. 173–89. I am preparing a critical edition of the entire Latin text of *On the Formation of Preachers*.
[7]Cf. Tugwell, *Early Dominicans*, pp. 2–3.
[8]Jerome, *Ep.* 58:5; the same point is made in *Ep.* 14:8.
[9]Jerome, *Contra Vigilantium* 16
[10]PG 61:53–4.
[11]Cf. above, ch. 2 nn 12 and 27.
[12]Jerome, *Contra Vigilantium* 15.
[13]Cf. Tugwell, *Way of the Preacher*, Appendix III.
[14]Jacques de Vitry was worried about the Franciscans on just this score: not only mature men but young men 'who should have been confined and

tested for a time in the discipline of the cloister' go wandering about all over the place (R. B. C. Huygens, ed., *Lettres de Jacques de Vitry* [Leiden 1960], pp 131–2). Later Cardinal Hugh of St Cher (himself a Dominican) complained that young Dominicans were being sent out without first being given time to 'mature in their cloisters' (in J. J. Berthier, ed., *Humberti de Romanis Opera de Vita Regulari* [repr. Turin 1956], II, p. 509).

[15]RNB Prol.:2, RB title.

[16]This point is raised against the Dominicans by John Pecham in C. L. Kingsford, A. G. Little and F. Tocco, ed., *Fratris Johannis Pecham: Tractatus Tres de Paupertate* (Aberdeen 1910), p. 128; cf. Pecham, *Canticum Pauperis*, Bibliotheca Franciscana Ascetica Medii Aevi IV (Quaracchi 1949), p. 188.

[17]Dominican Primitive Constitutions, Prologue (Tugwell, *Early Dominicans*, p. 457).

[18]FP 260–75.

[19]FP 197, 201–2, 204.

[20]The 'overflow' model is found in Bernard, *Super Cantica* 18:3; Humbert himself quotes it in FP 167, but in him it is severely relativised by other considerations elsewhere in the book.

[21]FP 191, 195–6.

[22]Cf. Bologna Canonisation Process 24, 26 (Tugwell, *Early Dominicans*, pp. 73–4); *Nine Ways of Prayer* 4 (ibid., pp. 96–7); Jordan, *Libellus* 62.

[23]FP 192.

[24]FP 193.

[25]The idea that Dominic's apostolic life represents an 'increase' from his contemplative life as a canon appears in the earliest liturgical office of St Dominic, in the 1st antiphon of the 2nd nocturn of Matins (the text remained unchanged until the most recent Dominican breviary, and is still found in the new *Proprium Ordinis Praedicatorum*, [Rome 1982], p. 298, antiphon 2 C). St Thomas provides the classic formulation of the doctrine that the highest life is a contemplative life which results in 'giving to others what you have contemplated' (*Summa Theol.* II^{a}II^{ae} q. 188 a.6). Cf. also Raymund of Capua, *Life of Catherine of Siena* 119–21.

[26]FP 194.

[27]FP 237.

[28]Bernard, *Super Cantica* 12:9.

[29]Bonaventure, *Legenda Maior* 12:1, 13:1.

[30]Jacques de Vitry, *Sermo primus ad Fratres Minores*, ed. cit., p. 117a.

[31]FP 34–6.

[32]FP 47 (Luke 6:37–8, Jeremiah 15:19).

[33]FP 48.

[34]Humbert, ed. cit., I, pp. 57–60.

[35]*Super Ev. Iohannis*, ed. cit., 1908, 1942.

[36]*Summa Theol.* II^{a}II^{ae} q. 180 a.1.

[37]*Quaestiones Disp. Quodl.* IV a.19.

[38]Humbert, ed. cit., I, p. 57.

[39]FP 34.

[40]FP 23–32.

[41]St Thomas, *De Veritate* q. 10 a.10; Bonaventure, I *Sent.* d.17 p.1 q.3.

[42]This is the well-known phrase which St Dominic had inserted into the

constitutions: Primitive Constitutions II 31; Bologna Canonisation Process 41.

[43]Peraldus, *Summa de Virtutibus*, Caritas ch. 7.

[44]St Thomas, loc. cit.

[45]William of St Thierry, *De Contemplando Deo* 3–4; cf. *Meditationes* 12:8–9.

[46]Pecham, *Tractatus Tres*, ed. cit., p. 129.

[46a]FP 99.

[47]FP 261.

[48]Jordan of Saxony, *Libellus* 104.

[49]Constantine of Orvieto, *Legenda S. Dominici* 44.

[50]MOPH I, p. 150. This passage is cited by Dietrich of Apolda, *Libellus de Vita S. Dominici* 273 (ed. in *Acta Sanctorum*, August, I. Antwerp 1733, repr. Brussels 1970), and the shockingness of the idea of an order founded primarily in order to preach is vividly illustrated by the fact that an interpolated version of Dietrich's text, probably produced in Italy towards the end of the thirteenth century, rewrites this section to make it say that the order was founded primarily for the sake of the salvation of the friars and only then for the sake of preaching. A critical edition of Dietrich is in preparation.

[51]FP 448–84.

[52]FP 563; the second part of FP consists of nearly 300 sermon outlines for an amazing range of possible preaching situations – including a sermon for prostitutes and one for a tournament.

[53]FP 235–6.

[54]FP 2.

[55]FP 140.

[56]FP 3.

[57]FP 79.

[58]People are to be appointed 'preachers' in accordance with the 'grace of preaching' God has granted them (Primitive Constitutions II 20; early 14th century German customary, *Archivum Fratrum Praedicatorum* 1 [1931], p. 103 no. 21); Dominic asks the pope to secure the services of various people whom he believes to have a 'grace of preaching' (MOPH XXV, p. 125). Jordan of Saxony complains in his 1233 Encyclical about people who have received a 'grace of preaching', but refuse to preach (*Archivum Fratrum Praedicatorum* 22 [1952], p. 184; Tugwell, *Early Dominicans*, p. 123). It is common to find outstanding Dominicans celebrated for their 'grace of preaching'. The term was not original to the Dominicans; cf. Gregory, PL 76:832D, 834B, 965A; *Glossa Ordinaria* to Judges 7; Odo of Canterbury, *In Libros Regum*, ed. cit., p. 21. It is found in Franciscan writers too, e.g. Eccleston, ed. cit., pp. 38, 58. On the 'grace of preaching', cf. Tugwell, *Way of the Preacher*, esp. ch. 5; Jean-Pierre Renard, *La Formation et la Désignation des Prédicateurs au début de l'Ordre des Prêcheurs* (Fribourg 1977), pp. 146–65; Guy Bedouelle, *Dominique ou la Grâce de la Parole* (Paris 1982), esp. ch. 6. (There is an excellent German edn of Bedouelle, which constitutes a revised version of the book: *Dominikus*. Graz 1984.)

[59]Tugwell, *Early Dominicans*, p. 5.

[60]FP 233.

[61]The 'grace of preaching' can be regarded as a grace given to the

hearers, rather than to the preacher: cf. Gregory, PL 76:920C; Humbert, FP 210; John the Teuton, MOPH V, p. 11:22–3.

[62]Humbert, *De Dono Timoris*, Prologue (Tugwell, *Early Dominicans*, p. 375).

[63]Cf. St Catherine's vision of Dominic 'proceeding' from the Father like the Word (Raymund of Capua, *Life* 204–5; Tommaso Caffarini, *Libellus de Supplemento*, ed. G. Cavallini and I. Foralosso [Rome 1974], pp. 38–9).

[64]FP 197, 199, 301–37, 519–49.

[65]FP 37–8.

[66]FP 182–205, 166–81.

[67]FP 6–22, 58–78.

[68]Humbert, ed. cit., II, pp. 33, 36.

[69]It was almost certainly Humbert who introduced community spies (*circatores*) into Dominican life. They first appear in the constitutions of the Dominican nuns at Montargis, which were probably composed by Humbert (*Archivum Fratrum Praedicatorum* 17 [1947], p. 79), and we may infer that it is due to Humbert that his first General Chapter as Master of the Order in 1254 instituted *circatores* for the friars too (MOPH III, p. 71). It was the responsibility of these officials to monitor conventual discipline. Cf. above, ch. 7 n 51.

[70]Cf. Humbert, ed. cit., II pp. 45–6 (Tugwell, *Early Dominicans*, pp. 141–5).

[71]Cf. Domenico Cavalca, *Specchio di Croce*, ch. 7; Catherine of Siena, *Dialogo* VII (ed. G. Cavallini [Rome 1968], p. 17); Giovanni Dominici, *Induite novum hominem*, text cited in *Memorie Domenicane* N.S. 1 (1970), p. 81.

14

Some Themes in English Piety

The Fourth Lateran Council in 1215 called for a revitalisation of preaching in the church and for a more systematic use of the sacrament of penance.[1] The two major orders of friars, the Franciscans and the Dominicans, soon established themselves as a powerful force which the church could draw on in the implementation of the council's hopes. Although the Franciscans were not at first a clerical order, they soon came to be one, assuming, like the Dominicans, the role of preaching and hearing confessions as one of their normal functions.

In view of the bias towards objectivity which we noticed in the previous chapter, it is not surprising that the Dominicans made a substantial contribution to the literature generated by the new concern for the sacrament of penance. Within a few years of the death of St Dominic, textbooks designed for the use of confessors had been produced by the Dominicans in Bologna and Paris, by Conrad of Höxter in Germany and by St Raymund of Peñafort in Barcelona.[2] By the middle of the thirteenth century William Peraldus had produced his substantial *Summa on Vices and Virtues*,[3] and by 1272 St Thomas Aquinas had completed the massive treatise of systematic moral theology which makes up the second part of the *Summa Theologiae*.[4]

It was not only moral theology in general which blossomed in this period; there was a great concern to apply moral theology to the various particular situations of different classes of people. This is found in some of the handbooks for confessors,[5] and it accounts for the sermons *ad status*, in which the specific obligations and temptations attendant upon different social, economic and professional roles are spelled out.[6]

Peraldus' *Summa* was enormously successful, and not only among the better educated;[7] his influence has been recognised in Dante and in Chaucer,[8] and he was a major source for the popular vernacular Italian writings of Domenico Cavalca.[9] His work was translated into French, Flemish and Italian,[10] and it underlies the Anglo-Norman *Manuel des Péchés*, which was translated into English by Robert Mannyng under the title, *Handling Sin*.[11]

152

Another Dominican work, this time written for the lay penitent rather than for the confessor, was also influential: Laurence of Orleans' *Somme le Roi*, written for Philip III of France in 1279, has been described as 'one of the most popular books of its kind';[12] it was translated into English for the first time in 1340 by a monk of Canterbury (this is the famous *Ayenbit of Inwit*)[13] and six other English versions of it are known.[14]

Unpromising as it might appear, the concern to clarify and apply the objective rules of human morality, with specific reference to confession and amendment of life, was not without its effect on imaginative literature. The rather bizarre story of *Sir Gawain and the Green Knight* is designed precisely to set up a moral test-case, teasing out with some subtlety the practical implication of what it means to be faithful, to maintain 'truth' with all the complexities that word has in medieval English (faith in God, belief in christian doctrine, fidelity to obligations), and the poet is clearly interested in the precise requirements for making a good confession.[15] And a great deal of the dramatic tension in *Piers Plowman* comes from Langland's passion to see both civil society and the church properly ruled by the objective principles contained in the Law.[16] Langland is also clearly interested in the application of the moral law to different *status*; knights, for instance, belong to an 'order' in their own way as much as religious do, and if they desert its obligations they are 'apostates' like runaway religious: by 'reason' (in accordance with right ordering) it is their job to guard 'truth' by pursuing and punishing transgressors:

> That is the profession apertly that appendeth for knights,
> And not to fast on Fridays for five score winters. . . .
> For David in his days dubbed knights
> And did them swear on their sword to serve Truth ever,
> And whoso passed that point was *apostata* in the order.[17]

It is the function of 'law and *lewte*' (meaning both loyalty and – in accordance with etymology – 'lawfulness'),[18] as established by 'the king and the commons and kind wit the third' ('kind wit' meaning 'natural reason'), to ensure that 'each life knows his own', that is to say, knows its own place and role in the scheme of things.[19] In the first part of passus VI Langland tries to spell out what this means for various categories of people.[20]

The belief in the objectivity of the moral order, as applied to society as well as to individuals, is supported by, even if it does not depend on, the belief that all law ultimately derives from the 'eternal law', which is no other than the divine Word of the Father, and that the moral commandments given in God's law are identical with the precepts of the unchangeable natural law written into our very constitution as human beings. This is indeed the doctrine of St Thomas,[21] and it goes with his conviction that the created order as a whole makes sense, precisely because it is the product of God's mind: the 'truth' inherent in things is caused by the intellectual act of God in creating them, and it is such as to cause understanding in the human mind.[22]

The Dominicans were, perhaps, more confident than most others in the marriage of reason and religion. Fourteenth-century Nominalism, associated particularly with the Franciscan William of Ockham, effectively sealed their divorce and denied the objective intelligibility of creation and of the moral law.[23] Even before this, the Franciscan theologians had been more concerned to stress the direct dependence of particular situations on the absolute will of God than the normative patterns which enable us to some extent to comprehend what is going on.[24]

The Franciscan influence on English poetry has become a commonplace of criticism,[25] though it has recently been suggested that it is not as all-pervasive as has sometimes been implied.[26] Be that as it may, the poets were evidently sensitive to the ways in which God's will cuts across the expectations which seem reasonable to our minds.

Langland has an extended passage in which the dreamer (the poet himself) is presented to Nature to admire the wonderful intricacies and orderliness of creation.

> But what moved me most and my mood changed
> Was that Reason regarded and ruled all the beasts
> Save man and his mate; many time me thought
> No reason ruled them.

This prompts the dreamer to break out into a bitter accusation against Reason, but Reason in turn rebukes him, pointing out that it is 'none of his business' why certain things are or are not tolerated. No creature can shape itself, and what God does is his own affair – and all that he does is good. And before attacking other people, the dreamer ought to look to himself. At this point the dreamer blushes and wakes up.[27]

There is a similar confrontation in the *Pearl*. The poet has lost his young daughter (symbolised by the pearl), and reason is insufficient to calm his grief and his anger. His 'wretched will', unable to abandon its 'woe', prevents him from being comforted by Christ.[28] His daughter appears to him in a dream, and explains that she is now a queen in heaven. The poet cannot swallow this either: it seems unjust that a girl who had never done anything to please God, who had not even learned how to say her prayers, should receive such honour. What about people who have laboured long in the rigours of this world?

> That courtesy is too free of deed
> If it be true as thou dost say.
> Thou lived not two year in our land. . .
> And queen made on the first day!

The poet refuses to beieve that God would 'twist so wrongly astray'.[29]

The girl tries to explain the situation in terms of the parable of the labourers in the vineyard, but the poet is still unconvinced: surely God himself has said that he gives people exactly what they deserve; but if what the girl says is right, then the one who works less earns more![30]

Eventually the vision of heaven becomes so glorious that the dreamer, maddened beyond endurance, tries to rush into it and wakes up sadly to reflect, 'It was not at my prince's pleasure.' The moral is not hard to see: it is madness to strive against the Lord and to propose anything which is against his pleasure.[31]

In another work of the same poet Jonah has to learn a similar lesson. Jonah finds himself disagreeing with God the whole way through. The words God bids him go and speak to the Ninevites he finds 'a marvel message a man for to preach among enemies so many', so he resolves to 'approach it no nearer' come what may.[32] But he soon finds that he was wrong to think that he could 'escape from the power of the Lord' simply by going to sea.[33] In the belly of the whale he is duly brought back to 'thinking on the Lord': 'now he knows him in care that knew him not in happiness'.[34] But when he has delivered God's threat to the Ninevites and they have repented and been spared, Jonah gets angry with God again, and resolves to have nothing more to do with a teaching 'which makes me a liar like this'.[35] And the last straw is when God destroys the 'woodbine' under which he had been sheltering: 'With all mischief that thou may,' he says to God, 'never thou me sparest.'[36] Whether Jonah ever gets the message is not made clear, but there is no doubt what the poet wants us to see; the whole tale of Jonah is an *exemplum* to illustrate the moral announced at the beginning of the poem:

> If a destiny is appointed for me, which I am due to have,
> what good is it for me to be indignant or make resistance?
> Or if my liege-lord wants to bid me either ride or run
> to Rome on an errand for him, what would grumbling do
>   for me
> except to look for more trouble?[37]

Neither Langland not the Gawain-poet presents God's will as simply arbitrary; the point is rather that it is a jolt to our ideas of what is reasonable to discover that God is, on the one hand, much more tolerant and much more generous than we are, and that, on the other hand, he is extremely demanding.[37a]

A much sharper tension is suggested between reason and faith in some slightly later lyrics.

> A God and yet a man?
> A maid and yet a mother?
> Wit wonders what wit can
> Conceive this or the other.
>
> A God, and can he die?
> A dead man, can he live?
> What wit can well reply?
> What reason reason give?
>
> God, Truth itself, doth teach it;
> Man's wit sinks too far under
> By reason's power to reach it.
> Believe and leave to wonder![38]

This is the attitude favoured in the seventeenth century by Sir Thomas Browne, who thought that 'to beleeve only possibilties is not faith, but meere Philosophy' and who complained, 'Me thinkes there be not impossibilities enough in Religion for an active faith.'[39] In his view it 'is no vulgar part of faith to believe a thing not only above, but contrary to reason, and against the arguments of our proper senses'.[40] But Browne himself is evidence that this attitude does not necessarily exclude a rational theology; one of the 'two books from whence I collect my Divinity' is precisely 'Nature, that universal and publick Manuscript'. We should not 'disdain to suck Divinity from the flowers of Nature'.[41] And Browne is keen to

> compose those fewds and angry dissensions between affection, faith, and reason. . . . As Reason is a rebell unto Faith, so passion unto Reason: As the propositions of Faith seeme absurd unto Reason, so that Theorems of Reason unto passion, and both unto Faith; yet a moderate and peaceable discretion may so state and order the matter, that they may bee all Kings, and yet make but one Monarchy, every one exercising his Soveraignty and Prerogative in a due time and place'.[42]

A far more radically negative attitude to reason is found, for instance, in a fifteenth-century poem which begins, 'Why, why, what is this why?' and in which every stanza ends with the refrain:

What is this why?
To ask why, I hold but folly;
It is none other certainly
But virtus verbi Domini.

The poet rules out not only questions about points of revealed doctrine and miraculous events, but also questions about nature.[43] Another poet is even more drastic, and recommends that we should not waste time trying to understand nature, social conditions, current affairs, biblical stories or anything: it is enough simply to comment, 'This was done by the Lord (*hoc factum est a domino*).'[44] Such an attitude is certainly a far cry from the position of St Thomas, who thought that it makes faith more meritorious if we love revealed truth enough to expend some intellectual energy on it and try to find rational arguments in support of it.[45]

Nobody, of course, wanted to deny that ultimately (at least in this life) our minds are defeated by God. We can know *that* God is, but we cannot know *what* he is, and even with the benefit of revelation we only have more pointers towards God and a mind aided by grace to appreciate the evidence better, but we still do not know *what* God is and so are 'joined to him as to one unknown'.[46] But very different consequences could be derived from this. The Dominicans on the whole maintained that, in spite of all the difficulties, it is precisely the *mind* which is most intimately involved in our final beatitude[47] and that the wide-ranging intellectual discipline of theology is therefore an integral part of our approach to God in this life.[48]

The Franciscan emphasis was rather different. St Francis, as we have seen, appears to be suspicious of theological study as liable to interfere with devotion. His more learned followers plainly could not accept that, but they do not follow St Thomas either in his belief that beatitude consists essentially in the *mind's* intellectual enjoyment of God. In their view, beatitude consists essentially in the *will's* loving enjoyment of God.[49] And other Franciscans seem to have retained the belief that intellectual activity is not part of the spiritual life at all – James of Milan, for instance, whom we have already met.

Whether or not it is due to Franciscan influence, there is no doubt that a great many of the English vernacular poems seem to be primarily addressed to the will and the emotions, and not to the intellect.[50] And it is easy to see how this was appropriate to the renewal of penance: the preaching of penance involved not just instructing people in some detail about their moral duties, but also inspiring them to turn away from sin.

It has been recognised that a great many of the vernacular lyrics are meditation poems, meant to be used by the faithful,[51] but it should not be forgotten that at least part of the impetus which led to their creation came from the preachers.[52] The affective, imaginative piety which the Cistercians developed was popularised by the preachers' use of it as a pedagogical tool. Some poems are best seen as a form of homiletic conversion literature, in which the situation is deliberately overdramatised. In spite of the personal form, such poems are not to be taken as autobiographical:[53] the depiction of a dramatically wicked sinner confronted with the passion of Christ is meant to facilitate the return of real, but probably more modest, sinners to Christ in the sacrament of penance. The basic problematic is usually presented in very simple terms: how can a sin-hardened heart learn to weep and to love? And the answer is equally simple: by coming face to face with Christ, usually with Christ in his passion.

Although Barsanuphius would probably not have approved, this kind of dramatisation can be very effective. One lyric, for instance, gives us a visionary picture of our Lady with her dead son, entirely divorced from any context, leaving the reader faced immediately and starkly with the scene depicted:

Suddenly afraid, half waking, half sleeping,
And greatly dismayed – a woman sat weeping.

With favour in her face far passing my reason,
And of her sore weeping this was the encheason:
Her son in her lap lay, she said, slain by treason.
If weeping might ripe be, it seemed then in season.
    'Jesu!' so she sobbed –
    So her son was bobbed*   * = buffeted
    And of his life robbed –
Saying these words, as I say thee:
'Who cannot weep, come learn at me.'

I said I could not weep, I was so hard hearted.
She answered me shortly with words that smarted:
'Lo, nature shall move thee; thou must be converted;
Thine own father this night is dead – lo, thus she
                    thwarted* –   * = replied
    'So my son is bobbed,
    And of his life robbed.'
    Forsooth then I sobbed,
Verifying the words she said to me:
'Who cannot weep, come learn at me.'[54]

Another poem, found in the preaching book of the Franciscan John Grimestone, makes the reader identify himself or herself with Eve confronted by the infant Jesus:

Lullay, lullay, little child,
Thou that were so stern and wild,
Now art become meek and mild,
    To save what was forlore.*   * = lost

But for my sin I wot* it is   * = know
That God's son suffreth this;
Mercy, Lord! I have done amiss,
Indeed I will no more.

Against my father's will I ches*   * = chose
An apple with a rueful res;*   * = impulse
Wherefore mine heritage I les,*   * = lost
And now thou weepest therefor.

An apple I took of a tree,
God it had forbidden me;
Wherefore I should damned be,
    If thy weeping ne were.*[55]   * = were it not for
                                 thy weeping

Sometimes the drama is reduced to the barest essentials:

When I see on rood
    Jesu my leman,*   * = beloved
And beside him stand
    Mary and Johan,
And his back swungen,*   * = beaten
And his side stungen,*   * = pierced
    For the love of man,
Well ought I to weep
And sins forlet,
    If I of love can,*   * = if I know anything
If I of love can,   of love
If I of love can.[56]

In other lyrics the focus is more on the sinner, as in a poem which
purports to be the prayer of an old man, who has indulged in every
possible kind of sin and is now forced by his condition to recognise
that

Mirths helpeth me no more;
Help me, Lord . . . .

What is the best recourse
But to praise him that hath us bought,
Our Lord that all this world hath wrought,
    And to fall at his feet?[57]

One very popular way of presenting the call to conversion is to imagine Christ himself calling to us from the cross. Thus in one poem he contrasts his own situation with that of the carefree worldling:

> Jesus doth him complain
> And speaketh to sinful man:
> 'Thy garland is of green,
> Of flowers many one;
> Mine of sharp thorns,
> Mine hue it maketh wan.'

The poem concludes with a simple appeal:

> 'Sweet brother, well might thou see
> These pains strong in rood tree
> Have I suffered for love of thee. . . .
> Be thou kind, for charity,
> Leave thy sin and love thou me,
> Heaven bliss I shall give thee,
> That lasteth aye and ever.'[58]

Appeals of this kind were a well established part of English piety. The author of the *Ancrene Riwle* in the thirteenth century describes how Christ 'woos' us. The author has already shown at length how much Christ has done for us to demonstrate that his love surpasses the love of friends, the love between man and woman, the love of a mother for her child and even the love between soul and body. Now Christ himself pleads his case:

> If your love is to be given, where could it be better bestowed than on me? Am I not fairest of all things? Am I not the richest of kings? Am I not the most nobly born? Am I not the wisest of all? Am I not the most courteous of men? Am I not the most generous?[59]

And so he goes on, proving that on all counts he is the ideal bridegroom. The same claim to love is celebrated again in a related text, which may indeed be by the same author,[60] this time in the form of a rather gushing address to Christ, which begins:

> Jesus, my Jesus, my beloved, my darling, my Lord, my Saviour, my honeydrop, my balm; sweeter is the thought of you than honey in the mouth. Who would not love your lovely face? What heart is so hard that it would not melt at the thought of you? Ah, who would not love you, lovely Jesus, for in you are all things together which might ever make anyone lovable to another? Fairness and lovely face, flesh white under its clothes, makes many

a man be loved the more; some are made loved and honoured by their gold and riches . . .

The author, as we should expect, goes on to extol in enthusiastic terms the surpassing excellence of Christ from all points of view.[61]

This is not quite the same sort of thing as the more homiletic appeal to sinners to abandon their sins, but it is still to be regarded as conversion literature. The addressee is being invited to *choose* Christ and this means rejecting other possible or actual suitors. The love of Christ is clearly seen as being in competition with other possible loves.

This is, indeed, a widespread topic.

> All other love is like the moon
> That waxeth and waneth as flower in plain,
> As flour that faireth and fadeth soon,
> As day that passeth and endeth in rain.

The only love which is entirely blissful is that which 'rests on heaven's king'.[62]

The traditional image of the soul being wedded to Christ is sharpened, at least for dramatic and homiletic purposes, by this depreciation of creaturely enjoyments.

> Jesu, that art king of life,
> Teach my soul, that is thy wife,
> To love best no thing in land
> But thee, Jesu, her dear husband.

> For other joy and other bliss,
> Woe and sorrow forsooth it is
> And lasts but a little while,
> Man's soul for to beguile.[63]

In the late thirteenth century a Franciscan, Thomas of Hales, wrote a 'love rune' at the request of some nun, in which he warns her that 'this world's love is nothing but frenzy', and commends Christ to her as the only worthwhile lover:

> He is fair and bright on hue,
> of glad cheer, of mood mild . . .

The list of his good qualities is much the same as in the *Ancrene Riwle*.[64] Richard Rolle gives similar advice; 'If thee list love anything, love Jesu Christ, that is the fairest, richest and wisest, whose love lasts in joy endless'.[65]

Perhaps the most famous instance of this theme comes in the peroration at the end of Chaucer's *Troilus and Criseyde*. Troilus, having been betrayed by Criseyde, dies on the battle field and, from the vantage point of heaven, sees that 'this little spot of earth' is not worth bothering about. So, the poet draws his moral, 'young fresh folks' in whom love is burgeoning should set their hearts exclusively on Christ, who is the one lover guaranteed never to let us down.

> And since he is the best for us to love
> And the least proud, why seek pretended loves?[266]

The conversion *to* the love of Christ either involves or results from a conversion *from* other loves, and this, inevitably, creates a context in which it is difficult to give any positive account of creation. It is not clear why God made this world, if it is to be regarded simply as a deception and a distraction.

It also appears that the love which is directed to Christ is motivated essentially by exactly the same considerations which would motivate any other love. In one sense, this is probably an important observation. The pseudo-Dionysius, for instance, had refuted on philological grounds the distinction that evidently some people were making even then between *erôs* and *agapé*, and had then developed a magnificent demonstration of the continuity of all love, from God's own love to the most perverted 'loves' of the sex-maniac.[67] But the point of this demonstration was to show that all love, however deformed, is in some way derived from divine love, from the 'love which moves the sun and the other stars' (*l'amor che move il sole e l'altre stelle*).[68] It is this philosophical doctrine of love which undergirds the common application of metaphors taken from human love to the love which subsists between us and God.

But the medieval tradition we have been looking at seems to be wide open to the risk of simply transferring carnal love to Christ, taking carnal rather than divine love as the norm; the metaphor becomes confused with reality, instead of shedding light on it. There seems to be a Freudian misapplication of sexual and emotional energy, rather than a real Jungian sublimation, and it is difficult to resist the suspicion sometimes that a fantasy love-affair with the Lord is being used as a device for evading the difficulties which beset real human love.

The sexual imagery is sometimes unusually forthright. Richard Rolle says to a nun, 'I will become that messenger to bring thee to his bed, that has made thee and bought thee',[69] and Margery Kempe 'hears' Christ say to her,

> 'It is fitting that a wife should be homely with her husband . . . therefore must I needs be homely with thee and lie in thy bed with thee. Daughter, thou desirest greatly to see me and thou mayst boldly, when thou art in thy bed, take me to thee as for

thy wedded husband, as thy dearworthy darling . . . and therefore
thou mayst boldly take me in the arms of thy soul and kiss my
mouth, my head and my feet as sweetly as thou wilt.'[70]

In both cases there is also a strong suggestion that the transference
of love to Christ is connected with emotional and sexual difficulties.
The beginning of Margery's religious experiences coincides with a
violent and apparently sudden distate for lying with her husband,
and when she has eventually persuaded him to let her make a vow
of chastity it is suggestive that he says to her, 'As free may your
body be to God as it hath been to me.'[71]

Richard Rolle seems to have suffered from particularly troublesome passions, and it is not surprising that he saw conversion chiefly
in terms of the re-orientation of our emotions. He evidently had
some crisis while he was an adolescent, and this has plausibly been
interpreted as an acute sexual temptation;[72] Rolle himself refers to
the episode in these terms: 'When adolescence had already wakened
in my youth and I was flourishing wretchedly, the grace of the
Creator came to me, restraining the urgency of temporal beauty
and turning me towards a desire for unbodily embraces.'[73] He was
an extremely affectionate young man[74] and he was evidently much
troubled by lust;[75] when he first became a hermit he passed through
an acute sexual temptation[76] and even after that his fascination with
femininity sometimes got him into trouble.[77] It is suggestive that
his notion of heavenly bliss includes 'the fullest possible beauty of
girls'.[78] If he insists on the necessity for the lover of Christ to 'flee
from women',[79] it is surely because of his own difficulties in coping
with women's charms. He takes it as axiomatic that we are all in
love with something, and the choice he offers us is a stark one: 'If
the soul loves a creature, it loses God and goes with what it loves
to death. . . . But whoever loves his Maker rejects everything that
is in the world.'[80]

Rolle explicitly admits that he was quite incapable of self-control;
the only remedy for lust was the 'kiss' of God's love.[81] The essential
grace which converts the heart is charity, 'the dearest sweetness,
radiantly inebriating the minds you capture for love',[82] leaving the
heart 'occupied (*occupatum*) by overflowing love'[83] – 'occupied' in a
quite precise sense: the seat is occupied, so nobody else can come
and sit there. It is precisely in the seat of lust that Rolle locates the
sweetness which God gave him: 'Now I receive sweet sound where
before the liver of lust lay (*ubi iecur iacuit cupidinis perverse*).'[84] In
Rolle's doctrine it seems clear that divine love is the antidote for
unruly passions quite precisely because it fully engages the
emotional, not to say sexual, energy which would otherwise be at
the mercy of the unruly passions.[85]

The same moral seems to be implicit in a story told by Caesarius of Heisterbach († 1240) about a Cistercian monk who was delivered from sexual temptations by a visionary experience in which Christ leaned down from the cross to give him a hug: 'in that tight embrace he crushed all his overwhelming temptations'.[86]

Because it is only the intensity of religious affections which is keeping at bay the tumult of unmanageable secular affections, the religious emotions have, of course, to be continual, and Richard Rolle accordingly insists on this. As we have seen, he regards the perfection of love as consisting in the sensations of heat, sweetness and angel-song, and even when he is at his lowest the contemplative ought to be enjoying at least one of these three.[87] Rolle refers to 'continual heat',[88] and claims that 'the comfort . . . departs never';[89] whatever he is doing, the heavenly singing always accompanies him.[90] And it is precisely this continual consolation which makes the contemplative 'impervious to the enemy's arrows'.[91] 'No one can remove you from this contemplation because even if the world rages and the devil roars and the flesh groans, they cannot detach you from the *sweetness* and practice of the contemplative life.'[92]

Because of Rolle's straightforward identification between the sensation of loving God and the reality, he cannot help but make the sensation something to be deliberately aimed at and cultivated: we are to 'try to feel his love'.[93] And the feeling in turn becomes our guide: we are 'led by sweetness',[94] and this guidance is taken to be infallible.[95] It is easy to see why his critics thought that Rolle was simply abandoning people to their own subjective opinions about life.[96] And Rolle himself certainly acted on his own criterion; he opted for a solitary life, for instance, because he found that the presence of other people interfered with his 'joy'.[97]

It is on the basis of this criterion that Rolle warns against excessive bodily austerity. Many people, he says, have hindered themselves by 'over much penance . . . and made them so feeble that they may not love God as they should'.[98] Bodily exhaustion interferes with the sensation of heat, sweetness and song in which 'loving God as we should' essentially consists.[99]

Apart from the psychological difficulties we may have about this kind of spirituality, with its 'trying' to feel and its insistence on sustained intense emotion and with its rather naive understanding of love, there is a further problem too. St Bernard had taught that we begin, quite properly, with a 'carnal' love for the humanity of Christ, but then we should move on towards a spiritual love of the Godhead.[100] But it is not at all clear how the very human and affective devotion, which could, it seems, be very easily inspired by the thought of the passion and other such imaginative meditations, is to develop into a love of the Godhead. Margery Kempe had been weaned easily enough from her addiction to vast quantities of vocal prayers,[101] and she became highly proficient at imaginative meditation; but it is a very different story when she is told to move on to the Godhead. When the Father said to her, 'Daughter, I want to have you wedded to my Godhead,' she tells us:

> The creature [herself, that is] kept silence in her soul and answered not thereto, for she was full sore afeard of the Godhead and she knew no skill of the dalliance of the Godhead, for all her love and all her affection was set in the manhood of Christ and thereof knew she good skill and she would for nothing be parted therefrom.[102]

And her attempts to cope with the Godhead in the imaginative way at which she was so proficient are decidedly maladroit, as when she arranges a kind of tea-party for the Trinity and lays out three cushions for the three Persons to sit on.[103]

Affective, imaginative piety could certainly make christianity very vivid to people, and it provided an easy, human, access to Christ and to his Mother and the saints, but it ran the serious risk of reducing God to the dimensions of essentially unchanged human affections. The gospel was coopted into the joys and pains of everyday life, but it is not clear that it did not lose in the process its capacity to raise people above themselves to the mystery of God. Redemption itself can become little more than a lark, as in a rather attractive carol which is first known from the fifteenth century:

> Out of your sleep arise and wake,
> For God mankind now hath y-take
> All of a maid without any make;*   * = blemish
> Of all women she beareth the bell.*   * = she takes
>   Nowell!   the cake
>
> And through a maiden fair and wise
> Now man is made of full great prize;
> Now angels kneel to mankind's service,
> And at this time all this befel.
>   Nowell!
>
> Now man is brighter than the son,
> Now man in heaven on high shall wone,*   * = dwell
> Blessed be God this game is begun,
> And his mother is empress of hell.
>   Nowell![104]

Abbreviations

CB XIII	Carleton Brown, *English Lyrics of the Thirteenth Century*. Oxford 1932.
CB XIV	Carleton Brown, *Religious Lyrics of the Fourteenth Century*. Oxford 1957.
CB XV	Carleton Brown, *Religious Lyrics of the Fifteenth Century*. Oxford 1939.
EEC	R. L. Greene, *The Early English Carols*. Oxford 1977.
Gray, *Selection*	Douglas Gray, *A Selection of Religious Lyrics*. Oxford 1975.

Notes

[1]Lateran IV, constitutions 10, 21.

[2]On the Bologna *Summa de Poenitentia* by Paul of Hungary (in collaboration with the brethren) and the Parisian *Flos Summarum*, as well as Conrad and Raymund, cf. William A. Hinnebusch, *History of the Dominican Order* II (New York 1973), pp. 236–40, 248–52.

[3]On Peraldus and his popularity, cf. A. Dondaine, 'Guillaume Peyraut: Vie et Oeuvres', *Archivum Fratrum Praedicatorum* 18 (1948) pp. 162–236.

[4]On the context for the Secunda Pars and its success, cf. Leonard Boyle, *The Setting of the 'Summa Theologiae' of Saint Thomas*. Toronto 1982.

[5]Cf. for example P. Michaud-Quantin, 'Textes Pénitentiels Languedociens au XIIIᶜ siècle', *Cahiers de Fanjeaux* 6 (1971), pp 167–8.

[6]A good Dominican example is provided by the model sermons in the first section of the second part of Humbert's *Formation of Preachers*.

[7]Cf. Dondaine, art. cit., pp. 187–8.

[8]Cf. J. A. Burrow, *Medieval Writers and their Work*, p. 110.

[9]This has been demonstrated in detail for Cavalca's *Pungilingua* by A. Olga Rossi in her unpublished doctoral dissertation submitted to the University of California, 'The Sources of Domenico Cavalca's *Pungilingua*'.

[10]Thomas Kaeppeli, *Scriptores Ordinis Praedicatorum Medii Aevi* II, (Rome 1975), p. 142; S. G. Axters, *Bibliotheca Dominicana Neerlandica Manuscripta 1224–1500* (Louvain 1970), pp. 153–4.

[11]W. A. Pantin, *The English Church in the Fourteenth Century* (repr. Toronto 1980), pp. 224–5.

[12]Ibid., p. 226.

[13]The Early English Text Society edn, with commentary and glossary, is now at last complete (OS 23, 278. 1866/1965, 1979).

[14]Pantin, op. cit., p. 226.

[15]Cf. J. A. Burrow, *A Reading of 'Sir Gawain and the Green Knight'*, London 1965.

[16]Cf. Myra Stokes, *Justice and Mercy in Piers Plowman*. London 1984.

[17]*Piers Plowman* I, 94–104 (all references are to the B text, in the edn of George Kane and E. Talbot Donaldson. London 1975). Commentators and translators all take *o friday in fyue score wynter* to mean 'on one Friday in a hundred years', but the C text makes it plain that Langland is not commenting on the paltriness of the penance they do, he is saying that their business

is to serve Truth rather than to undertake penitential practices. This is why I have presumed to disagree with so many experts. (I am grateful to Professor J. A. Burrow for encouraging me in my dissent.) For the general idea that all christians are 'regulars', belonging to an 'order', cf. Jacques de Vitry, *Historia Occidentalis* XXIV, ed. cit., pp. 165–6.

[18]Cf. Stokes, op. cit., p. 102.

[19]*Piers Plowman* Prol. 121–2. The reading *ech lif to knowe his owene*, adopted by Kane and Donaldson, and also in the edn by A. V. C. Schmidt (London 1978), seems preferable to the more common reading *ech man*. The idea goes back ultimately to Plato's definition of justice as ἰδιοπραγία in *Republic* 433.

[20]*Piers Plowman* VI, 1–151; cf. Stokes, op cit., pp. 192–7.

[21]*Summa Theol.* I^{a}II^{ae} q.93 a.1 and 3, q.94 a.3 and 5, q.99 a.2.

[22]*De Veritate* q.1 a.2; cf. J. Pieper, *The Silence of St Thomas* (Chicago 1965), pp. 50–6.

[23]Cf. Douglas Gray, *Themes and Images in the Medieval English Religious Lyric* (London 1972), pp. 28–9.

[24]Cf. Decima Douie, *Archibishop Pecham* (Oxford 1952), p. 25; Étienne Gilson, *Jean Duns Scot* (Paris 1952), p. 613.

[25]E.g. EEC, p. clvi; Gray, op. cit., p. 24. There is no doubt in some few cases that particular lyrics can be connected with the Franciscans, but it is less safe to suppose a direct link between the Franciscans and what is taken to be a 'Franciscan' mood in a much larger range of carols and lyrics; after all, some of the certainly Franciscan lyrics, like those of William Herebert, are straightforwardly liturgical or doctrinal, and the devotional mood is not confined to Franciscans. No Franciscan influence is normally posited on Langland (who had a hearty dislike of the friars) or on the Gawain-poet, and none is likely; but there too there is an affinity between Franciscan interests and the concerns of the poets.

[26]Gregory Joseph Schrand, *The Franciscans and Dominican Aesthetics in Middle English Religious Lyric Poetry*. Doctoral diss., Rice University 1982.

[27]*Piers Plowman* XI, 321–406.

[28]*Pearl* 51–6.

[29]Ibid., 409–88.

[30]Ibid., 589–600.

[31]Ibid., 1153–64, 1199–1200.

[32]*Patience* 81–6.

[33]Ibid., 109–12.

[34]Ibid., 293–6.

[35]Ibid., 428.

[36]Ibid., 484.

[37]Ibid., 49–53.

[37a]It is one of Ockham's doctrines that God is free to save even those who have not been prepared by grace: I *Sent.* d.17 q.1.

[38]CB XV, no. 120.

[39]Sir Thomas Browne, *Religio Medici*, I, 48; I, 9.

[40]Ibid., I, 10.

[41]Ibid., I, 16.

[42]Ibid., I, 19.

[43]EEC, no. 334.

[44]Gray, op. cit., p. 162.

[45]*Summa Theologiae* II^aII^{ae} q.2 art. 10.

[46]Ibid., I q.12 art. 12 and 13.

[47]Ibid., I q.12 art. 1, I^aII^{ae} q.3 art. 4; on St Albert, cf. Walter Senner, 'Zur Wissenschaftstheorie der Theologie im Sentenzenkommentar Alberts des Grossen', and Edouard Henri Wéber, 'L'Interprétation par Albert le Grand de la Théologie Mystique de Denys Ps-Aréopagite', in Gerbert Meyer and Albert Zimmermann, ed., *Albertus Magnus: Doctor Universalis.* Mainz 1980.

[48]*Summa Theologiae* II^aII^{ae} q.180 art. 3 and 4.

[49]On Bonaventure, cf. Étienne Gilson, *The Philosophy of St Bonaventure* (London 1940), pp. 468–9; Antonio Briva Mirabent, *La Gloria y su Relación con la Gracia según las Obras de San Buenaventura.* Barcelona 1957. On Duns Scotus, cf. Gilson, *Jean Duns Scot*, p. 601.

[50]Schrand, op. cit., points to some lyrics, however, which seem to be aimed more at the intellect; these he regards as 'Dominican'.

[51]Cf. Gray, op. cit., p. 37.

[52]Cf. Rosemary Woolf, *The English Religious Lyric in the Middle Ages* (Oxford 1968), pp. 373–4; S. Wenzel, *Verses in Sermons* (Cambridge, Mass. 1978), pp. 121–32.

[53]Exactly the same has to be said about the *Life* of Henry Suso, which is neither credible nor edifying if taken as genuine autobiography (cf. Jeanne Ancelet-Hustache in her introduction to Bx. Henri Suso, *Oeuvres Complètes.* Paris 1977). Suso himself points out in the Prologue that the *Life* is a didactic *exemplum* (ed. Bihlmeyer, p. 3). Cf. Christine Pleuser, 'Tradition und Ursprünglichkeit in der Vita Seuses', in E. M. Filthaut, ed., *Heinrich Seuse* (Cologne 1966), pp. 135–60.

[54]Gray, *Selection*, no. 24.

[55]CB XIV, no. 59.

[56]Gray, no. 33.

[57]CB XIV, no. 6.

[58]CB XIV, no. 126.

[59]*Ancrene Riwle* M 398 (Salu, pp. 175–6).

[60]E. J. Dobson, *The Origins of 'Ancrene Wisse'* (Oxford 1976), pp. 154, 367–8.

[61]W. Meredith Thompson, ed., *The Wohunge of ure Lauerd*, Early English Text Society 241 (1958), pp. 20ff.

[62]CB XIV, no. 49.

[63]Mabel Day, ed., *The Wheatley Manuscript*, Early English Text Society OS 155 (1921), p. 4.

[64]CB XIII, no. 43.

[65]Rolle, *English Writing*, ed. cit., p. 75.

[66]Chaucer, *Troilus and Criseyde* V, 1814–48. On the curious literary prehistory of this passage, cf. C. S. Lewis, *The Discarded Image* (Cambridge 1967), pp. 32–4.

[67]*Divine Names* IV, 11–20.

[68]Dante, *Paradiso* XXXIII, 145. On the pagan philosophical background to this, cf. G. Quispel, 'God is Eros', in William R. Schroedel and Robert

L. Wilken, ed., *Early Christian Literature and the Classical Intellectual Tradition* (Paris 1979), pp. 189–205.

[69]*English Writings*, p. 61.

[70]Margery Kempe, p. 90.

[71]Ibid., pp. 11–12, 25.

[72]Cf. C. Horstman, *Richard Rolle of Hampole* II (London 1896), p. vi[2]; however Horstman is wrong to imply that Rolle lost his virginity: see Rolle, *Melos*, ch. 39.

[73]*Incendium* ch. 15.

[74]*Melos* ch. 34.

[75]Ibid., ch. 31.

[76]Ibid., ch. 19; *English Prose Treatises*, ed. G. G. Perry (London 1921), pp. 5–6.

[77]*Incendium* ch. 12.

[78]*Melos*, ch. 11.

[79]Cf. ibid., ch. 21 and 43; *Incendium* ch. 24 and 29.

[80]*Emend. Vitae* ch. 6.

[81]*Melos*, ch. 23.

[82]*Incendium* ch. 16. Cf. ibid., ch. 37; *Melos* ch. 6 and 8; *Super Apocalypsim*, ed. Nicole Marzac (Paris 1968), p. 138.

[83]*Melos*, ch. 31.

[84]Ibid., ch. 19; cf. ibid., ch. 44.

[85]Ibid., ch. 14; *English Writings*, p. 109:1–3.

[86]*Dialogus Miraculorum* VIII, ch. 13.

[87]*Incendium*, ch. 11; cf. ibid., ch. 37.

[88]*Melos*, ch. 36.

[89]*English Writings*, p. 90.

[90]*Melos*, ch. 6.

[91]*Incendium*, ch. 14. This was one of the doctrines attacked by Rolle's critics; cf. Thomas Basset, *Defensorium*, ed. Michael Sargent, *Analecta Cartusiana* 55:1 (1981), pp. 196–7.

[92]*Super Apocalypsim*, ed. cit., p. 150.

[93]*English Writings*, p. 52 ('try to feel his love'); *Melos*, ch. 46 ('the saints strive to feel the flame . . .'), ch. 50 ('let us apply ourselves, with all the force we can, to being refreshed by the sweetness . . .').

[94]*Melos*, ch. 36 and 42; *English Writings*, p. 89.

[95]*Incendium*, ch. 11.

[96]Basset, ed. cit., p. 200.

[97]*Incendium*, ch. 27.

[98]*English Writings*, p. 96.

[99]*Incendium*, ch. 11.

[100]Bernard, *Super Cant.* 20:6–9.

[101]Margery Kempe, p. 17.

[102]Ibid., p. 86.

[103]Ibid., pp. 210–11.

[104]EEC, no. 30.

15

The Cloud of Unknowing

It is not known who wrote *The Cloud of Unknowing*, in spite of much scholarly speculation about the author.[1] He was probably contemporary with, and possibly also acquainted with, Walter Hilton († 1396), since there appears to be a reciprocal influence between them.[2] Apart from *The Cloud*, he wrote several other works, of which the *Book of Privy Counselling* and the *Epistle on Discretion of Stirrings* are the most important; he also certainly wrote an *Epistle of Prayer* and two translations (of a rather loose kind), one of Pseudo-Dionysius' *Mystical Theology* and one of Richard of St Victor's *Benjamin Minor*. He is also generally credited with an *Epistle of Discretion of Spirits*, consisting chiefly of some texts from Bernard neatly woven together.[3]

The main sources of his doctrine are, at least in outline, clear enough. He adopts Guigo's fourfold schema, almost certainly from Guigo himself.[4] But his understanding of the four rungs of the ladder is profoundly affected by trends of piety which had been gathering force since Guigo. The role of reading is accordingly reduced: instead of ensuring the doctrinal foundation of the whole spiritual ascent to God, it is merely something without which beginners and proficients will not 'well' be able to meditate, just as they will not 'well' be able to pray without meditation.[5] And meditation has come to mean essentially affective meditation.

> What man or woman that weeneth to come to contemplation without many sweet meditations of their own wretchedness, the Passion, the kindness and the great goodness and the worthiness of God coming before, surely he shall err and fail of his purpose.[6]

This kind of meditation is situated within something like Bernard's idea of 'carnal love' of Christ's humanity, and our author regards it as desirable to move on from there to the contemplative life which is concerned with the Godhead.[7] And this moving on is understood in the light of the kind of non-intellectual Dionysianism which we find in Thomas Gallus (whom our author cites as 'the abbot of St Victor')[8] and Hugh of Balma.[9] A certain unclarity in our author's terminology results from the complexity of the traditions he draws on. Although he does not hesitate to call the highest state of life 'contemplative',[10] yet 'contemplation' has to be left behind in favour of a 'blind stirring of love unto God'.[11]

This is not the only way in which our author appears to have been more hindered than helped by his sources. His inherited schema obliges him to regard the contemplative life as something to which one progresses after being exercised in 'many sweet meditations', yet he is clearly very sceptical of the value of such meditations: in themselves they 'profit little or nought'.[12] In this life any attempt to focus the mind sharply on spiritual things is inevitably 'meddled with some manner of fantasy',[13] that is to say, it involves some confusion between bodily and spiritual reality,[14] and this is precisely the 'unknowing' which is 'oft-times cause of much error';[15] the attempt to approach God by 'travail' in our 'wits' and in our 'imagination' is almost certainly going to mean a working 'against course of kind (nature)', a 'manner of working, the which is neither bodily nor ghostly'.[16] Yet meditation on the passion of Christ and other such subjects involves precisely this kind of 'subtle and quaint imaginations and meditations'. So, although our author insists that these things are necessary before we come to the higher part of the contemplative life,[17] it is not at all clear why, since it is not at all clear how they can possibly lead to anything except error. We have to use these preliminary 'means', yet, it turns out, they are after all not means to the perfection of the devotion which our author is commending.[18]

Our author's doctrine actually makes much more coherent sense if we take him to be offering us, not, as he claims, a *higher* spiritual path, which we should not presume to enter until we have passed the appropriate entrance examination, but simply an *alternative* spiritual path which, other things being equal, is exposed to fewer hazards than the current devotional path.

In the *Book of Privy Counselling* the author attempts a theological explanation of why meditation is necessary, but it is rather infelicitous in its consequences. On the basis of John 10:1–9, where Christ identifies himself as the door through which we must enter and be saved, the Cloud-author suggests that we enter through that door by meditating on the passion, with the proper affective response of contrition and compassion;

whoso entereth not by this door, but climbeth otherwise to perfection . . . is not only a night thief but a day skulker. A night thief he is, for he goeth in the darkness of sin, more leaning in his presumption to the singularity of his own wit and his will than to any true counsel or to this common, plain way touched before. A day skulker he is for, under colour of clear ghostly living, privily he picketh the outward signs and words of contemplation and hath not the fruit.[19]

This effectively coalesces the role of Christ himself with the role of meditation on 'the pain of his manhood', and our author's main point is to get us to move on from such meditation: 'What thereof if this be the door? Shall a man then when he hath the door ever stand thereat or therein and come no further in?'[20] This illustrates the doctrinal weakness of a whole tradition of spirituality: whereas devotionalism finds it hard to move on from the humanity of Christ to God, this more theocentric piety finds it difficult to ascribe to Christ anything more than a rather temporary significance.[21]

What the Cloud-author is really interested in is not the preliminaries, but the contemplative life itself. And he is very concerned that we should be under no illusions about what is involved in turning our attention to God himself. Though it is good to think about God's kindness and about the joys of heaven, yet

It is far better to think upon the naked being of him, and to love him and praise him for himself. But now thou askest me and sayest, 'How shall I think on himself and what is he?' And to this I cannot answer thee but thus: 'I wot never.'* For thou has brought me with thy question into that same darkness and into that same cloud of unknowing that I would thou were in thyself. For of all other creatures and their works, yea, and of the works of God himself, may a man through grace have full head of knowing, and well to be able to think on them; but of God himself can no man think. And therefore I will leave all that thing that I can think, and choose to my love that thing that I cannot think. For why, he may well be loved, but not thought.[22]

Nothing less than God can actually satisfy us,

For he is even meet to our soul by measuring of his Godhead;[23] and our soul even meet unto him by worthiness of our creation to his image and to his likeness. And he by himself without more, and none but he, is sufficient at the full and much more to fulfil the will and the desire of our soul. And our soul, by virtue of reforming grace, is made sufficient at the full to comprehend all him by love, the which is incomprehensible to all created knowable might, as is angel and man's soul.[24]

To say that our soul can 'comprehend all him by love' does not,

* = I have no idea.

I think, mean more than that 'he may well be loved, but not thought'; I do not believe that our author has any doctrine, such as that of William of St Thierry, that love itself becomes a kind of understanding of God. He is only making the much more common-place, and much less hazardous, observation that we cannot in this life know God as he is in himself, though we can know his works, but we can love God in himself, in that God himself can be the object of our desire.

Since God cannot be 'thought', attending to him in himself cannot involve any clear object for the mind to focus on; it can only be 'a blind beholding unto the naked being of God himself only'.[25] 'Lift up thine heart unto God with a meek stirring of love and mean himself and none of his goods.'[26] However the obscureness of the object of our desire makes the desire itself mysterious: 'yet it is no will, nor no desire, but a thing thou wost never what, that stirreth thee to will and desire thou wost never what.'[27]

Our author is plainly sensitive to the impropriety of simply trying to transfer our love to God as if this did not require a radical transformation in the nature as well as in the object of our love. If we cannot grasp God in our understanding, we cannot 'feel him in sweetness of love' in our affections either.[28] It is not only our inquisi-tive minds which are baffled by the 'naked entent unto God.'[29] Once we feel such a 'naked entent' it would be inappropriate 'to go back in feeding of thy wits . . . so that thou mightest by such beholding feed and fill thine affection with lovely and liking feelings in God and ghostly things and thine understanding with ghostly wisdom of holy meditations in seeking after the knowing of God.'[30]

The Cloud-author is not simply hostile to the use of the mind. As we have seen, he is conscious that 'unknowing is oft-times cause of much error'. He evidently regards it as important that we should be clear-headed. What he is opposed to is any attempt to do with any of our natural powers what they are just not created to do. If we are concerned with 'the self substance of God', then we are not concerned with anything, 'bodily or ghostly', that the mind can engage itself with.[31] Our bodily senses are meant to be the means whereby we have knowledge of bodily things; when they are faced with things they cannot handle, 'then we may be verily certain that those things been ghostly things and not bodily things'. In the same way it is when our spiritual powers are defeated that we know that we are dealing with God himself.[32]

It is important not to be misled by the kind of things that spiritual writers say. Our author devotes several very funny, but also very serious, pages to the antics of pseudo-contemplatives who, owing to their 'unknowing', fail to appreciate the metaphorical nature of spiritual language. When they hear that 'a man shall draw all his wits within himself, or how he shall climb above himself they try to put this into practice in a way which is neither genuinely bodily nor genuinely spiritual; it is simply 'a working against nature'.

> They turn their bodily wits inwards to their body against the course of kind, and strain them, as they would see inwards with their bodily eyes and hear inwards with their ears and so forth of all their wits, smell, taste and feel inwards. And thus they reverse them against the course of kind and with this curiosity they travail their imagination so undiscreetly that at the last they turn their brain in their heads.[33]

Because of this danger of misunderstanding, the Cloud-author prefers not to say that we should 'gather' our 'mights and wits' within ourselves:

> Thus will I bid thee. Look on no wise that thou be within thyself. And shortly, without thyself will I not that thou be, nor yet above nor behind nor on one side nor on other. 'Where then', sayest thou, 'shall I be? Nowhere by thy tale!' Now truly thou sayest well, for there would I have thee. For why, nowhere bodily is everywhere ghostly. Look then busily that thy ghostly work be nowhere bodily. . . . And though all thy bodily wits can find there nothing to feed them on, for them think it nought that thou dost, yea! do on then this nought. . . . Travail busily in that nought with a waking desire to will to have God that no man may know. For I tell thee truly that I had rather be so nowhere bodily, wrestling with that blind nought, than to be so great a lord that I might when I would be everywhere bodily, merrily playing with all this ought as a lord with his own.[34]

Because of the risk of being misunderstood – a risk all the more acute in the prevailing context of imaginative, affective piety – our author prefers to be frankly enigmatic. But, as he discovered, that too could be misunderstood. Evidently some people found *The Cloud* so abstruse 'that scarcely it may be conceived of the subtlest clerk or witted man or woman in this life'. The author finds it both sad and amusing that his writing has been considered so elevated. Nothing could be further from what he intended. His essential message is, in his view, 'little mastery for to think', and it should be within the capacity of 'the lewdest man or woman that liveth in the commonest wit of kind in this life'.[35]

The misunderstanding perhaps forced the author to explain more clearly what he regarded as the essence of the 'naked entent unto God'. In the *Book of Privy Counselling* he to some extent removes a confusion that was present in *The Cloud*. He had perhaps not made it sufficiently clear that, in its own way, the will is as helpless before God as the mind is. He now explains that the

> naked entent . shall be nought else to thy thought and to thy feeling but a naked thought and a blind feeling of thine own being, as if thou saidest thus unto God within in thy meaning, 'That that I am, Lord, I offer unto thee, without any looking to any quality of thy being, but only that thou art as thou art, without any more.'[36]

This is so simple that if people find it difficult, it can only be because they are looking for something clever that is just not there.[37] And to make sure that we do not suppose that we are to look for our 'being' in some refined elevation of ourselves, the author reminds us that he is telling us to think and feel *that* we are, not *what* we are. He wants us to 'come down into the lowest point of thy wit . . . and think on the lewdest manner'.[38] In a vivid phrase, he says, 'Take good, gracious God as he is, plat and plain as a plaster, and lay it to thy sick self as thou art.'[39]

Assuming that we have confessed our sins and done what we can to make amends (by penance and the intention not to sin again), we should not be bothered any further with *what* we are, any more than we can profitably probe *what* God is.

> Bear up thy sick self as thou art unto gracious God as he is, without any curious or special beholding to any of all the qualities that belong to the being of thyself or of God, whether they be clean or wretched, gracious or natural, godly or manly. It chargeth not now in thee but that thy blind beholding of thy naked being be gladly borne up in listiness of love, to be knitted and oned in grace and in spirit to the precious being of God in himself only as he is, without more.[40]

It makes things much clearer, once we are told that it is our being that is to be united with God, rather than any of our faculties. But this apparent simplification of the author's doctrine makes rather sharper another perplexing ambiguity, which I do not think he ever really resolves.

The difficulty is that he is recommending both a comprehensive attitude and a specific activity, without ever sorting out the relationship between them.

It is the activity (or 'work') which formally engages the author's attention, though my suspicion is that this is due more to his doctrinal and personal situation than to the logic of his teaching.

The essence of the 'work' is precisely the 'naked entent unto God', the blind stirring of love towards the being of God. But this, in itself, is a 'work' only in a rather peculiar sense, in that it is not something that we produce by any deliberate act of will. 'If it be truly conceived, it is but a sudden stirring, and as it were *unavisid* [coming without warning], speedly springing unto God as sparkle from coal.'[41] There is nothing we can do to enable ourselves to feel such stirrings; 'the ableness to this work is oned to the work itself, without separation, so that whoso feeleth this work is able thereto and else none.' Quite precisely 'the presence thereof ableth a soul for to have it and for to feel it'.[42] And we must resist the temptation to try to encourage such stirrings if we do feel them. 'Beware in this work and travail not in thy wits nor in thine imagination in no wise.'[43] Particular meditations will hinder, not help this 'work', so it is wrong to use them to try to 'feed and increase thy purpose'.[44] The 'work' must be allowed to look after itself: 'Let it be the worker and thou but the sufferer; do but look upon it and let it alone. Meddle thee not therewith as thou wouldest help it, for dread lest thou spill all.'[45]

Strictly speaking the naked orientation of our 'entent' towards God is produced in us by God himself, and he does not want our help.[46] But if we are to be focused simply on God, whom we cannot think, leaving our minds in complete darkness, in a 'cloud of unknowing', there has to be another cloud too:

> If ever thou shalt come to this cloud and dwell and work therein as I bid thee, thee behoveth, as this cloud of unknowing is above thee, betwixt thee and thy God, right so put a cloud of forgetting beneath thee, betwixt thee and all the creatures that ever have been made.[47]

This is where our 'travail' comes in.

> A travail shall he have, whoso shall use him in this work, yea surely, and that a full great travail, but if he have a more special grace or else that he have of long time used him therein. But I pray thee, wherein shall that travail be? Surely not in that devout stirring of love that is continually wrought in his will, not by himself but by the hand of almighty God. . . . Surely his travail is all in treading down of the mind of all the creatures that ever God made and in holding of them under the cloud of forgetting.[48]

This travail, however, must not be misunderstood. There must be no question of forcing ourselves to do something against our natural bent. We may be beguiled into forcing ourselves by a misguided desire to 'feel the love of our God'.[49] Our author repeatedly makes it clear that the 'naked entent' is indeed something which we feel, so it is important that he should clarify what he does not mean by this. To this end he exploits the punning possibilities of a medieval proverb.

For God's love be ware in this work and strain not thine heart in thy breast over-rudely nor out of measure, but work 'more with a list than with any lither strength'. For ever the more listly, the more meekly and ghostly. . . . Learn thee to love listly with a soft and demure countenance, as well in body as in soul, and abide courteously and meekly the will of our Lord and grab not overhastily, as it were a greedy greyhound, hunger thee never so sore.[50]

'More with a list than with any lither strength' basically means 'more with cunning than with brute force', but 'list' can also mean 'zest, enjoyment' and our author exploits this possibility by using the adverb 'listly' (zestfully).

But cunning comes into it too. Instead of trying to force our mind away from interfering thoughts, the author suggests two 'sleights' we might use. The first is to take no notice of thoughts but, as it were, look over their shoulders – a modern image could be derived from what we all do spontaneously in the theatre or cinema when there is someone in front blocking our view. Another 'sleight', when we feel that we simply cannot 'put down' our thoughts, is to give up trying: 'and therefore thou yieldest thee to God in the hands of thine enemy'. This is 'nought else but a true knowing and a feeling of thyself as thou art, a wretch and a filth, far worse than nought, the which knowing and feeling is meekness and this meekness deserveth to have God himself mightily descending to venge thee of thine enemies.'[51] It is also, of course, and perhaps more importantly, a way of putting into practice the naked offering of ourselves which is recommended in the *Privy Counselling*.

The two poles of this work are our own being and the being of God. Our hope is to come to the 'feeling of the being of God';[52] quite what that means we shall consider shortly. But at first we cannot attain to the feeling of God, so our author says, 'Lap and clothe the feeling of thy God in the feeling of thyself.'[53] There are several points in this. First there is a practical point: there is nothing difficult about feeling our own being, in the basic sense which is intended (we can hardly claim to be unable to perceive our own existence).[54] And the naked entent unto God means in the first place an all-encompassing offering of our own being to God. But there is also a more speculative point: 'He is thy being and in him thou art that that thou art . . . evermore saving this difference betwixt thee and him, that he is thy being and thou not his.'[55] Thus to feel our own being is already, in some sense, to feel God's being. However, the feeling of our own being is not meant to be some form of metaphysical narcissism. We are meant to 'knaw' on the feeling of our own being [56] – maybe the implied metaphor is that this is the 'bone' thrown to us, as if we were troublesome dogs, to keep us quiet for a bit – until we are capable of something better. But this feeling of our own being is in fact an important part of the contemplative life, as it focuses all that separates us from God. Even if we succeed in forgetting all other creatures, we shall still find ourselves getting in the way, and other creatures can in any case only hinder us because we are ourselves in the way.[57] Thus just as the shift to contemplative life means abandoning discursive, imaginative ways of approaching God, so it also means abandoning a discursive view of what separates us from God. The 'meditation' of contemplatives can be reduced to two simple words, 'God' and 'sin' ('not breaking nor expounding these words with curiosity of wit').[58] And this 'foul stinking lump', sin, is 'none other thing than thyself'.[59]

When meditation is simplified to this extent, it merges imperceptibly with prayer. There is no real separation between the recommended monosyllabic 'meditation' and the prayers 'which rise evermore suddenly unto God, without any means or any premeditation' and which, 'if they be in words, as they been but seldom, then been they in full few words, yea, and in ever the fewer the better. Yea, and if it be but a little word of one syllable, me think it better than of two and more according to the work of the Spirit.' This allows our author to give an added, though not alien, significance to the tradition of short prayer.[60]

The feeling of self as the quintessential obstacle preventing us from attaining to the feeling of God is obviously parasitic upon the desire for the feeling of God. And the only way to be rid of it is to feel it to the full as a 'strong and a deep ghostly sorrow', which is described in rather paradoxical terms. It is a sorrow so intense that by comparison all other sorrows are a joke; the person who feels it 'often he goeth nigh mad for sorrow, in so much that he weepeth and waileth, striveth, curseth and banneth'. Yet at the same time it is quite different from the sort of sorrow which we can work up by self-dramatisation. Our author inserts in this context one of his frequent warnings against 'rudely straining' the body or the spirit. And he is careful to point out that there must be no desire 'to unbe', which would be 'devil's madness and despite unto God'. 'But him listeth right well be, and he meaneth full heartily thanking to God for the worthiness and the gift of his being, though all that he desire unceasingly for to lack the witting and the feeling of his being.'

This sorrow 'cleanseth the soul, not only of sin, but also of pain that he hath deserved for sin. And thereto it maketh a soul able to receive that joy, the which robs a man of all witting and feeling of his being.' The meekness involved in the painful 'feeling' of our own being is an essential precondition, but the actual forgetting of self comes entirely from God's grace.[61] And this grace is given to different people in different ways. Some people lose the feeling of self only rarely, and perhaps only in a state of actual rapture; other people lose it more or less whenever they like, and without at the same time losing the ability to perform the ordinary functions of life. But, whatever form it takes, this is the 'perfection' of the 'work' of the contemplative.[62]

We must now come back to the question of what is meant by the 'feeling of God'. Unfortunately the Middle English 'feel' is every bit as ambiguous as the Modern English; the main difference is that the word had not yet acquired the bias towards emotional 'feelings' which is characteristic of modern usage. The author is explicit that we cannot 'feel' God as he is in himself[63] and that in this life our union with God is always in the 'cloud of unknowing'.[64] It is clear that the feeling involved in the 'work' is not any form of real knowledge.[65] But it is also clear that the 'feeling' is not essentially affective either: the 'naked' feeling of him by 'ghostly one-ing to his love' is 'unclothed and not lapped in any of these sensible feelings, be they never so sweet nor so holy, that they may fall in this life'.[66] Our author, like Rolle, is aware that it takes a lot of energy to sustain prolonged 'sweet feelings and weepings', and, unlike Rolle, he sees this as a reason for not 'leaning too much on them, for fear of feebleness'.[67] So it seems that we have to fall back on the basic (and least interesting) meaning of 'feeling': consciousness or awareness. And it seems likely that there is no essential difference between the 'feeling' of God and the 'feeling' of the perfection of the 'work' (any more than Guigo means by the 'sensed experience' of the Lord anything other than an acute awareness of our own desire for him). The 'feeling of God' is what is left when the feeling of self has gone. And this is, in the nature of the case, something rather obscure. In chapter nine of *The Cloud* no distinction appears to be made between the 'feeling' of God and the 'feeling' of the blind stirring of love, and apparently we cannot even 'see' the latter clearly, all we can do is 'grope and feel it' in this life.[68]

The author does hint that occasionally God may 'send out a beam of ghostly light, piercing this cloud of unknowing that is betwixt thee and him, and show thee some of his privity', but since God's 'privity' is something which 'man may not, nor can not, speak', we can only follow our author's example and leave it at that, as a mysterious hint.[69]

As a particular activity, the contemplative's 'work' is, in the nature of the case, something that is only done 'for a time'.[70] On the other hand, the author also says that 'I would that thou shouldst never cease of this work the whiles thou livest', though he slightly qualifies it by saying that 'thou shouldst evermore have it either in earnest or in game, that is to say, either in work or in will'.[71] He recognises that fraternal charity will sometimes make it necessary to abandon for a time 'the height of this work', but to abandon the work entirely 'may not be without great sin'.[72]

It is not hard to see why it would be 'great sin' to abandon the 'work' entirely. After all, the essential attitude expressed by the 'work' is central to christianity. The 'entent unto God' is really nothing but that charity which is the heart of any christian life, whose loss means the cessation of the life of grace. 'Charity is nought else . . . but love of God for himself above all creatures, and of man for God even with thyself.'[73] Not only is this precisely what is expressed in the 'naked entent', but it must also be said that without the 'naked entent' there cannot be any real perfection of charity or of any other virtue. 'For the defailing in this working a man falleth deeper and deeper in sin, and further and further from God; and by keeping and continual working in this work only, without anything more, a man evermore riseth higher and higher from sin and nearer and nearer to God.'[74]

> It destroyeth not only the ground and root of sin, as it may be here, but thereto it getteth virtues. For if it be truly conceived, all virtues shall be subtly and perfectly conceived and felt comprehended in it, without any meddling of the intent. And have a man never so many virtues without it, all they been meddled with some crooked intent, for the which they been imperfect.[75]

The naked entent is precisely that directing of all one's interests and activities to God which is what makes them christian; this is why the simple offering of self, in which the naked entent is expressed, 'shall be the chief of all thy doings in all thy doings, whether they be active or contemplative'.[76]

There seems to be no reason, therefore, to regard the 'work' as belonging exclusively to 'contemplatives'. Yet the Cloud-author is most insistent on the special grace involved in being a contemplative, as distinct from the common vocation to be a christian. Only *some* people are called to perfection.[77]

It is not too hard to see what our author is afraid of. His doctrine is in large measure concerned with basic right motivation, and it would make nonsense of it if it were to be adopted for the wrong motives. He does not, to use a slightly anachronistic phrase, want to be seen as simply recommending a new 'method' of piety, which might be taken up simply out of superficial curiosity.[78] And he is clearly suspicious of people who follow certain practices simply because they have noticed other people following them.[79] And the sort of people who would be most likely to get excited about his teaching for the wrong reasons would surely be, in the fourteenth century, people who had learned their piety in the school of devotionalism. And, as his repeated warnings against forcing ourselves 'against course of nature' show, the worst mistake that could be made would be to transfer the techniques of devotionalism to a sphere where they can only do harm. Our author has no desire to encourage people to construct fanciful heavens for themselves and then take them by storm, and persuade themselves that they are 'contemplatives' simply because they manage to induce paranormal sensations in themselves.[80]

Against this background, it becomes intelligible that our author should have wanted to posit a complete discontinuity between the practice of meditation and the practices proper to the contemplative life, and that he should have wanted to ascribe the contemplative life to a distinct grace of its own. He is not wanting to imply that the contemplative life is 'supernatural' in such a way as to make it contrary to what is natural to us; rather the reverse, in fact. The 'stirring of love' which is the essential characteristic of the contemplative life is easily ascribed to a special grace because it arises spontaneously, and the fraudulent imitation of it is what is unnatural. The author invites his readers to practise his doctrine only if it suits their 'disposition in body and soul'.[81]

The Cloud-author takes it for granted, I suspect, that his readers are already engaged in some form of affective, imaginative piety; his concern is, in effect, to get them out of it. But he does not want to get them out of it only to leave them in something worse, which is what would happen if they tried to focus simply on God, without being capable of the radical simplification which such focusing involves and without being ready for a complete 'noughting of self' and 'all-ing of God'.[82] Hence his precautions. For those who are capable of the proper attitude, the inherited tradition provided a very simple device for authorising their change of piety: they can be seen as moving on from the purgative way to the unitive way, from meditation to contemplation.

For our purposes it might have been clearer if the author had presented his teaching in a slightly different manner. He does not take it upon himself to challenge devotionalist piety as such, he allows it to have its own propriety provided that at least some people move on from it. But he drops substantial hints that suggest that it might have been much better if most people had never got into it in the first place. At the very least there is a serious risk that a religion which puts too much stress on affectivity will degenerate into a mere quest for sensations,[83] and that a piety which relies heavily on imagination will be motivated 'not by . . . a meek, blind stirring of love, but by a proud, curious and imaginative wit'.[84]

If we disregard the élitest segregation of contemplatives, the Cloud-author can be read as teaching us all something of what it means to take God seriously. And one of the first things is that we must take our own pious practices much less seriously. This is because, strictly speaking, there are absolutely no 'means' by which to 'get God'.[85] It is God who stirs our will to himself, 'without means either on his side or on thine'. No 'means' can bring us to this point; 'all good means depend on it, and it on no mean'.[86] 'Mean unto God get thee none but God.'[87]

Since we cannot work out for ourselves any way of 'getting God', we should in general avoid tying ourselves down to any particular regime of life, unless we are clearly called to do so by grace. Committing ourselves unnecessarily to set practices will mean that we are often unable to respond to the real demands of actual situations and that, 'under colour of holiness', we shall enslave ourselves 'in full and final destroying of the freedom of Christ.'[88] We do not have to make any definitive choice between such options as eating and fasting, speaking or keeping silence, living alone or with other people. None of these things is God, none of these necessarily leads to God. Therefore we should choose God who is 'hid betwixt them', and in that way we shall be 'silently speaking and speakingly silent, fastingly eating and eatingly fasting' and so on.[89]

No amount of calculation will enable us to find exactly the right formula to govern such things as our diet and timetable. But if we continually direct our intention towards God, then everything else will simply fall into place. Our author recommends 'recklessness' about external practices.[90]

He also recommends 'recklessness' about sensible consolations. There is a kind of 'sweetness' which is not suspect, in that it springs simply from the 'abundance of ghostly gladness and of true devotion in the spirit'; all other mysterious sensations are highly ambiguous. But there is no need to try to diagnose which come from a good angel and which come from an evil angel. And we do not even need to distinguish carefully between bodily and spiritual consolations. If we are really concerned simply with God, then we shall not object to having our senses pampered from time to time, but equally we shall not mind being left without such consolations.[91] The substance of all perfection is precisely a good will, consisting essentially in a 'meek stirring of love'.[92]

We should work 'with a list' rather than with 'lither strength', and this means that we should regard our relationship with God in somewhat playful terms. Reason, in our author's view, is not competent to deal directly with God, and 'ever when reason defaileth, then list love live and learn for to play'.[93] 'I trow, whoso had grace to do and feel as I say, he should feel God gamesomely play with him, as the Father doth with the child.'⁹⁴

If we accept our author's advice, then, precisely because we shall not be forcing any of our natural powers to do anything which is unnatural to them, we shall find our whole lives spontaneously becoming decorous and well-ordered. There are no means that lead to pure love of God: pure love of God is itself the means to everything else. Human beings are the 'seemliest creature in body that ever God made',⁹⁵ and if we genuinely direct our intention towards God the whole time then our outward appearance and behaviour, as well as the movements of our soul, will all be governed 'full seemly'.⁹⁶

All this is good, wholesome doctrine. It should be claimed back from the 'contemplatives' for the use of the church as a whole.

Bibliography and Abbreviations

Editions used
Phyllis Hodgson, ed., *The Cloud of Unknowing and Related Treatises*. Salzburg 1982. References in the notes are given to this edn; for *The Cloud* itself chapter nos. are also given (which apply equally to all other edns), but for the other works there is no standard way of indicating particular passages, so I give only the page and line references to Hodgson.
Phyllis Hodgson, ed., *The Cloud of Unknowing*, Early English Text Society 218. 1944.
Phyllis Hodgson, ed., *Deonise Hid Diuinite*, Early English Text Society 231. 1955.

Recommended translations
Justin McCann (several edns).
James Walsh, Classics of Western Spirituality. 1981.

Abbreviations
Cloud	*The Cloud of Unknowing*
Hid Divinity	*Deonise Hid Diuinite*
Hodgson¹	Phyllis Hodgson's 1982 edn
Hodgson²	EETS 218
PC	*Book of Privy Counselling*
Prayer	*Epistle of Prayer*
Stirrings	*Epistle of Discretion of Stirrings*

Notes

¹Cf. the introduction to the edns by Phyllis Hodgson and the tr. by James Walsh.
²The 'other man's work' referred to in *Cloud* 48 (50:41) may well be

Hilton's *Scale*, as is suggested in a fifteenth-century annotation (cf. Walsh, p. 213[318]); conversely the end of Hilton's *Angel's Song* (ed. Toshiyuki Takamiya [Tokyo 1980], pp. 14–15) appears to be a comment on precisely this passage of the *Cloud* (cf. Hodgson[1], pp. lxxxiv–v). Cf. J. P. H. Clark, *Downside Review* 98 (1980), pp. 108–9.

[3]For the corpus of writings, cf. Hodgson[2], pp. xii–xiv.

[4]The 'other man's work' referred to in *Cloud* 35 (39:27) is almost certainly Guigo (cf. Walsh, p. 187[245]); this is where the fourfold schema is explicitly stated. It is also likely that the definition of prayer in *Cloud* 39 (42:32–3) is from Guigo, SC 2, and that the passage in PC 96 on the 'coming and going' of God derives from SC 9–10, which also probably underlies *Prayer* 106:14–17. It is tempting to see an echo of SC 6 (*in sensu experientiae*) in *Cloud* 9 (19:16) (*fele in experience*).

[5]*Cloud* 35 (39:28–36). Walsh gives *goodly* a stronger sense and takes the author to mean that 'there can be no *profitable* reflection without previous reading' and no '*true* prayer without previous reflection', which would be closer to Guigo; but *may not goodly* in Middle English regularly means 'can hardly' (Sherman M. Kuhn, ed., *Middle English Dictionary* [Ann Arbor 1956ff], s.v. *godli* adv. (2) 4), and Hodgson takes this to be the sense here (see her glossary). Hilton (*Scale* I, 15), writing for someone who could not read Latin, seems prepared simply to drop reading; the Cloud-author does not go as far as this. For those who cannot read, hearing (sermons and so on) is just as good. He also observes that it is inconceivable that, without reading or hearing, 'a soul that is blinded in custom of sin should see the foul spot in his conscience' (40:1–3).

[6]*Cloud* 7 (15:16–20).

[7]Cf. ibid., 17 (26:13–17). There is no hint of such a progress from manhood to Godhead in Guigo.

[8]*Hid Divinity* Prol. (119:9–10).

[9]An influence of Hugh of Balma on the Cloud-author has often been alleged, but this has recently been challenged: A. Minnis, 'The Sources of *The Cloud of Unknowing*: A Reconsideration', in Marion Glasscoe, ed., *The Medieval Mystical Tradition in England* (Exeter 1982), pp. 63–75.

[10]Only once, I think, in PC 83:20–3, does the author even hint that the active/contemplative dichotomy is not, after all, terribly important.

[11]*Cloud* 9 (18:38–19:5).

[12]Ibid., 12 (21:32).

[13]Ibid., 8 (18:18–21).

[14]Ibid., 65 (65:28–31).

[15]*Prayer* 103:24–5.

[16]*Cloud* 4 (12:38–13:1).

[17]PC 90:12–16,29–35.

[18]*Prayer* 107:9–12.

[19]PC 91.

[20]PC 92:4–6.

[21]St Teresa of Avila was bothered by the tendency to leave the humanity of Christ behind – and she realised that this problem was connected with the abandonment of discursive thinking in contemplation: *Interior Castle* 6:7.

[22]*Cloud* 5–6 (14:4–22).

[23]*Mesuring* means 'making proportionate to' (cf. 22:28), which involves a sort of 'toning down' of the Godhead for our sake; nevertheless the play on *mete-mesuring* emphasises that there is a real proportion between God, precisely as God, and our soul. God is *mete to oure soule*, 'made to measure for our soul', as it were, even if this does require a *mesuring of his godheed*.

[24]*Cloud* 4 (10:22–9). 'Knowable might': intellectual faculty.

[25]Ibid., 8 (17:32–3).

[26]Ibid., 3 (9:12–13).

[27]Ibid., 34 (38:36–8).

[28]Ibid., 3 (9:33–4).

[29]Ibid. (9:31).

[30]PC 80:17–22.

[31]*Cloud* 67 (67:4–5).

[32]Ibid., 70 (69:29–70:4).

[33]Ibid., 51–2 (53:5–38). The satire and warning against false contemplatives continues to the end of ch. 56, the exposition of the metaphorical nature of such religious language occupies ch. 57–61, and this leads into an exposition of the powers of the soul (ch. 62–6).

[34]Ibid., 68 (67:30–68:10).

[35]PC 76:17–24.

[36]Ibid., 75:23–8.

[37]Cf. ibid., 76:32–7.

[38]Ibid., 76:38–77:6.

[39]Ibid., 77:27–8.

[40]Ibid., 77:19–23,34–42.

[41]*Cloud* 4 (12:22–4).

[42]Ibid., 34 (38:30–3).

[43]Ibid., 4 (13:7–8).

[44]Ibid., 5 (14:4–9).

[45]Ibid., 34 (39:2–4).

[46]Ibid., 2 (9:4–6).

[47]Ibid., 5 (13:24–7).

[48]Ibid., 26 (34:5–16).

[49]Ibid., 45 (47:20–3).

[50]Ibid., 46 (48:16–30).

[51]Ibid., 32 (37:1–22).

[52]PC 88:39–89:7.

[53]Ibid., 89:9–10.

[54]Ibid., 76:38–77:3.

[55]Ibid., 75:31–7.

[56]Ibid., 89:4.

[57]*Cloud* 43 (45:21–46:8).

[58]Ibid., 36 (40:22–7).

[59]Ibid., 43 (45:34–5).

[60]Ibid., 37–40 (40:39–44:14).

[61]Ibid., 44.

[62]Ibid., 71–2.

[63]Ibid., 14 (23:15–16).

[64]Ibid., 3 (9:36–7); 69 (69:11–12).

[65]PC 98:36–7.

[66]Ibid., 97:14–22.

[67]*Cloud* 50 (52:1–3).

[68]Ibid., 9 (19:6–10).

[69]Ibid., 26 (34:31–4).

[70]Cf. ibid., 8 (18:4), 9 (19:27), 40 (43:26).

[71]Ibid., 40 (44:22–4,29–30).

[72]Ibid., 25 (33:12–14).

[73]Ibid., 24 (32:19–21).

[74]Ibid., 4 (11:13–7).

[75]Ibid., 12 (21:32–22:2).

[76]PC 83:21–3.

[77]Ibid., 92:21–37. This élitist doctrine of perfection was authoritatively rejected by Vatican II, *Lumen Gentium* 39–40.

[78]Cf. *Cloud* 75 (73:19–24).

[79]Cf. *Stirrings* 113:1–17.

[80]Cf. *Cloud* 48 (50:27–9), 52 (53:39–42), 57 (58:26–36).

[81]Ibid., 74 (72:26–8).

[82]PC 84:27.

[83]*Cloud* 50 (52:3–4).

[84]Ibid., 4 (12:33–5).

[85]*Stirrings* 116:7–9.

[86]*Cloud* 34 (39:11–21).

[87]*Stirrings* 117:20.

[88]Ibid., 114:16–26.

[89]Ibid., 115:4–13.

[90]*Cloud* 42.

[91]Ibid., 48, 50.

[92]Ibid., 49.

[93]*Stirrings* 115:31–2.

[94]*Cloud* 46 (48:34–6).

[95]Ibid., 61 (63:20–1).

[96]Ibid., 54 (55:25–56:6).

16

Julian of Norwich

About the external circumstances of the life of Julian of Norwich very little is known. In May 1373, when she received her famous 'revelation of love',[1] after suffering a severe heart attack,[2] she was thirty and a half years old.[3] At the time, she appears to have been living at home as a laywoman.[4] We first hear of her as an anchoress in 1394[5] and thereafter there is spasmodic evidence of her being still alive up to 1416, including Margery Kempe's account of the 'holy dalliance' she had with Julian, to whom she had been sent for spiritual advice.[6] We know neither when Julian became an anchoress nor when she died.

Of her inner development we know rather more, thanks to her own writings. At some stage before she was thirty[7] she tells us that she 'desired three gifts by the grace of God'.[8] These gifts indicate clearly that at that time Julian's piety was of an affective, devotionalist kind. The first gift was 'mind of the passion', a commonplace of affective piety; in particular she wanted to have more 'feeling in the passion of Christ', and to this end she desired 'a bodily sight', so that she could more easily identify herself with those who were actually present on Good Friday and suffered with Christ.[9]

Secondly, Julian desired to fall seriously ill at the age of thirty. This is undoubtedly intended as' a form of bodily imitation of the passion of Christ.[10] Julian's motive is the same as that which prompted Suso to attach a wooden cross to his back, with sharp needles in it to pierce his flesh.[11]

Thirdly, Julian desired three wounds, inspired, as she tells us, by hearing the story of St Cecilia, who received three wounds in her neck.[12] The three wounds she wanted were contrition, compassion and 'wilful longing to God'. It may be remarked that these wounds coincide exactly with the three things which James of Milan regarded as the essential factors conducing to contemplation.[13]

Julian's third desire remained with her continually, but the other two, she says, 'passed from my mind'.[14] This probably reflects a movement away from 'carnal love' of the humanity of Christ towards something supposedly more elevated. It is interesting that when Julian is propped up in bed after her heart attack and the

187

priest offers her a crucifix to look at, she does not want to look at it, because 'me thought I was well, for my eyes were set upright into heaven'. She consents to look at the cross only for the purely medical reason that she thought it would involve less physical strain to look straight ahead than to go on looking upwards.[15] Later on the tension between her 'upward' piety and the continuing vision of the passion precipitates a crisis: Julian wanted to look away from the cross but did not dare to do so for fear of fiends.[16] But then she realises that there is nothing between the cross and heaven which could do her any harm, so either she has to look up or she has to find another reason for continuing to look at the cross. She very deliberately refuses to look away, choosing Jesus, in all his pain, as her heaven.[17] This is a decisive move, even if it is only long after-wards that Julian appreciates its full significance: the 'upward' movement towards God, towards heaven, is redirected towards the suffering humanity of Christ. *That* is where heaven must be sought.

Probably within a few years of her showings Julian wrote the first version of her book, the Short Text.[18] She was still far from having absorbed the meaning of her revelation, and in particular she still viewed herself and her readers from within a distorting perspective which she later abandoned. She appears to have thought of herself as a 'contemplative', and she certainly addresses herself to people 'that desire to live contemplatively'.[19] And she seems to have a conventional enough notion of what it means to 'live contempla-tively'. Contemplatives are people who are not 'occupied wilfully in earthly business', and who gladly 'nought [despise] all thing that is made, for to have the love of God that is unmade'. They seek that spiritual repose which can only be had when the soul is 'noughted for love'.[20]

The 'contemplative' evidently aspires to 'pass unto God by contemplation'; the vision of Christ is a necessary preliminary to this, but it is only proposed to us as something to look at 'if' we cannot 'look into' the Godhead.[21]

Julian's self-presentation in the Short Text exploits several 'contemplative' commonplaces. She insists that she is not to be regarded as a 'teacher': 'I am a woman, lewd [uneducated], feeble and frail.'[22] This may be regarded as a typical 'modesty formula',[23] but it should be noticed that the implications of such formulae were not in fact totally modest. By denying his or her own authority, the writer could lay claim to a much greater authority, on the pretext of simply passing on a teaching received from someone else.[24] In particular it could be claimed that it is characteristic of God to use unlearned people to be the bearers of his message.[25] People are led to abandon 'the common doctrine and counsel of holy church' by their 'pride and curiosity of kindly wit and letterly cunning [natural intellectual inquisitiveness and educated know-how]';[26] the 'contemplative' life, on the other hand, is a safe, simple life which is not exposed to any such hazards.[27]

Julian is well-mannered enough not to make fun of other people's intellectual abilities, but she turns against herself the conventional 'contemplative' suspicion of intellectual curiosity. She had, as she tells us, often wondered why God did not prevent sin, but now she accuses herself of folly and pride because of this attitude of questioning God's wisdom.[28] God has shown us our Saviour and our salvation, and we should be content with that, and not pry into God's 'privy counsels'.[29] True to her own precepts, Julian accepts the answers that the Lord gives her and does not pursue her questioning any further.

She also declares that there was nothing in any of the showings which disturbed her or drew her away from the teaching of the holy church.[30] Her orthodoxy is quite untroubled.

That, no doubt, was where Julian intended to leave the matter, but the matter was not prepared to be left there. The revelation continued to exercise her mind, and some fifteen years after the revelation of 1373 she seems to have finished a new, much longer, version of her book, and even then she felt that she had only made a beginning.[31] It was not until 1393 that she completed the Long Text.[32]

The most significant development that occurred between the completion of the Short Text and the writing of the Long Text is that Julian freed herself from the 'contemplative' straitjacket and came to terms with herself as an intelligent woman with a probing and insistent mind. She is still prepared to accuse herself of 'folly' in wondering why God did not prevent sin, but she no longer accuses herself of pride; and the foolishness for which she blames herself seems to reside more in the grumbling attitude with which she asks her question than in the question itself.[33] And it is noticeable that this time she is much less easily satisfied by the Lord's assurances, and pursues her questioning much further and far more rigorously.

She is still well aware that we must respect God's 'privities', but she is also convinced that God intends us to. seek knowledge. If something is, for the moment, meant not to be revealed to us, then God shows it to us precisely as something still 'closed'; that is to say, we do not have to be shy of probing, because God himself shows us where the line is drawn beyond which we are not going to get any answers.[34]

Julian is as determined as she ever was not to be unfaithful to the doctrine of the church, but she is no longer able to claim simply that the showings posed no problems to her faith. There are several very serious problems, and she does not shirk them.[35]

Since writing the Short Text Julian has become much more confident of her own intellectual powers, and she no longer has any ideological anxieties about using them. As she now sees it,

> By three things man standeth in this life, by which three God is worshipped and we be sped, kept and saved. The first is use of man's kindly [natural] reason, the second is the common teaching of holy church, the third is the inward gracious working of the Holy Ghost, and these three be all of one God ... and all are sundry gifts, to which he will that we have great regard and accord us thereto.[36]

Reason, which is grounded in God,[37] far from being in any way opposed to faith, is one of the sources of our faith.[38] This means that when the showings are over and the revelation is entrusted to faith for its preservation,[39] there is no justification for excluding from faith a genuine intellectual effort to appropriate and explore the doctrinal significance of the showings.

It is noticeable that Julian no longer considers it necessary to insist that she is not a teacher, nor does she now describe herself as a 'lewd woman', writing only because God wants her to. She says that the revelation was made 'to a simple creature unlettered',[40] but she does not say that she is still unlettered at the time of writing. Whatever kind of education she has picked up since 1373,[41] there is no mistaking the new tone of authority with which she writes. She can no longer simply claim to be passing on someone else's teaching; it has become her own teaching.

In the Short Text Julian never makes it clear quite what the relationship is between her revelation and the public teaching of the church, except to claim that there were no problems. In the Long Text she admits that there are problems, but nevertheless insists that the content of the revelation is identical with that of 'the faith, neither more nor less'.[42] The revelation is an elucidation of the public doctrine of the church, and as such it could only be addressed to the church as a whole. Granted the prevailing usage of the word, it is unlikely that Julian still thought of herself as a 'contemplative', and she seems to have lost interest in the élitist pretensions which such a word made possible,[43] but in any case she evidently realises that her task is to present a vision of christian truth which, if it is true at all, must be true for everybody.

The finesse of Julian's method can be seen at once in her rehandling of the first showing. The vision begins with the sight of the crucifix bleeding, but what strikes Julian most is the astounding readiness of God, 'who is so reverent and so dreadful', to be intimate ('homely') 'with a sinful creature living in this wretched flesh'.[44] It is just this intimacy which will be our supreme joy in heaven, but in this life we normally know about it only by faith; it is only by a special gift of grace that we can sometimes begin to perceive it more directly.[45]

The meaning of the revelation as a whole (and Julian always treats the sixteen showings as constituting one revelation) is love,[46] but the particular nuance which is brought out in the first showing (which Julian takes to be foundational for all the rest)[47] is that the love in question is the utterly preposterous love between God, who is all great, and creatures who are, in themselves, almost nothing. Julian's attention is drawn to our Lady, whose 'wisdom and truth [fidelity]'[48] are clearly exemplary for us: by them she appreciated with wonder 'the greatness of her maker and the littleness of herself'.[49]

In the course of the first showing,[50] Julian tells us,

He showed a little thing, the quantity of an hazelnut, lying in the palm of my hand, as me seemed, and it was as round as a ball. I looked thereon with the eye of my understanding and thought, 'What may this be?' And it was answered generally thus, 'It is all that is made.' I marvelled how it might last, for me thought it might suddenly have fallen to nought for littleness. And I was answered in my understanding, 'It lasteth and ever shall, for God loveth it, and so hath all thing being by the love of God.'[51]

The implications of this vision of the littleness of all that is made are, of course, highly ambiguous. In the Short Text the exposition is tilted fairly unambiguously in one direction: since we can never have real bliss until we are 'so fastened to (God) that there might be right nought that is made between' God and us, it follows that we should 'nought all thing that is made for to have the love of God that is unmade'.[52] This moral still stands in the Long Text, but there it is complemented by a much greater emphasis on the other side of the picture: God loves all that is made, and his love is immediately at work in all of it. We must not be impressed by creatures in themselves, but equally we do not have to turn aside from them in order to meet God's love. In a splendidly down to earth passage which evidently shocked one of the pious copyists, Julian illustrates the way in which God's love 'cometh down to us to the lowest part of our need' by reminding us of how our bodies digest food and then eliminate the residual waste matter: and 'it is he that doeth this'.[53] Later on, in her famous comments on divine motherhood,[54] Julian makes it clear that ordinary human motherhood is not just an image of divine love, it is a real part of the operation of divine love.[55]

The subtle attitude we should adopt towards creatures is illustrated in a section which Julian added to her account of the first showing in the Long Text. Reflecting on contemporary forms of prayer, Julian comments that we tend to have insufficient confidence in God's goodness, and so we approach him in a wheedling manner, as if we had to persuade him to be well-disposed towards us by reminding him of the passion or of our Lady or whatever. But God is already well-disposed towards us, and we should do him better worship by going straight to the point; we ought to 'pray to himself of his goodness'. 'Means' are not needed. But at the same time all the means which people use are good and we are right to use them, but we should understand that they are not ways of procuring God's favour, they are precisely gifts of his favour. 'Wherefore it pleaseth him that we seek him and worship him by means, understanding and knowing that he is the goodness of all.'[56]

A full presentation of Julian's doctrine would require a detailed exposition of each of the showings in turn, which is unfortunately beyond the scope of this book. At the risk, therefore, of oversimplifying and overschematising her teaching, we must concentrate on some of the salient points contained in the final version of the Long Text, ignoring both the pedagogical excellence of the way in which the successive showings progressively build up and refine Julian's christian vision and several interesting elements in that vision.

Julian came to see that the divine intimacy, revealed in the first showing, is the fundamental fact which undergirds our whole life.

> I saw that God began never to love mankind; for right the same that mankind shall be in endless bliss, fulfilling the joy of God as regards his works, right so the same mankind hath been in the foresight of God known and loved from without beginning in his rightful entent.[57]

Wher is our bodies were made from 'the slime of the earth', our souls are made 'of nought that is made'.

> And thus is the kind [nature] made rightfully oned to the maker, which is substantial kind unmade, that is God. And therefore it is that there may be nor shall be right nought between God and man's soul. And in this endless love man's soul is kept whole, as all the matter of the revelation meaneth and showeth. In which endless love we be led and kept of God, and never shall be lost. . . . And right the same that we shall be without end, the same we were treasured in God and hid, known and loved, from without beginning.[58]

Julian, like St Thomas, has a strong doctrine of the complete efficacy and all-pervasiveness of God's creative act. God does everything that is done, even what is done by creatures.[59] And because his will is unchanging, this means that creatures must indefectibly attain to their foreordained goal.[60] In the case of human beings Julian goes even further:

> For the great endless love that God hath to all mankind, he maketh no departing in love between the blessed soul of Christ and the least soul that shall be saved. For it is full easy to believe and trust that the dwelling of the blessed soul of Christ is full high in the glorious Godhead; and truly, as I understand, in our Lord's meaning, where the blessed soul of Christ is, there is the substance of all the souls that shall be saved by Christ.[61]

In God's purpose, humanity is first and foremost the humanity of Christ. And in some sense we were all made at once, in the humanity of Christ, inseparably united to God in him, endlessly loving him and enjoying him. This means that in all the elect there is an indefectible 'godly will', which never swerves from God.[62] This is what we really are, our 'substance', and it unfailingly does God's will.[63] 'Ever more it doeth that it was made for: it seeth God and it beholdeth God and it loveth God.'[64] Thus, in one sense, we must say that 'we are more truly in heaven than on earth'.[65]

If we view everything simply from the point of view of God's act, which cannot help but be effective, then we have to conclude that 'everything that is done is well done'.[66] And, from this point of view, it is tempting to infer that it is only a 'blind judgment' on our part to reckon that some things are not well done.[67] But Julian realises that this would be oversimple: sin is a real damage,[68] and it is the church, not just our blindness, which judges some deeds to be evil.[69] Although Julian accuses herself of folly in wondering why God did not prevent sin at the outset, she comes to see that it is absolutely imperative to have an answer to the question of how God sees sin, of how it is possible to hold together the divine satisfaction with all that is done ('All is well')[70] and the inescapable recognition that all is not well.[71]

Julian is aware of the metaphysical proprieties involved in any discussion of sin. She knows that 'sin hath no manner of substance or any part in being'.[72] But it cannot be denied that sin is an important part of our lives, as we actually experience them. Julian's contention is that sin is known precisely in the pain that it causes.[73] This is, in fact, how God sees sin: he sees our sin simply as pain in us.[74] Julian could not see any hint that God blames us for our sins (and therefore, as she shrewdly points out, it would be quite wrong for us to blame God for our sins).[75] In one sense, this is a necessary doctrine: granted that God is unchanging, if there were any wrath in him at all, then that would entail an eternal and ceaseless anger, and this would be incompatible with our being created out of love. So Julian concludes, 'If God might be wroth a touch [for a moment], we should neither have life nor stead nor being'.[76] But in that case, what becomes of forgiveness? 'Our soul is oned to him, unchangeable goodness, and between God and our soul is neither wrath nor forgiveness in his sight.'[77]

Julian solves this particular problem by relocating wrath: it is not in God, it is in us: it is we who are not always 'in peace and love', even though objectively 'peace and love are ever in us'.[78] Using the word 'forgive' in a way which is no longer current in modern English, Julian says that there is no wrath in God for him to 'forgive' (i.e. forgo, give up), it is our wrath which he 'forgives' (that is to say, forgiveness and mercy work in us to dispel our own inner disquiet at ourselves).[79]

But this does not really deal with the essential difficulty: if God does not blame us, why should the church blame us, why should we blame ourselves? And even if we reinterpret the discussion of sin so as to turn it into a general discussion of 'all that is not good', including all the pain of all God's creatures,[80] what is the point of all this pain?

This life is undeniably painful. But if we could see God clearly, then there could be no pain, no disorder, no sin.[81] If we undergo pain and fall into sin, it is in some way because God does not show himself clearly to us. Or rather, it is because he shows himself to us in a particular way: if he were to show us 'his blissful cheer [countenance] ... all thing should be to us joy and bliss', but because he shows us 'cheer of passion, as he bare in this life his cross, therefore we be in disease and travail with him as our kind asketh'.[82] Reflecting on the darkness of the second showing, Julian understood that the darkness was 'a figure and a likeness of our foul black death which that our fair, bright blessed Lord bare for our sin'.[83] There is a certain circularity here: it is our death which Christ bore on the cross, yet somehow it is only because he shows himself under the modality of passion that there is any death for him to bear. The problem of sin and pain actually turns out to be the problem of this life as a whole. Julian's brooding on the difficulty of reconciling God's judgment that 'all is well' with the church's judgment that all is not well leads her to a much broader observation, that it is seemingly a necessary facet of life in this world that we should not see God clearly the whole time:[84] it is not just God's attitude to sin that we need to discover, it is God's view of this life as such.

It is made clear that our acceptance of the terms of this life is something to do with God's glory and the increase of our own bliss[85] and, even before she cracks the difficult fourteenth showing, Julian is able to suggest various ways of making sense of this. There is, first of all, a commonplace ascetic comment: we can learn humility from our feebleness and sinfulness.[86] Also there is some 'property of blessed love that we shall know in God, which we might never have known without woe going before'.[87] Julian echoes St Paul in asserting that the reward that awaits us in heaven far transcends anything we might have deserved by any amount of 'pain and travail' on earth.[88] And we are rewarded specifically for all our pains, including the pains caused by our sins – Julian rather daringly says that in heaven sin will be a glory, not a shame.[89]

Julian is quite clear that the puzzle over our own pain, including sin, can only be resolved by reference to the passion of Christ. She sees that in principle all pain is enfolded in his passion. There is no separation between the pains he suffered in his own body on the cross and the pains which he continues to suffer in his members until the end of the world.[90] 'For every man's sin that shall be saved, he suffered; and every man's sorrow, desolation and anguish he saw and sorrowed, for kindness and love.'[91] His humanity *is* 'all mankind that shall be saved'[92] and there is a real ontological link between his suffering and the suffering of all of his creatures, so that our whole life in this world can be viewed in this light: 'Thus was our lord Jesus pained for us, and we stand all in this manner of pain with him and shall do till that we come to his bliss.'[93] This means that the essential penance which we undertake 'with mind of his passion' is, quite simply, this life: 'for I tell thee, howsoever thou do, thou shalt have woe . . . and then shalt thou truly see that all thy living is penance profitable'.[94]

The problem, then, is why there is this whole dimension of pain, Christ's and ours. It is true that Christ's pain is caused by our sin,[95] but it is also true to say that it is only because he shows us 'cheer of pain' that we are in pain. We cannot make sense of any of it unless we can discover precisely the role of all this pain in God's intention. As Julian came to see very clearly, there are only two possibilities: either sin (and pain) are simply brought to nothing in God's eyes, or in some way they do enter into the divine perspective.[96] At first Julian was prepared to accept that this whole life, from the point of view of eternity, is simply 'nought', but later she was not satisfied with this.[97] If this life really comes to nothing, then life is simply a waste of time. In the Long Text Julian assures us that this is not so: nothing will be lost,[98] time is not wasted.[99]

The answer that Julian eventually receives is based on a rather opaque little story of a lord and a servant. This was the part of the fourteenth showing which she was slowest to understand, but when she did understand it, it provided the key to all the rest. In the story, she saw a lord sitting in a barren wilderness, with a single servant standing to one side, waiting to hurry away to fulfil his master's bidding. When the time came, the servant rushed off, eager to accomplish his task, and fell, doing himself a serious hurt. The worst pain of all was that he could no longer see his master looking at him with unchanging love, tinged now with pity. The lord, meanwhile, plans to give the faithful servant a special reward because of what he has suffered.[100]

Julian understood at once that this must be an allegory of the fall of Adam, but she saw that there were some points which did not fit Adam as a single individual.[101] She was forced to accept that there is a double meaning in the servant: he is not only Adam, he is also Christ. And, because of the union established at the very beginning of creation between the soul of Christ and the souls of all the elect, Christ cannot be separated from Adam. So Julian has to say, 'When Adam fell, God's Son fell . . . Adam fell from life to death, into the vale of this wretched world, and after that into Hell; God's Son fell with Adam into the vale of the maiden's womb.'[102] The fall of Adam and the Incarnation are essentially one and the same story.

Julian appears to accept what is sometimes taken to be the Scotist view, that the Incarnation was always intended by God.[103] But at the same time there is not the slightest hint in Julian of any notion of a possible Incarnation which would not at the same time be a redemption, any more than there is anything said about the fall except in the perspective of redemption.[104]

In the terms of the story of the lord and the servant, the fall occurs precisely because of the servant's eagerness to carry out his master's will. As applied to Adam/Christ, this means that Adam's fall is exactly coincident with the mission of the Son of God. And, although the imagery gets rather confused, it seems clear that the mission of the Son of God could not be accomplished without some sort of fall. The servant is sent to fetch a treasure which is on the earth, he is sent to dig something out of the earth which his master wants, he is also, it seems, to achieve something which will enable the lord to take his seat in his glorious palace, instead of sitting on the barren earth.[105]

It is the last part of the servant's mission which is most clearly explained: the Father's chosen dwelling place is the human soul, and this only becomes fit to be his dwelling place as a result of the Son's redeeming work.[106] Our souls are presented to the Father, united with the humanity of Christ, at the Ascension.[107] It is also, presumably, our souls which are the 'treasure in the earth' which is to be prepared as a food fit for the lord's table.[108]

But this food has to be dug out of the earth. It cannot be fetched without a 'fall'. At the level of substance, we are never separated from God, but God wants us to be more than substance: we are meant to be 'double', sensuality as well as substance.[109] And it is in our sensuality that God wishes to dwell.[110] 'Sensuality' does not just refer to our body; Julian, following normal usage, talks about our soul as 'sensual':[111] sensuality means our whole life, as lived within the terms of the body, the terms of this world. Whereas our substance is indefectible, sensuality is precisely the sphere within which we 'fail'.[112] Sensuality would be impossible without some separation from the clear beholding of God, because, as Julian has already explained, if we could see God clearly we should not be subject to the limitations of sensuality. It is because of this unavoidable element of failure associated with sensuality that it is necessary to talk about 'mercy and grace', which 'restore' sensuality 'by process of time'.[113] Time is of no concern to substance, it is only sensuality which has a history, and this history represents a genuine 'increase'.[114]

The reason why Christ suffers and we suffer is that the intended dénouement would not be possible without this kind of story to lead up to it. Julian's doctrine is reminiscent of that of St Irenaeus: God could have made Adam perfect all at once, but if he had done so he would not have created Adam, he would have created something else.[115] And the reason why we have to go through the laborious business of living in the flesh, of living in this world, is that God's purpose is precisely the 'salvation of the flesh'.[116] Julian is making much the same point, only she is more courageous than Irenaeus, in regarding sin as an inevitable part of the story. Sin is 'necessary',[117] because without it there would not be sensuality. Sin enters into the divine perspective, it is not 'wasted', because what God wants is precisely saints who have been sinners.[118] This life, sin and all, does have a real significance, even *sub specie aeternitatis*, because our final bliss and the worship we bring to God depend on our being precisely *this* kind of creature.

In the light of this doctrine the significance of Julian's choosing Jesus as her heaven becomes much more apparent: choosing Jesus as our heaven, precisely in his pain, is right for us because our heaven is one in which there must be no separation between our substance and our sensuality.[119] This life is a responsibility which we must not shirk.[120]

But if sin is a necessary part of this life, if sin is to be 'worship' to us in heaven, should we not therefore go out and sin for all we are worth? Julian's theology seems to bring her to precisely the problem which St Paul was forced to deal with.[121] And she has an excellent response to it. The inference that we should positively cultivate sin is wrong for the simple reason that we do not want to go out and sin. Whether we are consciously aware of it or not, we do not like sin.[122] Sin is the 'sharpest scourge' with which we are afflicted.[123] Because of the limitations of our sensuality, there is a 'beastly will' in us, which cannot help but will evil;[124] our wills are oppressed, so that sometimes we cannot help but sin.[125] But sin is a constraint upon our godly will, not something that we could or should choose for its own sake. In Julian's view, we need to be comforted in face of our sins;[126] and the basic comfort is the assurance that even if we do nothing but sin, we still cannot thwart God's purpose.[127] And this is true of frequent, grievous sins[128] and even of mortal sins.[129] None of them can stop God loving us or accomplishing his purpose.

The eternal contentment which is expressed in 'All is well' is imaged in time by the assurance that 'All shall be well', and, as Julian realised, this has to be taken at its face value: *all* shall be well and all manner of thing shall be well; not the least thing will be forgotten.[130] But it is precisely here that Julian discovers a seemingly insuperable difficulty: our faith teaches us that some people may be damned, so how can all be well?[131]

Julian tries for all she is worth to get an answer to this question, but she gets little except the assurance that there is a deed which the Trinity will do at the end of time which will make it plain that God can and will make all things well. What this deed is will not be known until it is done; until then, it is known neither in heaven nor on earth.[132] In the meantime, nothing is revealed about damnation, and it is therefore not a subject about which our minds can be profitably occupied, for lack of data.[133] There is, however, a single hint dropped: in heaven there is 'no more mention made of them (the damned) before God and all his holy ones than of the devil'.[134] We are referred back to the fifth showing, where Julian saw the powerlessness of the fiend. She saw that God 'scorns' the devil, but she also saw that there was no wrath in God towards him. The sight made her burst out laughing, and she realised that such laughter is quite proper, but yet she noticed that she did not see Christ laughing.[135] The point seems to be that God does not react to the devil at all. If we apply this to the damned, then it seems that at least one way of trying to cope theologically with damnation has to be ruled out: damnation does not enter into the picture of salvation at all, hell is not part of the same scenario as heaven, so we do not have to imagine the saints somehow enjoying the sight of hell.[136] It is, I think, evidence of Julian's rare tact as a theologian that she is content to accept that what is revealed to us is a doctrine of salvation;[137] we simply do not have any way of making damnation intelligible, however much we have to accept that it is a possibility.

If this is true, then it follows that we cannot work on any assumption other than that we are destined for salvation. We cannot know, of course, strictly speaking, that we are among the elect, but it is impossible to handle any other supposition. God wants us to live in hope.[138]

Julian's mature doctrine provides us with a vision by which we can make sense of life as it actually is, and consequently exhortation plays a much less prominent role than interpretation. The main exhortation which Julian addresses to us is the warning not to be taken in by foolish dread masquerading as modesty.[139] The essential moral dynamism of the christian life is vested in faith, which flows from our substance into our sensuality; and from faith cóme the virtues (obedience to the commandments) and the seven sacraments.[140] Rather than trying to move us on beyond this to some higher realm, Julian is more concerned to help us make sense of the many ways in which we tend to fall below the basic standards of christian living.

The doctrine of substance and sensuality allows Julian to reinterpret ontologically the devotionalist aspirations with which she started. Mind of the passion and bodily identification with the passion are generalised to include the whole of our earthly life as such: simply by accepting the limitations of life in this world, we are sharing in the passion of Christ, and it is in learning by faith to see God at work in all of it that we learn to recognise the Trinity in the passion. Similarly the three 'wounds' are all found to be ontologically grounded in the act of God and in the love of God, 'continued' by grace into our own natures.[141] Contrition is a fact: by virtue of our godly will, which is kept in Christ, we do not like sin and our own sins pain us. Compassion is a fact: by virtue of the penality of our lives we do 'stand' in the passion of Christ. Longing for God is an inescapable condition of our natural will, and it is inseparable from the 'thirst' which Christ has to draw us wholly into bliss.[142]

The essential qualities which devotionalism sought to feel turn out to be essential facts about us, but, precisely because we cannot perceive our substance in this life, except by faith,[143] we shall not normally be able to *feel* them. In the seventh showing Julian was taken through a rapid oscillation of feeling, from extreme consolation to total desolation, and the changes were so rapid that they could not be ascribed to any change in her; as she says, there was no time for her to have committed a sin between the consolation and the desolation. The purpose of this exercise was to emphasise the point that God keeps us equally securely whatever we feel like, in weal and in woe.[144] It is precisely because we attend to our own 'feelings' (our own perceptions, our own subjective experience) that we make life such a misery to ourselves.[145]

But Julian's doctrine is more subtle than we might have expected. She does not say that our perceptions, our feelings, are of no significance at all. It is 'the feeling of pains in sorrow and mourning' which we are told not to 'follow'.[146] The feeling of consolation is genuinely a revelation of the state of affairs which pertains at the level of our substance, and does not need to be spurned or distrusted. The important thing is that we appreciate by faith that the shift in our own feeling does not in any way mean that we have somehow lost God's love or his safe-keeping. The facts are more important than our feelings, but our acknowledgment of these facts is already, in an obscure way, due to the clear vision which our substance already enjoys.

Thus Julian, reflecting on the very dark vision which constituted the second showing, comes to see that even our seeking of God presupposes some kind of self-revelation on his part. There is no essential discontinuity between seeking and seeing. When we do not see, we must appreciate that in some sense we do see. 'He will that we believe that we see him continually, though that us think that it be but little.'[147]

In the last analysis, the all-important thing is faith, not 'feeling'. 'Above the faith is no goodness kept in this life, as to my sight, and beneath the faith is no health of soul.'[148] Julian has no doctrine of any progression leading from faith to feeling, such as Hilton's notion of 'reformation in faith and feeling'.[149] What is constant is the objective reality, which we know about by faith, and it is on that that we must take our stand. By special graces we may sometimes see more clearly, we may have some 'feeling' which makes God's love and our own inseparable union with him less opaque to us; but such special graces are, in the nature of the case, unpredictable and cannot be used as evidence of progress, any more than the lack of them can be taken as evidence of spiritual immaturity.

Julian has come a long way from her initial devotionalism and she has broken completely with the élitism of the 'contemplatives'. But precisely because she is now taking her stand on the common doctrine of the church, she offers us a vision which will make sense of any kind of christian life. Her break with affective piety allows her to be more, not less, sympathetic towards human emotions. She proposes to us a way of 'enjoying God' which does not oblige us to do violence to the necessarily erratic nature of our emotions. Where affective piety can make sense only of some emotions, Julian's doctrine can cope with them all. Just as creatures have to be 'noughted' if they are to be properly appreciated, so the only fruitful way to take emotions seriously is to take them lightly. By taking her stand on faith and on the understanding of doctrine, Julian can cope with any kind of subjective experience of the christian life which may occur. She was remarkably unflustered by Margery Kempe, for instance. Her theological vision gives us space within which to be human, within which to accept the insufficiencies as well as the sufficiencies of life. In her view, we do not need to flee from the ordinary terms of our existence in this world in order to accept and rejoice in our salvation, because our redemption is a redemption *of* this life, not a redemption *from* it.

Bibliography and Abbreviations

Editions of Julian

Edmund Colledge and James Walsh, ed., *A Book of Showings to the Anchoress Julian of Norwich*. Toronto 1978. References are given to this edn, by chapter no. (which is transferable to other edns) and by page and line nos.

Marion Glasscoe, ed., *Julian of Norwich: A Revelation of Love* [LT only]. Exeter 1976.

Reference is made in some of the notes to the MSS of LT, whose readings can be found in the edns cited: Parisinus (Paris, B.N. Fonds anglais 40), and the two Sloane MSS (British Library, Sloane 2499 and 3705). The task of producing a coherent critical text remains to be done; basically Colledge and Walsh is an edn of Parisinus, and Glasscoe is expressly an edn of Sloane 2499.

Editions of Tauler

F. Vetter, *Die Predigten Taulers*. Berlin 1910.

Théry: *Sermons de Tauler*, French tr. Hugueny, Théry and A. L. Corin, 3 vols. Paris 1927–35.

Colledge and Ciantar: John Tauler, *Spiritual Conferences* [selected texts], tr. Eric Colledge and Sister M. Jane [Ciantar]. St Louis, Mo. 1961.

Abbreviations

LT Julian's Long Text.
ST Julian's Short Text.

Notes

[1]LT 1–2 (281:2, 285:3–4).
[2]For the diagnosis, see Colledge and Walsh, p. 69.
[3]LT 3 (289:2).
[4]During her sickness her mother is at her bedside, with some others: ST 7 (224:14), 10 (234:29). The priest who is sent for to give her the last rites is called 'my curate [my parish-priest]': ST 2 (208:23). Colledge and Walsh, p. 44, argue that this does not exclude the possibility of her being a nun, possibly a Benedictine at Carrow; but there are no grounds for supposing that she was a nun (cf. Glasscoe, p. vii), and even though it is true that

some monasteries of nuns had secular chaplains, it would surely be odd for an individual nun to refer to 'my curate', as Julian does.

[5]Colledge and Walsh, p. 33.

[6]Ibid., pp. 33–5; Margery Kempe, pp. 42–3.

[7]'In my youth' in ST 1 (204:45), LT 2 (288:38–9) is ambiguous, but probably means that it was in her youth that Julian conceived the desire for a sickness, rather than that she desired to fall sick during her youth, though the reading of the Sloane MSS at LT 2 (285:6) would support the latter interpretation. But in any case 'youth' could mean anything from adolescence to just before the time of the revelation.

[8]LT 2 (285:4–5).

[9]LT 2 (285:5,7–286:16). On the devotionalist context, cf. supra ch. 14. See also Rosemary Woolf, *The English Religious Lyric in the Middle Ages* (Oxford 1968), pp. 19–66; Douglas Gray, *Themes and Images in the Medieval English Religious Lyric* (London 1972), pp. 122–45; J. A. W. Bennett, *Poetry of the Passion* (Oxford 1982), pp. 32–61.

[10]LT 2 (285:6, 286:20–287:39). For the interpretation see Wolfgang Riehle, *The Middle English Mystics* (London 1981), p. 28.

[11]Suso, *Life*, ch. 16.

[12]ST 1 (204:46–53), LT 2 (285:6, 288:40–3).

[13]*Stimulus Amoris* ch. 4.

[14]LT 2 (288:45–6).

[15]LT 3 (291:22–8).

[16]LT 19 (370:2–5); cf. LT 3 (291:30–2), ST 2 (209:36–7), with Colledge and Walsh's comment on the likely iconographical background.

[17]LT 19 (370:6–371:11). Cf. Suso, *Life* ch. 13, for a similar return to the passion from the delights of the Godhead. Suso, like the author of *The Cloud* (PC 91:3ff), uses John 10:9 ('I am the door') to indicate the necessity of passing to the Godhead through contemplation of the passion.

[18]It is impossible to date ST, but ST 11 (237:3–4) implies that some time has elapsed since the actual showings; on the other hand the development of Julian's thought between ST and LT suggests that a good many years of hard work have intervened between the two texts.

[19]ST 4 (215:42).

[20]ST 4 (215:40–216:53). Cf. *Imitation of Christ* III 31:7, 'The reason why there are so few contemplatives to be found is that there are few people who know how to separate themselves entirely from creatures.' On 'self-noughting', see Riehle, op. cit., pp. 64–6, but it should be noted that English writers on the whole keep clear of the doctrine, found in the German writers, of a real reduction of the soul to 'nothing', a real dispossession of oneself and one's faculties (e.g. Eckhart, *On Detachment*; Tauler, *Qui manducat meam carnem* [Sermon 31 Théry, 60f Vetter]). For English writers being 'noughted' often means only a total abandonment of self-love and love of creatures: e.g. Hilton, *Scale* II, ch. 27; *Privy Counselling* 84:20–41. Thus Julian, in a linguistically rather odd phrase, talks of being 'noughted of all that is made' (cf. 'noughted of our deadly flesh', ST 13 (245:58), LT 27 (406:20) – the ST text shows that the reading of the Sloane MSS is to be preferred to that of Parisinus).

[21]ST 13 (242:3–4, 243:26–8). In 243:27 *schalle se hire* must be mistaken,

in spite of Colledge and Walsh's attempt to make sense of it; *hire* must be emended to *hine* or *hym*. It is the vision of Christ in his humanity which is the prelude to the vision of God. Cf. *Imitation of Christ* II, 1:24, 'If you do not know how to contemplate high, heavenly things, rest in the passion of Christ and dwell willingly in his sacred wounds.'

[22]ST 6 (222:40–2).

[23]On 'modesty formulae', see E. Curtius, *European Literature and the Latin Middle Ages* (London 1953), pp. 83–5. Thus Gower, *Confessio Amantis*, Prol. 52, calls himself a 'burel clerk', and the author of *The Cloud* refers to his 'boistous beholding' (ch. 1, 7:30).

[24]Cf. A. Minnis, *Medieval Theory of Authorship* (London 1984), pp. 172–3. Hadewijch uses this ploy at the beginning of *Poems in Couplets* (1:5–16). For a hagiographical variant of the same theme, see André Vauchez, *La Sainteté en Occident aux derniers Siècles du Moyen Age* (Rome 1981), p. 610[79.]

[25]E.g. Mechthild of Magdeburg, *Fliessende Licht* II, 26.

[26]*Cloud of Unknowing* 56 (58:1–2).

[27]James of Milan, *Stimulus Amoris* ch. 11. Cf. the famous contrast drawn by Peter of Celle between monastic wisdom, which is learned *sine studio et lectione*, and the learning of the schools (Letter 1:73, PL 202:520A). On the anti-intellectualism which came to be typical of the Devotio Moderna, see R. R. Post, *The Modern Devotion* (Leiden 1968), pp. 320–1.

[28]ST 13 (244:41–5). Julian is asking the same question as Langland (cf. *Piers Plowman* B XI 374–5).

[29]ST 14 (247:17–248:39).

[30]ST 6 (223:55–6).

[31]LT 86 (731:2–3, 732:14). The index to LT (LT 1, pp. 281–4) seems to belong to a phase before the final completion of LT, as it stands now, as it does not allude at all to ch. 51–63; it is probable that, at least in outline, a draft of the whole of LT, except for these chapters, was completed round about 1388.

[32]LT 51 (520:86). This still leaves open the possibility that Julian went on revising the text even after 1393.

[33]LT 27 (404:6–405:11).

[34]LT 46 (494:40–6). LT 30 is taken over largely unchanged from ST 14, but in LT 33–4 she develops the point in a much more nuanced way (429:28–431:14), and returns to it again in LT 36 (437:18–438:33). Cf. also LT 32 (424:26–9).

[35]See especially LT 32 (424:37–425:48), 45 (487:13–488:30), 50 (511:10–512:38).

[36]LT 80 (707:2–8). In 707:8 Parisinus' *accordyng* must be emended to *accorden* (Parisinus habitually corrupts the infinitive into the participle). The Sloane MSS read *attenden us*, but I am not convinced that such a reflexive use of *attenden* is possible.

[37]LT 56 (574:39), 80 (707:6).

[38]LT 55 (566:14–15).

[39]LT 70 (652:18).

[40]LT 2 (285:2).

[41]Colledge and Walsh, pp. 43–59, argue for an impressive degree of literary formation; Riehle, perhaps more plausibly, argues that Julian

picked up her theological education from conversations with clerics in Norwich (op. cit., p. 29). On the basis of a very few texts, Colledge and Walsh argue that Julian was able to read the bible in Latin; they also cite a great many passages in their commentary and in the introduction to their translation, designed to prove Julian's dependence on William of St Thierry, but none of their citations is at all cogent. It has so far proved impossible to demonstrate any real literary sources for Julian.

42LT 7 (316:65–7).

43Where before she addressed herself to contemplatives, she now simply says 'us', and she drops the restrictive reference to those 'occupied in worldly business': LT 5 (301:24). Cf. also LT 73 (668:28–669:40), which discusses in terms of 'us' an unhelpful attitude which was previously ascribed to 'many men and women' and discussed largely in terms of 'them': ST 24 (274:18–25). In LT Julian seems much happier to identify herself with the 'common [citizenry]' of the church: LT 61 (607:57–61).

44LT 4 (296:16–19).

45LT 7 (315:52–67). In 315:56 the Sloane reading, weten, is preferable to Parisinus' know; the point is not that we cannot 'know' the homeliness of God, but that we cannot directly perceive it. For weten in this sense, cf. Cloud 44 (47:6), and notice LT 11 (336:5) where Julian uses seeyng to correspond to ST 8 (226:3) wittande; cf. also LT 51 (516:33).

46LT 86 (732:15–733:20).

47LT 6 (309:63–4).

48Truth is always a difficult word in Middle English; for Julian it seems to mean primarily 'faithfulness'. Cf. LT 60 (595:16).

49LT 4 (297:31–6).

50It may be significant that in ST Julian reports the vision of the 'hazelnut' before she mentions our Lady, whereas in LT our Lady comes before the 'hazelnut'.

51LT 5 (299:9–300:16).

52ST 4 (213:18–21, 215:43–4), taken over into LT 5 (300:19–22, 301:24–6), but in LT Julian eliminates the suggestion that creation actually is 'nought'.

53LT 6 (306:35–307:39); this passage is omitted in the Sloane MSS.

54In view of the exaggerated claims which are sometimes made for Julian's doctrine of divine motherhood, it should be pointed out that it is a relatively common doctrine in the later middle ages, and it is particularly common with male writers. Cf. Caroline Walker Bynum, Jesus as Mother (University of California Press, 1982), pp. 110–69.

55LT 60 (599:49–58).

56LT 6 (304:2–306:29).

57LT 53 (557:26–30).

58LT 53 (558:41–560:56).

59LT 11 (336:7, 338:19–21). Cf. St Thomas, De Pot. q.3 a.7; c. Gent. III 67.

60LT 11 (339:39–340:49).

61LT 54 (561:2–8). Julian is evidently aware of the standard doctrine that all the elect are predestined in the predestination of Christ: cf. St Thomas Aquinas, Summa Theologiae III q.24, a.4.

[62]LT 58 (582:2–11). On the godly will, cf. LT 37 (443:15–20). Julian's doctrine rests on the scholastic commonplace formulated, for example, by Peter Lombard in *Sent*. II d.39 cap. 3: 'The higher spark of the reason (*scintilla rationis*), which could not be extinguished even in Cain, as Jerome says [*in Ezek*. 1:7], always wills good and hates evil.' On this doctrine in the twelfth and thirteenth centuries, see Odon Lottin, *Psychologie et Moral aux XIIe et XIIIe siècles*, II i (Louvain 1948), pp. 105–349; Timothy Potts, *Conscience in Medieval Philosophy*. Cambridge 1980. German spiritual writers, under the influence of Neoplatonism, developed the notion of the *scintilla*, making of it, as Julian does, something in us which continually enjoys union with God, whether or not 'we' are conscious of it. Cf. Tauler, *Beati oculi qui vident* (p. 350 Vetter; II, pp. 360–1 Théry); *Quod scimus loquimur* (p. 300 Vetter; II, p. 68 Théry; p. 142 Colledge and Ciantar).

[63]LT 57 (576:2–5).
[64]LT 44 (484:14–15).
[65]LT 55 (566:13–14).
[66]LT 11 (338:18).
[67]LT 11 (339:35–7).
[68]LT 29 (412:8–10).
[69]LT 45 (487:18–26).
[70]LT 34 (431:24).
[71]LT 50.
[72]LT 27 (406:26–7).
[73]LT 27 (406:28).
[74]LT 39 (452:35–6).
[75]LT 27 (407:35–8).
[76]LT 49 (505:5–506:16).
[77]LT 46 (493:37–8).
[78]LT 48 (500:6–7), 39 (453:42–3).
[79]LT 48 (500:7, 504:47–9), 49 (507:22–30).
[80]LT 27 (405:15–19).
[81]LT 10 (326:21–7), 47 (496:16–21).
[82]LT 21 (380:18–381:23).
[83]LT 10 (327:36–328:38).
[84]LT 47 (498:37–8).
[85]LT 47 (498:39).
[86]LT 28 (409:11–410:20).
[87]LT 48 (503:46–504:47), 59 (589:2–4).
[88]LT 14 (352:13–20); cf. Rom. 8:18.
[89]LT 38.
[90]LT 31 (419:34–420:40); cf. LT 17 (364:50–2).
[91]LT 20 (376:19–21).
[92]LT 51 (537:254–6).
[93]LT 18 (367:14–369:37).
[94]LT 77 (692:30, 693:36–40).
[95]LT 52 (550:51–2).
[96]LT 50 (511:19–20).
[97]ST 20 (264:23–5); contrast LT 64 (622:28–30), where it is not this life which disappears, but only the pain of life.

⁹⁸LT 32 (422:9). Even our sins are not wasted: LT 39 (452:30–5).
⁹⁹LT 62 (611:10–11). Julian's dogmatic demonstration that time is not wasted contrasts with *The Cloud*'s ascetic anxieties about wasting time (*Cloud* 4, 11:18–40).
¹⁰⁰LT 51 (513:2–518:61).
¹⁰¹LT 51 (519:67–71). In 519:70 Parisinus' *thre knowynges* is nonsensical and the Sloane reading *onknowyng* must be adopted.
¹⁰²LT 51 (532:211–534:223).
¹⁰³LT 53 (557:29–558:35).
¹⁰⁴Cf. LT 78 (696:2–5).
¹⁰⁵LT 51 (529:185–532:210, 543:312–544:314).
¹⁰⁶LT 51 (525:144–526:152).
¹⁰⁷LT 55 (565:2–6).
¹⁰⁸The 'food' which delights God is human souls: e.g. Humbert of Romans, FP 24; Tauler, *Qui manducat* (p. 312 Vetter; II, p. 93 Théry).
¹⁰⁹LT 56 (575:58–9), 58 (585:39–40).
¹¹⁰LT 55 (567:24–9). Julian's doctrine is drastically different from that of the German spiritual writers, for whom God dwells in our highest part, or in our essence: e.g. Tauler, *Hic venit ut testimonium* (p. 331 Vetter; II, pp. 253–4 Théry; p. 119 Colledge and Ciantar).
¹¹¹Cf. LT 56 (572:21–2); 'sensual soul' is used several times in the course of the fourteenth showing, e.g. LT 57 (580:43).
¹¹²LT 57 (576:2–577:9).
¹¹³E.g. LT 57 (577:9–11), 63 (616:22).
¹¹⁴'Increase' is an important notion in the fourteenth showing: cf. LT 58 (586:46, 588:67).
¹¹⁵Irenaeus, *Adversus Haereses* IV, 38.
¹¹⁶Ibid., esp. V, 2–3. Cf. Simon Tugwell, 'Irenaeus and the Gnostic Challenge', *The Clergy Review* 66 (1981), pp. 127–30, 135–7.
¹¹⁷LT 27 (405:13). When Julian says that sin is *behouely* (or *behovabil*), she may only mean that sin is 'useful'; but the general context of her thought supports the stronger interpretation of the word, 'necessary'.
¹¹⁸Julian illustrates the *felix culpa* theme by reference to saints whose glory is all the greater for their having once been sinners: LT 38.
¹¹⁹LT 55 (568:44–569:59).
¹²⁰In LT 64 (620:10–12) Julian is much more severe towards her own desire to be 'delivered from this world' than she is in ST 20 (263:1–8).
¹²¹LT 40 (456:26–30); cf. Romans 6:1.
¹²²LT 40 (457:31–41).
¹²³LT 39 (449:2–3).
¹²⁴LT 37 (443:17–18).
¹²⁵LT 47 (496:18): our will is 'overlaid [oppressed]'.
¹²⁶LT 34 (431:22–3).
¹²⁷LT 36 (438:37–9).
¹²⁸LT 39 (453:40–2).
¹²⁹LT 72.
¹³⁰LT 32 (422:7–9).
¹³¹LT 32 (424:37–425:48).
¹³²LT 36.

[133]LT 33.

[134]LT 33 (428:12–13).

[135]LT 13.

[136]For a classic attempt to situate the sight of the damned with reference to the joys of the blessed, cf. St Thomas, *Summa Theol.* Suppl. q. 94.

[137]Cf. LT 36 (439:44–440:48).

[138]LT 65 (627:2–6).

[139]LT 73 (668:28–669:42).

[140]LT 57 (578:26–579:38).

[141]Cf. LT 18 (366:4–5) for the 'substance of kind love continued by grace'.

[142]LT 51 (538:260–6), 75 (679:9–10).

[143]LT 46 (490:2–3).

[144]LT 15.

[145]Cf. LT 51 (515:20–2).

[146]LT 15 (356:32–5).

[147]LT 10 (325:11–16, 326:27–327:29).

[148]LT 71 (655:12–13).

[149]Cf. Hilton, *Scale* II, 5.

17

Jean-Pierre de Caussade

To move from Julian of Norwich, writing at the end of the fourteenth
century, to the Jesuit Jean-Pierre de Caussade in the eighteenth
century is to move almost into a different world. The brave new
church of the Tridentine reformation emerged from the dramas and
traumas of the sixteenth century with new anxieties and with new
certainties. It was a church of 'law and order' and piety, like
everything else, was progressively tidied up into well-marked stages,
with disciplined spiritual exercises proper to each stage. Well-
trained directors were expected to rule over the souls of those who
sought a 'spiritual life'. The natural and the supernatural were
segregated into a far more rigid apartheid than ever before, and
strict immigration procedures controlled admission into the realm
of 'supernatural prayer'. Just as, doctrinally, the church had
retreated to a bastion of securely demarcated orthodoxy, and felt
nervous about venturing outside it, so too in spirituality people felt
confident of certain well-mapped devotional exercises, like spiritual
reading, visits to the blessed Sacrament, mental prayer with its
orderly succession of points and acts, meticulous self-examination
and so on, but any move outside this safe enclosure was dogged by
the fear of illusion. Eventually – but this was still controversial in
the early eighteenth century – the camp was enlarged to take in the
'mystics', but only on condition that they stuck to the official paths
on their way up Mount Carmel.

No doubt many people were nourished and well nourished by
the prevailing piety, with its intricate technicalities and systems.
But all the same, it was rather too well policed. Those who wanted
something more simple, more free, were suspected by the hard-
headed of illusion and vanity, and if they overcame this obstacle
they fell into the clutches of the 'mystical theologians', who wanted
to know exactly their degree of supernaturalness and their qualifications for moving on to more 'advanced' forms of prayer.

This is, no doubt, something of a caricature, but these do genuinely seem to be the problems facing the people for whom Jean-
Pierre de Caussade was writing, and indeed facing Caussade
himself.

Born in 1675, Caussade entered the Jesuit noviciate in 1693 and was immediately plunged into an academic career of teaching and study, which lasted until 1720 (he was ordained in 1704). Thereafter, until his death in 1751, he was primarily engaged in spiritual direction. Prominent among those who benefited from his direction were the Visitation nuns of Nancy, to whom we owe most of his surviving works.

Caussade leaves us in no doubt what the kernel of his message is: 'I wish I could cry out everywhere, "Abandonment! Abandonment!" [self-abandonment to God, that is]. And then what? Abandonment again, but abandonment without limit and without reserve.'[1] The key to all spiritual growth is, in his view, a total and peaceful resignation of ourselves into the hands of God. Our perfection is his business, not ours.[2]

Some of Caussade's confrères evidently found this doctrine dangerously simplistic,[3] and his known indebtedness to Fénelon[4] left him vulnerable to suspicions of 'quietism'.

Caussade had no intention of surrendering the simplicity he loved so well, but it was presumably because of the suspicions of his enemies that the only book he published was surrounded by so many precautions. It began as a manuscript Treatise on Prayer of the Heart, which somehow fell into the hands of Caussade's enemies, who referred it to Rome. The Roman censors were actually quite encouraging, and Caussade drafted a new version. But he then consulted another Jesuit, Paul Gabriel Antoine, who, like Caussade himself, was a valued director of the nuns at Nancy. With Antoine, Caussade prepared a final version of his book, in which the undisputed orthodoxy of Bossuet was repeatedly invoked to support his doctrine. The book was published anonymously in 1741, under the title, *Spiritual Instructions*.[5]

Caussade was brought to the notice of a much wider audience in 1861, when Henri Ramière, s.j. published, under the name of Caussade, a little book entitled *Abandonment to Divine Providence*, to which, in subsequent editions, he added a growing collection of Caussade's letters. The work was quickly established as a religious bestseller, which it remains to this day.

Unfortunately considerable mystery surrounds this work. Ramière edited it from a manuscript emanating from the nuns of Nancy. This manuscript was not in any way due to Caussade himself; it was, supposedly, put together by one of the nuns from letters and 'advice' given to her by Caussade. It was copied by another nun, who added an introductory warning that the doctrine contained in it was not suitable for general distribution. So matters remained for a hundred years. In 1853, when the question of publication was first raised, a Jesuit who was consulted, Louis Hilaire, opined after a careful study of the text that its doctrine was unsound and that Caussade could not be the author. Nevertheless, encouraged by the more positive comments of others, Ramière went ahead with the publication, though, to guard against the suspicion of quietism, he rearranged the material with considerable freedom and omitted some passages which he found hazardous.

It was not until 1966 that the text of the original manuscript was published, in an edition by Michel Olphe-Galliard, s.j.[6]

In 1981 Olphe-Galliard returned to the question of authorship and concluded, contrary to his own previous belief, that Hilaire was right and that the *Abandonment* cannot be by Caussade.[7] The first chapter of the book certainly derives from a letter by Caussade, though with some significant alterations; the rest, in the view of Olphe-Galliard, appears to be a treatise by some unknown follower of Mme Guyon – which throws us right into the heart of quietism!

The doctrinal and stylistic arguments proposed by Olphe-Galliard are impressive, but his account of the genesis of the *Abandonment* is difficult to swallow. And I am not convinced that the doctrinal arguments make it impossible to believe that the bulk of the *Abandonment* derives, however indirectly, from Caussade's teaching. It is, of course, possible that some of it was not original to Caussade. It is known that he was interested in some spiritual writings which the nuns possessed, including at least one from the circle of Mme Guyon[8] (though he does not seem to have known this), and he may have passed on to Mme de Rottembourg a commendation of other such texts, which she then worked into her compilation of Caussade material.

It is, at present, impossible to say exactly what the real relationship is between Caussade and the *Abandonment*, but we can say for certain that the *Abandonment*, whatever its prehistory, belongs as it stands in the context of a Visitation convent profoundly marked by the teaching of Caussade. And we can, I think, continue to take it as reflecting, at least in its broad outlines, the authentic teaching of Caussade, even if it has been distorted somewhat by more dubious influences.

In this chapter, bearing in mind that the *Abandonment* is the popular and most accessible work associated with Caussade, I shall try to provide a context for it from the more certain works of Caussade, with only occasional references to the *Abandonment* itself.

The keynote of his doctrine, as has already been said, is self-abandonment to the providence of God.

Let us not make a 'providence' for ourselves, by our own hard work and our own anxious and blind foresight; such a providence will be as deceptive as God's providence is enlightened and full of assurance. We should rely solely on his fatherly care and abandon ourselves entirely to it to look after our temporal and spiritual interests, and even our eternal interests.[9]

Caussade knows very well that it is normal for spiritual writers of the time to dwell at length on the dangers of illusion, but he refuses to follow suit, because he reckons that this anxiety is not only commonplace, but also frequently counterproductive.[10] Fears and doubts are a symptom of self-will and lack of detachment, in fact.[11]

Against the allegation that it is dangerous to abandon the disciplined routine of conventional piety with all its works and exercises, Caussade indicates that it may be dangerous not to abandon it. He warns against being 'enslaved by devotional practices, whether bodily or interior'.[12] 'Believe me,' he writes to one nun, 'You have too many practices already. What is needed is rather a progressive inner simplification.'[13] Too many people identify spiritual prowess with 'being perpetually busy in heaping up meditation upon meditation, prayer upon prayer, reading upon reading' instead of 'learning from simple souls the great secret of knowing how, from time to time, to hold yourself back a little in peace and silence, attentive before God'.[14] This mistake leads to unnecessary discouragement on the part of those who are not good at this kind of hectic piety. Worse still, it encourages people to place their trust in their own good works, instead of in the mercy of God and the merits of Christ – which is nothing but self-love and pride.[15] We can come to be as dangerously attached to our own will in matters of piety and holiness as we can in worldly things, and such 'pious pigheadedness' is still self-love, however 'spiritualised'.[16] Nothing is more contrary to the Spirit of God than this kind of hidden, probably unconscious, vanity, which makes us rely more on our own lights and resolutions and will-power than on God's grace, and which lures us all unawares into telling ourselves complacently how much we are doing for God, for our salvation, for perfection.[17]

The desire for reassurance that we are spiritually in good shape springs simply from self-love. Like worldly 'worshippers of their own beauty', we want to be able to admire ourselves in our spiritual looking-glasses.[18] We attach ourselves to all that can be felt and recognised as holy in ourselves.[19] But really this preoccupation with ourselves is uncalled for, especially the preoccupation with locating exactly our own supernatural status.

> I see that God has sensibly hidden from you the little bit of good he made you do during your sickness; otherwise a thousand vain complacencies would have ruined it all . . . God has sustained you against your weaknesses, and all that remains for you is to

thank him for it, without all this probing to discover if it has all
really been supernatural. Leave that to God. Try simply to forget
yourself and think only of him . . . God asks of us that we should
accomplish our duties, he does not require us to find out whether
there is any merit in it or not. Under the pious pretext of making
progress in God's way, you think too much about yourself, you
fuss too much about yourself.[20]

According to Caussade it is a waste of time trying to discover
how far we have progressed into 'mystical death', because we shall
never succeed in getting an answer and it would not do us the
slightest bit of good if we did.[21] What does it matter whether our
prayer is 'active' or 'infused', so long as it is prayer?[22] Caussade
shows no interest at all in elaborate, stratified notions of progress
in prayer; he does not mind how we pray, so long as our prayer is
rooted in a simple, attentive, total reference of ourselves to God,
which he calls 'prayer of the heart',[23] and this is so simple that
there is no need of any anxious deliberation as to whether or not
we are really 'called' to it.[24] Far from being a particularly exalted
kind of prayer, this is the 'most humiliating' kind of prayer.[25] If we
reach the point of feeling that we do not know how to pray at all,
so much the better![26]

People in quest of some 'imagined elevation'[27] cannot begin to
realise just how ordinary and how utterly unimpressive the life of
real submission to God is. Its watchword is 'Fiat', always and
everywhere 'Fiat',[28] and Caussade presents our Lady, not surprisingly, as the model for such a life; but he stresses particularly the
ordinariness of her life.

There is little that is extraordinary in the blessed Virgin. Her life
is very simple and, outwardly, very commonplace. She does and
she suffers what people in her state of life do and suffer. She goes
to visit her cousin, and the other members of the family do just
the same; she retires to a stable – a consequence of poverty. She
returns to Nazareth, and Jesus and Joseph live there with her,
working to earn their livelihood. That is the daily bread of the
holy family! But what is the bread which nourishes the faith of
Mary and Joseph? What is the sacrament of their sacred
moments? What is open to view is much the same as what
happens to everybody else, but the invisible secret which faith
discovers there is nothing less than God working very great deeds.
O Bread of angels, heavenly manna, pearl of the gospel, sacrament of the present moment, you give God under the appearances
of such vulgar things as the stable, the crib, the hay and the straw.
But who do you give him to? *Esurientes reples bonis* . . . God reveals

himself to little ones in the most little things, and the great, who fasten on to the husks only, never find him even in great things.[29]

Caussade acknowledges that there are extraordinary phenomena in some people's lives, but they do not interest him. The way that he recommends has nothing extraordinary about it at all – that is why fear of illusion in it is simply a bogy dreamed up by wilful ignorance.[30] In a splendid paragraph the *Abandonment* says:

> When God gives himself like this, everything commonplace becomes extraordinary, and that is why nothing appears extraordinary. This way is extraordinary in itself, and so it does not need to be decorated with marvels which do not belong to it. It is a continual miracle, revelation, rejoicing, apart from a few faults; but it is characteristic of it that it has nothing marvellous that can be seen; instead it makes everything that can be seen, everything most commonplace, into a marvel. That is what the blessed Virgin practised.[31]

What we can expect to be most conscious of, if we really entrust ourselves to God, is our own failures.

> Your lively feeling of your own poverty and of your own darkness delight me, because they are a definite indication to me that the divine light is growing in you, without your knowing it, to form in you a great depth of interior humility. The time will come when the sight of this wretchedness, which horrifies you now, will fill you with joy and keep you in a delightful peace. It is only when we have reached the bottom of the abyss of our nothingness and are firmly established there that we can 'walk before God in justice and truth'[32]. . . . The fruit of grace must, for the moment, remain hidden, buried as it were in the abyss of your wretchedness underneath the most lively awareness of your weakness.[33]

So Caussade can write to one nun, 'Rejoice every time you discover a new imperfection.'[34]

The essential quality we need to learn is interior peace,[35] and this requires above all else that we should learn how to put up with ourselves.[36] If we find ourselves getting impatient, we must bear our impatience patiently, if we lose our tranquillity, we must bear the loss with tranquillity, if we get angry, we must not get angry with ourselves for being angry, if we are not content, we must be content not to be content.[37] We must be detached from everything, even from detachment; we must abandon into God's hands even our self-abandonment.[38] The last thing we should do is try to *feel* our own submission to God.[39]

All that matters is that we should place our confidence in what

God does, and let him get on with it[40] and, as Caussade never tires of reminding us, much of what God does in us he does without our knowledge.

These impressions one has of being separated from God [Caussade wrote to one of his nuns], terrifying as they are, are what ˙we might call a completely hidden, crucifying, operation of divine love, purifying the soul of all self-love, as gold is purified by fire in the crucible. Oh how happy you are without knowing it! How cherished you are without realising it! What great things God is bringing to pass within you, all the more securely because the manner of it is so dark, so unknown. O my God, it is our weakness, our wretched self-love, our pride which reduce you to being unable to do great things in us except by hiding them from us and working, as it were, behind our backs, for fear that we should corrupt your gifts by appropriating them to ourselves by vain, secret, imperceptible complacency. There you have the whole mystery of this hidden way in which God leads us.[41]

Instead of trying to monitor, let alone interfere with, our own progress, we should leave it to God to shape us and perfect us in any way he likes. 'I want only as much perfection and as much interior life as it pleases God to give me, and only at the time appointed by him for it.'[42] To go flat out for whatever we regard as constituting progress is 'to want to perfect myself to suit me rather than to suit him, to have more regard to my own taste than to God's, in a word, to want to serve God according to my own fancy rather than in accordance with his will.'[43]

The trouble comes from taking too seriously our own *ideas* of progress and perfection (our 'dreadful ideas of perfection', as the *Abandonment* calls them).[44] Caussade's apparent anti-intellectualism is essentially a vehement refusal of rationalist piety, a total rejection of the possibility of *planning* the way to perfection for myself or for anyone else. It is because of our notions of what ought to be going on that we opt for *methods* of piety, that we overdramatise our contrition and devotion and so on. Caussade is not totally opposed to regulated piety, when it is appropriate,[45] but he points out that our fathers in the faith, and our Lady herself, had no 'method':[46] and he warns us against forcing ourselves.[47] He also points out that there is a dramatic kind of sorrow for sin which is actually nothing but pride;[48] the truest contrition is the least conscious of itself.[49] It is a big mistake to want to judge of spiritual realities by what we can feel and perceive.[50] Intense, demonstrative piety is all too 'natural', in Caussade's view.[51] Genuinely supernatural conditions are always characterised by complete serenity and peacefulness.

What Caussade is concerned with is not that we should succeed in achieving any particular spiritual condition, but that we should learn the proper 'way of viewing things'.[52] All the vicissitudes, interior and external, which make life so unpredictable and annoying, must be accepted as precisely the way in which God forms us, making us – if we are docile to all that God gives us – malleable to the working of the Holy Spirit.[53] To look for stability in this life is to resist the decree of Providence, subjecting all things to continual change.[54] 'Vicissitude' is a word which Caussade uses over and over again, and it suggests a vision of the christian life rather different from that associated with the word 'progress'.

What Caussade wants us to appreciate is that God gives himself to us in *everything*, in *all* the ups and down and ins and outs of life.

What is the secret of finding this treasure, this drachma? There is no secret at all. The treasure is everywhere; God, being God, offers himself to us the whole time, wherever we are. All creatures, whether they are our friends or our foes, pour out this treasure without stint, making it flow through all the faculties of our body and soul to the very centre of our hearts. Let us open our mouths and they will be filled. The action of God inundates the universe, penetrates all creatures, swims above all creatures; wherever they are, it is, going ahead of them, accompanying them, following them. All we have to do is let ourselves be carried away in its waves.[55]

It follows from this that 'it is easy to arrive at outstanding holiness by means of the simple duties of christianity'.[56] 'One can always find God anywhere, without any effort, because he is always present for those who seek him with all their heart, even though he does not always make them feel his divine presence.'[57] 'Self-abandonment to divine providence, as I understand it and recommend it, is not as heroic and difficult as you think.'[58]

In one sense, it requires nothing at all of us except to yield ourselves to the act of God, to be a canvas for God to paint on.[59] But it is wrong to infer that this leaves us simply passive. Passivity and activity come together: we do whatever needs to be done in a spirit of receptivity, of passivity before God, so we are 'passively active or actively passive'.[60] At each moment, we must discover what it is we are to do. 'Think only of the present, to enclose yourself there in nothing but the will of God, leaving the rest to his providence and his mercy.'[61]

Take no pains to be your own guide in all these different situations. You have only one thing to do, which is simple and very easy: to see where the deepest prompting of your heart is leading you, without consulting reason or reflection, which would spoil everything. Act constantly with this holy simplicity, good faith and rightness of heart, without looking back or on either side, but always looking straight ahead at the present time, the present moment.[62]

This is not as irrationalist as it sounds. Caussade points out elsewhere the irrationality of trying to guide ourselves by our own rational planning:

On the pretext of looking ahead to what might happen (so as not to tempt God, as they say), how much time people spend piling up thought upon thought, reflection upon reflection, plan upon plan. People wear themselves out with their anxious foresight, their woebegone worries, their precautions, which are quite useless because, when the time comes, things look quite different or we change our minds and feelings. People end up taking steps quite contrary, very often, to those they had thought of so uselessly in advance and decided on so pointlessly . . . . Let us think only of benefiting from the present moment according to God's order, leaving the past to his mercy and the future to his providence.[63]

This allows for mysterious hunches, but Caussade specifically denies that it is always necessary to wait for an interior inspiration before acting: the 'signified will of God' is to be recognised also in the duties of our state in life and also in the call of reason and good sense.[64] But we must learn not to rush into doing things simply out of our natural 'liveliness'.[65] We must try to seek out the 'order of God' in each moment, and do whatever that means for us. And sometimes there may be nothing for us to do, in which case we should do nothing.[66] God may leave us sometimes in a state of complete emptiness, in which case we must be content with this.[67] Our life, even our interior life, does not belong to us, it belongs to God.[68]

Bibliography and Abbreviations

All references are given to the page nos. of the editions by Michel Olphe-Galliard.

Ab.   L'Abandon à la Providence Divine. Paris 1966.
L   Lettres Spirituelles, 2 vols. Paris 1962, 1964.
OC   Traité sur l'Oraison du Coeur, Instructions Spirituelles. Paris 1981.

Notes

1 L I, p. 268.
2 L I, pp. 119, 153.
3 Cf. L I, p. 66.
4 Cf. L I, pp. 22–5.
5 Cf. Olphe-Galliard's introduction to OC.
6 J. P. de Caussade, *L'Abandon à la Providence Divine*, ed. Michel Olphe-Galliard. Paris 1966. For the history of the text, see the introduction to this edn.
7 *Bulletin de Littérature Ecclésiastique* 82 (1981), pp. 25–56.
8 Cf. OC, pp. 31–2.
9 L I, p. 95.
10 OC, p. 206.
11 L II, p. 58.
12 L II, p. 204.
13 L II, p. 21.
14 OC, p. 100.
15 L II, p. 25.
16 OC, pp. 186–7.
17 OC, p. 140.
18 L I, p. 311.
19 L II, p. 42; OC, p. 166.
20 L I, pp. 97–8.
21 L I, p. 169.
22 OC, p. 160.
23 OC, pp. 51, 94.
24 OC, p. 114.
25 OC, p. 82.
26 L I, p. 123; OC, pp. 86, 97.
27 OC, p. 83.
28 L II, p. 47.
29 L II, p. 153; *Ab.*, pp. 26–7.
30 OC, pp. 77, 206.
31 *Ab.*, p. 130.
32 L I, p. 96.
33 L I, p. 167.
34 L I, p. 58.
35 L I, p. 227; II, pp. 12–13.
36 L I, pp. 86–7, 158.
37 L I, pp. 88, 155, 198, 296; II, p. 40; OC, pp. 167, 174, 178–9.
38 L I, pp. 195, 197; II, p. 49.
39 L II, p. 19.
40 L II, p. 34.
41 L I, pp. 151–2.
42 L I, p. 234.
43 L I, p. 160.
44 OC, pp. 85, 164, 166; *Ab.*, p. 87.
45 E.g. L I, p. 70.

218   WAYS OF IMPERFECTION

⁴⁶L II, p. 152.
⁴⁷E.g. L I, p. 145.
⁴⁸OC, pp. 124–5.
⁴⁹L I, pp. 73, 163.
⁵⁰L I, p. 171; OC, p. 195.
⁵¹L II, p. 55; OC, p. 104.
⁵²L I, p. 64.
⁵³L I, p. 92.
⁵⁴L I, p. 275; OC, p. 197.
⁵⁵L II, p. 153; Ab., p. 27.
⁵⁶L II, p. 154; Ab., p. 28.
⁵⁷L I, p. 241; II, p.203.
⁵⁸L I, p. 67.
⁵⁹OC, p. 108.
⁶⁰OC, p. 115.
⁶¹L II, p. 31.
⁶²L I, pp. 92–3.
⁶³OC, p. 136.
⁶⁴OC, p. 192.
⁶⁵L I, p. 79.
⁶⁶L I, p. 273.
⁶⁷L II, p. 37; OC, p. 194.
⁶⁸L II, p. 37.

18

Thérèse of Lisieux

In several obvious ways Thérèse of Lisieux (1873–97) reminds us of Caussade. Like him she espoused a spirituality of abandonment. 'Abandonment is my only guide,' she wrote in the first of her autobiographical manuscripts.[1] Like him she appreciated that we have to take life one day at a time.[2] Like him she was inclined to be suspicious of the more gaudy varieties of holiness.[3] She revered Mère Geneviève all the more when she learned that she had never received any revelations, because that is 'the truest, the holiest kind of holiness . . . there are no illusions to be faced there.'[4] Like Caussade she celebrates the ordinariness of the life of our Lady: 'No raptures, no miracles, no ecstasies embellished your life, O Queen of the Elect.'[5] Even as a child she was distressed by the supernatural inquisitiveness of the Carmelites with whom she was destined to live: the good nuns were determined to turn the austere miracle which restored the ten year old Thérèse to health into a fussy apparition of our Lady. Thérèse herself never even claimed to have had a real 'vision', only that somehow our Lady smiled beautifully at her, but the nuns were anxious to know all the visual details, leaving Thérèse with the horrid feeling that she had told them a lie, so impossible was it to recognise in their silly prying what had actually happened to her.[6] If we may trust Mère Agnes, much the same thing happened again on Thérèse's deathbed: her sister Marie suggested to her that she would see troops of angels coming with Christ in all their beauty to fetch her; she retorted, 'All these images do me no good at all. I can only find nourishment in the truth. That is why I have never desired visions. On earth it is impossible to see heaven and angels as they really are.'[7]

It is a very moot point among commentators how far St Thérèse was at odds with the spirituality of her family and her fellow nuns,[8] but at least some element of disagreement and incomprehension cannot be denied. Mère Agnes reported that Thérèse detested the pious trivialities which find their way into religious life ('Elle détestait les petites dévotions de bonne femme . . .').[9] And Thérèse had no illusions about the nuns with whom she lived; she described them to Céline as 'a fine collection of old maids'.[10] On her deathbed, according to Mère Agnes, she complained that nobody understood her.[11] All this suggests both that Mère Agnes was not quite as disingenuous as has sometimes been suggested and that indeed she was perhaps not the best person to interpret her little sister to the world.

In 1896 Léonie, the nearest the Martin family came to having a black sheep, was suffering from scruples and Thérèse wrote to her to say, 'I assure you that the good God is much better than you believe.'[12] It seems that French catholics of the period were rather prone to project on to God their own sense of outrage and indignation in the face of the wickedness and unbelief and secularism of their contemporaries. Inevitably this resulted in a somewhat daunting kind of God, who had to be worshipped with anxiety and placated by heroic acts of reparation. Many of the French Carmelites were eager to offer themselves as 'victims' to divine Justice.[13] Thérèse evidently rejected this whole view of God and of christianity. In her view, it is a disastrous mistake to be intimidated by God. She ventures to turn the picture upside down: if anything, God is intimidated by us. She sees God as helplessly at our mercy precisely because he is a 'beggar for our love'.[14] So Thérèse writes to Léonie:

> I find perfection very easy to practise, because I have realised that all we have to do is take Jesus by the heart. Consider a child who has just upset his mother by losing his temper or disobeying her. If he goes and hides in a corner with a sullen look on his face and cries because he is afraid of being punished, his mother will certainly not pardon his fault. But if he comes to her and holds out his arms to her and smiles at her and says, 'Give me a hug, I'll never do it again', how can his mother resist taking him fondly and pressing him to her heart, forgetting his childish wickedness? Yet she knows perfectly well that her dear child will do it again as soon as the occasion arises, but that makes no difference; if he takes her by the heart again, he will never be punished.[15]

As an adolescent Thérèse had herself been tormented by scruples for more than a year, and she was finally freed only when Père Pichon, s.j. assured her in confession that she had never committed a mortal sin.[16] But later on she came to a rather different conclusion for herself: even if she had committed every possible sin, she would still have exactly the same confidence in God.[17] She no longer needed the assurance of her own virtue, because in one sense she came to see that it really makes no difference whether we are virtuous or not. Either way we are beneficiaries of exactly the same divine love, even if its method is different in the two cases. Thérèse uses the image of a doctor with two children: he clears all the obstacles from the path of one child, so that he never trips up; the other child he picks up after he has fallen over and tends him and heals him. There is no difference in the dependence of both children on their father.[18]

But there is more to Thérèse's position than this. By the end of her life she rejoices to find herself so imperfect.[19] Yet we also know that when she was, for all practical purposes, novice mistress, she was extremely demanding and did not allow any imperfections to go unremarked.[20] To understand Thérèse's attitude and in particular to understand this apparent contradiction, we must take another look at the kind of piety and morality which she was, however unobtrusively, repudiating. As a child she had been instructed by Pauline and then by Marie in 'a great number of practices'; Marie talked to her about 'the immortal riches which it was easy to accumulate each day'. Although she does not say so in so many words to Pauline (who would perhaps not have understood at all what she was talking about), she makes it clear that what she has retained from this fussily competent and acquisitive piety is not any notion of amassing spiritual riches (in a later poem she roundly declares, 'I am, alas, nothing but weakness in person, I have, as you know, God, no virtues'),[21] but the very different and far more serious principle of 'being holy by way of fidelity to the smallest things'.[22]

And this minute fidelity is transformed by Thérèse into a concern for the detailed tactfulness involved in fraternal charity. Thérèse has some extremely penetrating observations on the minutiae of actual human relationships,[23] and there is no lack of evidence that she was in practice a real expert in dealing lovingly with the petty annoyances caused to her by her community. But at the same time she insists that what this amounts to is not 'heroic virtue', but little 'nothings'.[24] And it is not God who will be hurt by failure – she was immediately convinced by the doctrine of Alexis Prou, of whom her fellow nuns disapproved heartily, that our faults cannot hurt God.[25] Nor will our failures interfere with our own holiness; Thérèse came to believe that genuine holiness is precisely a matter of enduring our own imperfections patiently.[26] Failures in charity hurt precisely the other people whom we are failing to love. In this perspective there is no room left for the moral narcissism which so often besets religious people.

The other kind of piety which Thérèse was unable to accept was the whole spirituality of heroic sacrifice. And she saw clearly what was wrong with it. In the first place it distorts the real situation which obtains between us and God. In July 1897 she wrote to abbé Bellière, 'How little known are the goodness, the merciful love of

Jesus! It is true, to enjoy these treasures it is necessary first to humble ourselves and recognise our nothingness, and that is what many souls are not willing to do.'[27] On the excellent authority of the gospel story of Mary Magdalen, Thérèse suggests that the Lord prefers the loving confidence of a sinner who comes to him in all humility to the unblemished purity of innocence.[28]

It is also wrong to suppose that we can, strictly speaking, do anything for God. In response to a request from Céline for a poem about how much she, Céline, has given up for the Lord, Thérèse writes a poem in which she reminds the Lord how much he has given up for her.[29] By contrast with the heroic souls who offer themselves as victims to divine Justice, Thérèse explains that it is precisely her feebleness which emboldens her to offer herself as a 'victim' to divine Love.[30] 'This is all that Jesus asks of us; he has no need of our works, but only of our love.'[31] Judged by the worldly criterion of usefulness, such love is nothing but foolish, it is simply a 'waste'.[32] But to suggest that we could do anything useful for God would be at best misleading. Thérèse prefers to talk in terms of 'casting flowers', as children do in a procession.[33] Her aim is simply 'to give pleasure to Jesus'.[34]

With a very fine instinct Thérèse indicates both the objective element in christian behaviour, which is concerned with the real effects of our behaviour on our fellow human beings, and the subjective element, which is concerned with our relationship with God. We can hurt (or help) other people, but to God we can only 'give pleasure', and that only because his love for us finds value in our 'nothings'.

Thérèse does not really mean us to believe that, in every possible sense, it makes no difference whether we are virtuous or not. The essential point is that, whether we are virtuous or not, it is dangerous for us to take our stand on our own virtues. To apprehend ourselves as virtuous or conversely to apprehend ourselves as lacking in virtue and so to lose heart is to misread our situation. It is precisely our weakness, fully acknowledged as such (to whatever extent we may or may not be protected by grace from its effects), which gives us our claim on God. In Mère Agnes' notebooks there is an exposition of Thérèse's way of spiritual childhood, which reflects her teaching even if it does not preserve her *ipsissima verba*, in which the essential point is precisely that when a child grows up it is sent out to 'earn its own living', but as long as the child is still a child, the father *has* to support it.[35]

From very early on in her life Thérèse wanted to be a saint, even 'a great saint'.[36] But she discovered what she was up against in 1890 when she confided in the Jesuit who was giving the Carmelites their retreat (Père Laurent Blino), 'Father, I want to become a saint.' The good priest was utterly scandalised by her 'pride' and 'presumption' and told her, 'Confine yourself to correcting your faults, to not offending the good God any more, to making some small progress every day and moderating your temerarious desires.' But Thérèse was not cowed. After all, Jesus himself tells us to be perfect.[37]

However Thérèse did realise that if perfection means the laborious, gradual process preached by Père Blino, then she was a nonstarter.

You know, my mother [she wrote to Mère Marie de Gonzague], that I have always wanted to be a saint, but, alas, I have always found, when I compared myself with the saints, that there was as great a difference between them and me as there is between a mountain with its summit hidden in the sky and an unnoticed grain of sand trodden underfoot by the people who pass by. But instead of getting discouraged, I said to myself: The good God would not inspire unrealisable desires, so I can, for all my littleness, aspire to sanctity. It is impossible for me to become bigger, so I must put up with myself as I am, with all my imperfections. But I will look for the means to go to heaven by a little way, which is direct and short, a completely new little way. We live in an age of inventions; in these days there is no longer any need to take the trouble to climb the stairs, rich people have a lift instead, which is much better. I too should like to find a lift to raise me up to Jesus, because I am too small to climb the rude ladder of perfection.[38]

The 'lift' which Thérèse found was the loving welcome extended by the Lord to the little ones. Perfection, as she wrote to Léonie in the letter already quoted, can thus be had very simply, though admittedly it is a rather different kind of perfection from that which Thérèse's contemporaries were normally looking for. Like Père Blino, most of them regarded perfection as a matter of acquiring spiritual 'grades' over a long period until eventually we have enough to graduate. But for Thérèse perfection is a matter of going straight to the essential point, the point being the love of God. Since he loves us 'madly' (à la folie),[39] how can he resist us if we simply present ourselves to him with all the confidence of children? Instead of conquering a reluctant deity by myriads of 'practices', Thérèse proposes simply to accept his love and let him take full responsibility for the consequences.

It seems that Thérèse had a tendency to go to sleep during times of formal prayer, and instead of feeling guilty about this, as she says (mischievously) that she should, she turns it into a symbol of her whole spirituality.[40] In the second of her autobiographical manuscripts, written for her sister Marie, she compares herself to a little bird which is distracted by all kinds of things but, instead of going off into a corner to weep and to 'die of repentance', it 'temerariously' (echoes of Père Blino!) abandons itself to its beloved Sun, relating all its infidelities and thinking thereby only to win more power (*empire*) over the Sun by attracting to itself more fully the love of him who came not to call the just, but sinners. 'O Jesus,' she exclaims, 'how happy your little bird is to be feeble and little. What would become of it if it were big? It would never have the audacity to come into your presence and then go to sleep!'[41] We must not be taken in by Thérèse's mock humility. She knows perfectly well what she is doing. It is precisely in being little and in having the audacity to go to sleep that faith and love are expressed. Being 'big' means growing out of faith. 'If I had amassed any merits,' she is supposed to have said, 'I should have despaired immediately.'[42] In a poem on St Cecilia she writes, 'With your heavenly song you unveil love, love which has no fear, which goes to sleep and forgets itself on the heart of its God, like a little child.'[43] Going to sleep is not a breach of charity, however much it may be a breach of pious etiquette, it is a privileged sign of charity.

It is also a form of imitation of Christ and participation in him. Thérèse is particularly fond of the thought of Jesus asleep in the boat while the tempest rages. 'To live by love, when Jesus sleeps, is to rest on the stormy seas. Do not be afraid, Lord, that I shall wake you up.'[44] Her preference for weakness is not a ploy to draw forth the manifest power of God to defend her, it is a response to the weakness of God, to the sleep of God. Her weakness is modelled on that of Christ: 'My beloved, your example invites me to lower myself, to despise honour. To charm you, I want to remain small; in forgetting myself, I shall charm your heart.'[46] Her devotion is drawn particularly to the helplessness of Christ as a baby, in his passion, when he is asleep. The devotion to the Face of Christ, which made her add 'of the Sacred Face' to her name, meant for her essentially devotion to the hidden face of Christ.[47] Thérèse grasps with profound intuition that redemption is not best seen as an act of divine power. The heart of it is the helplessness of God in face of his own love for us.

In a remarkable poem, Thérèse seems almost to be describing one of those dreadful love affairs which trap people in hopeless mutual dependence:

> Toi le Grand Dieu, que tout le Ciel adore
> Tu vis en moi, Prisonnier nuit et jour
> Ta douce voix à toute heure m'implore
> Tu me redis: 'J'ai soif . . . j'ai soif d'Amour! . . .'

Je suis aussi ta prisonnière,
Et je veux redire à mon tour
Ta tendre et divine prière:
'Mon Bien-Aimé, mon Frère
J'ai soif d'Amour! . . .'

[You, the great God, whom all heaven adores, you live in me, a prisoner night and day; the whole time your gentle voice implores me, you keep on saying, 'I am thirsty . . . I thirst for love.' I also am your prisoner, and I want to say back to you your own tender and divine prayer, 'My beloved, my brother, I thirst for love.']⁴⁸

This coincidence of human weakness with divine weakness, human thirsting with divine thirsting, provides an important key to the understanding of St Thérèse; in its light we can see how several apparently contradictory elements in her make-up can be harmonised.

Very early in her life Thérèse discovered her own capacity for love, and she realised how easily it could go astray. In her convent she could see how cloying and unhealthy human affection could become. She claims that she was protected by God's grace from any love for creatures – otherwise she would probably just have 'burned up completely'.⁴⁹ She was far from insensible to human affection – she once said that she could not understand saints who did not love their families⁵⁰ – but she realised that only God could satisfy the vastness of her capacity to love and be loved. But she came to see not only that God was the only one who could receive all her love, not only that God was the only one who could give her sufficient love, but that God must be both subject and object of all that loving. 'I will love you with the very same love with which you loved me, Jesus, eternal Word.'⁵¹ Unlike some of the late medieval devotionalists, Thérèse realised that it is not enough simply to transfer our own affections to God. It is by inserting our own loving into his loving (his loving à la folie) that we can safely give free rein to our own loving. Merely making God the object of our love does not essentially alter the nature of our covetousness.

And Thérèse was, as she acknowledges, exceedingly covetous. When she was a child, she recalls, her sister Léonie one day offered the two youngest girls the doll's dresses and things which she was now too old to want. She told them to choose what they wanted, and Céline duly made her selection. But Thérèse said, 'I choose the lot', and that, as she goes on to say, is the story of her whole life. Exactly the same greed makes her choose sanctity in toto, it is not enough for her to be 'half a saint'.⁵² But the childhood mémoires which she wrote for Pauline (Mère Agnes) do not reveal the whole story It is her sister Marie who is the recipient of Thérèse's far more extravagant confidences. In spite of her love of hiddenness and weakness, she is nevertheless haunted by the most preposterous ambitions. She wants to be another Joan of Arc (a role she played with evident success in some convent theatricals). And, as if that were not enough, she wants to follow all vocations. She wants to be a warrior, a priest, an apostle, a doctor, a martyr, she wants to accomplish all the most heroic deeds.

It was meditating on 1 Corinthians 12–13 which showed her how to fulfil this absurd ambition. She realised that 'love enfolded all vocations'; love lies behind all the different tasks undertaken by christians, love makes all the members of the Body of Christ do their various deeds. She would therefore do them all if she situated herself in the very heart of the church. She concluded, 'Love was my vocation'. She would be love in the heart of the church.[53] It was this discovery which led to her famous Act of Self-oblation to Merciful Love, which begins with the all-important declaration, 'O my God, blessed Trinity, I desire to love you and to make you loved.' And it is precisely in Christ's love that she offers her own love.[54]

The discovery of love as the key to all Thérèse's ambitions allows us, and probably allowed her, to understand how those ambitions can paradoxically merge with her weakness. God's love is shown precisely in the helplessness, the unobtrusiveness, of Christ. 'The uncreated Word of the Father, who exiles himself here below for you, my sweet Lamb, your little brother, Marie, will not speak to you. . . . This silence is the first pledge of his inexpressible love. Understanding his silent language, you will imitate him every day.'[55]

Even the stubbornness which was evidently characteristic of Thérèse as a child comes into its own here. It turns out to be nothing but the dogged perseverance, the desperation almost, of divine love. The 'almost invincible obstinacy' of her childhood[56] becomes the weakness of a love which refuses to give up.

But above all, the insertion of Thérèse's love into that of Christ makes sense of and justifies both her apostolic yearnings and her joy in suffering. On her own account, she suffered considerably during her early years, but later she came to love suffering,[57] which at first sight seems to place her squarely in the context of the rather masochistic piety which has been all too common, particularly among religious women. But we must take with complete serious-ness her own account of the matter: 'I have realised that suffering has charms, that it is by the cross that one saves sinners.'[58] And that is Thérèse's great desire. The most immediate way to give pleasure to Jesus is to make people love him (he is thirsty for love), to win for him the souls he died to save.[59]

The first major turning point in Thérèse's life came in 1886 at Christmas: she calls it 'my complete conversion'.[60] That was when she suddenly stopped being a weepy child ('I was truly insufferable because of my excessive sensitivity')[61] and grew up. But the very same grace which broke her morbid sensitivity 'made me a fisher of souls; I felt a great desire to work for the conversion of sinners. . . . In a word, I felt *charity* come into my heart, the need to forget myself in order to give pleasure.'[62] For the rest of her life Thérèse was insistent on the apostolic nature of her calling. She entered Carmel not to be a 'contemplative', but to be an apostle.[63] And at the end of her life she wrote to abbé Bellière, 'I admit that if I could not go on working for God's glory in heaven, I should prefer to remain in exile.'[64] According to Mère Agnes' reporting of Thérèse's deathbed conversations, Thérèse was planning to burgle heaven when she got there, no doubt to accomplish her desire to obtain favours for her friends.[65]

The 'first son' adopted by the new, apostolic, Thérèse was the hated murderer Pranzini, whose last minute conversion she seemingly obtained by her prayers.[66] From then on we find periodic signs of her readiness to espouse the cause of the pariahs who were beyond the sympathy of most catholics. But the real breakthrough did not come until Easter 1896. Until then Thérèse had enjoyed a radiant faith; heaven seemed to be so real and close that 'doubt was not possible, and already we had no further need of faith and hope' (Thérèse is referring to herself and Céline).[67] She was unable to conceive of anyone really being without belief. 'I thought that they spoke contrary to their real thoughts in denying heaven.'[68] But at Easter 1896 God gave her what she took to be a very special grace; suddenly she lost all her enjoyment of faith. 'He permitted my soul to be swamped by the thickest darkness, so that the thought of heaven which had been so sweet to me became nothing but a subject of battle and torment. This trial was not just to last for a few days, a few weeks, it was to last until the time appointed by the good God. That time has not yet come.'[69] From then until her death Thérèse lived in almost unmitigated spiritual darkness, hanging on only by making repeated acts of utterly opaque faith.

The most striking thing about this sudden transformation is that Thérèse sees it, not as the kind of 'dark night' any student of St John of the Cross might have predicted, but as a way of identifying herself totally with unbelievers and sinners.

Lord, your child has understood your divine light; she asks pardon for her brothers, she consents to eat for as long as you wish it the bread of sorrow, and she will not rise from this table, which is filled with bitterness, where poor sinners eat, until the day you have appointed. Further, can she not say in their name, in the name of her brothers, 'Have pity on us, Lord, for we are poor sinners'? . . . I told him that I am happy not to enjoy heaven on earth in order that he may open heaven for ever to poor unbelievers.[70]

Heroic souls who offer themselves as victims to divine Justice presuppose their own separation from the sinners who offend that justice; but Thérèse totally identifies herself with 'my brothers, the sinners'.[71] When she describes her own inner darkness, she says that it mocks her 'with the voice of sinners: "You dream of light . . . you believe you will one day emerge from the fog which surrounds you. Proceed, then, proceed! Enjoy death – which will not give you what you are hoping for, but only an even deeper night, the night of nothingness (*la nuit du néant*)."' At that point Thérèse breaks off, for fear of 'blaspheming'.[72] The temptation to unbelief is entirely authentic, evidently. There is nothing condescending about her self-identification with unbelievers; she knows exactly what their position is, because she is in it herself. She can make her acts of faith on their behalf because she is precisely where they are.

Her spiritual journey seems to be almost exactly the opposite of what we should have expected. Her way is almost a 'descent from Mount Carmel'. The intimacy of her love for God, which characterised her childhood, made way for aridity when she became a nun, and then finally she fell into this total darkness. Yet it was precisely in this way that she came to know the reality of love, and to enter into her apostolate of love. All that is left, finally, after the consolations have gone, is the desolate cry, 'I thirst (*j'ai soif*)!'

In the course of her account of the 'grace' of Easter 1896 she breaks into a direct address to Jesus, as she so often does in her autobiography; but this time she draws attention to it: 'My little story, which was like a fairy tale, has suddenly turned into prayer.'[73] The interruption in her narrative seems to be particularly significant here, and surely this is because it reflects the 'interruption' in her life, which cut off the fairy tale which she had been living before and turns it too into prayer. As a Carmelite she had certainly known all along that prayer was a central part of her vocation, but it seems that suddenly, in 1896, prayer takes on a new urgency. We have some evidence that she was not very good at her formal times of prayer (for which she uses the word *oraison*); as we have seen, she used to go to sleep quite often, and she was easily distracted. It was not during her times of prayer but during her everyday work that she usually received any 'lights' she needed.[74] It appears that her best use of the time of *oraison* was when she was able to get

interested in some passage of scripture.[75] The rosary was a torment
to her.[76] But in 1896 the fairy tale turns into prayer – and she uses
prière, not *oraison*. This suggests that she has to some extent, no doubt
unwittingly, rediscovered the original, primary sense of 'prayer' as
petition, as the cry for help which the creature addresses to the
creator precisely because the creature is helpless. The proprieties
of *oraison* had largely obscured the true nature of prayer, simply by
making it an exercise in which the practitioner could hope to become
reasonably competent, whereas prayer arises, if at all, from incom-
petence, otherwise there is no need for it. It is not at the top of
Mount Carmel that prayer is learned, but at the bottom. It is the
little ones who cannot master *oraison* who can engage in *prière*.[77] It
is seated at the sinners' table of sorrow that Thérèse learns the full
intensity of prayer, because there is nothing left to her except prayer.

When Pius XI canonised Thérèse he stressed that she was specially significant for our own time because she fulfilled her vocation
'without leaving the common order of things'.[78] This must not be
taken to mean that in her a harmlessly devout triviality was being
canonised. She is the saint of the 'common order of things' precisely
because she represented a total love of God and a total belief in
God in the very predicament where most people find themselves,
namely sin and unbelief. 'I have my faults, but I also have
courage.'[79] She dares to express the love which sinners do not dare
to and are not able to express. She makes herself sing the praises
of God even though 'blasphemy resounds even into my heart'.[80]
And so she expresses the worship which blasphemers are unable to
express. Unlike so many exponents of the ways of piety, she neither
bullies us nor teases us from any position of elevation; she simply
gets on with loving God *as one of us*. And in so doing she shows us
that precisely as sinners, as doubters, we are welcome to run to
God's love. Her acceptance of darkness identifies our darkness as a
thirst for God, and at the same time assures us that even in this
very darkness Christ is there thirsting for our love.

Bibliography and Abbreviations

All references are to the *Édition Critique des Oeuvres Complètes*, published by
Éditions du Cerf and Desclée de Brouwer. A complete English translation
is being produced by the Institute of Carmelite Studies, Washington, D.C.

DE   *Derniers Entretiens (Her Last Conversations)*. References are given to the
      date and no. of each saying (the dates are given in the European
      manner, with the day of the month coming before the month).
      Unless it is specified to the contrary, all references are to the Carnet
      Jaune (Yellow Notebook).

HA   *Histoire d'une Ame (Story of a Soul)*. References are given to the chapter

230   WAYS OF IMPERFECTION

(though earlier edns use different numbering) and folio no., as given
in the 1972 edn (the foliation differs by one page from that given
in the 1957 edn published by the Carmel of Lisieux, *Manuscrits
Autobiographiques*). I also give a page reference to the Institute of
Carmelite Studies translation.

LD   see LT.

LT   references to the letters contained in *Correspondance Générale (General
Correspondence)* are given in accordance with the numbering of the
letters by, to or about Thérèse in the critical edn and translation.

P   *Poésies*. References are given to the no. of the poem, followed, where
necessary, by either a stanza no. or line nos., in accordance with
the critical edn.

Notes

[1]HA VIII 83ʳ (p. 178); cf. P 52.
[2]HA VIII 76ʳ (p. 165), P 5.
[3]Cf. her comment on her autobiography,'There will be something there
for all tastes, except for extraordinary ways': DE 9.8.2.
[4]HA VIII 78ʳ (pp. 169–70).
[5]P 54:17.
[6]HA III 30ʳ–31ʳ (pp. 65–7).
[7]DE 5.8.4.
[8]The interpretation of Thérèse as being seriously at odds with her family
and fellow nuns is particularly developed by Ida F. Görres, *The Hidden Face*
(New York 1959), and Jean-François Six, *La Véritable Enfance de Thérèse*
(Paris 1972), and *Thérèse de Lisieux au Carmel*. Paris 1973. Against this
interpretation, cf. P. T. Rohrbach, *The Search for St Thérèse*. New York 1961.
For a recent balanced biography, see Guy Gaucher, *Histoire d'une Vie*. Paris
1982.
[9]Quoted from the canonisation process in Gaucher, op. cit., p. 167.
[10]Six, *Thérèse de Lisieux au Carmel*, p. 308.
[11]DE 11.7.1.
[12]LT 191.
[13]Cf. Six, op. cit., pp. 121–36.
[14]P 36:5, LT 145.
[15]LT 191.
[16]HA IV 39ʳ (p. 84), VII 70ʳ (p. 149).
[17]HA XI 36ᵛ (p. 259), DE 4.7.4, 11.7.6, 20.7.3.
[18]HA IV 38ᵛ–39ʳ (p. 84).
[19]HA VII 74ʳ (p. 158), DE 29.7.3.
[20]HA XI 23ʳ (p. 239).
[21]P 53:2.
[22]HA IV 33ʳ (p. 74).
[23]E.g. HA X 15ᵛ–18ᵛ (pp. 225–9).
[24]HA VI 68ᵛ (p. 144), LT 143.
[25]HA VIII 80ᵛ (pp. 173–4); cf. Six, op. cit., pp. 140–2.
[26]LT 243.

[27]LT 261.
[28]Cf. Six, op. cit., p. 219.
[29]P 24 (with the editors' introduction).
[30]HA VIII 84^r (p. 180), IX 3^v (p. 195).
[31]HA IX 1^v (p. 189).
[32]P 17:13.
[33]HA IX 4^{rv} (pp. 196–7).
[34]HA X 3^v (p. 208), DE 16.7.6 (p. 349).
[35]DE 6.8.8.
[36]HA IV 32^r (p. 72), LT 80.
[37]Six, op. cit., pp. 81–2.
[38]HA X 2^v–3^r (pp. 207–8). For Thérèse's childhood encounter with lifts, see LD 5–6 Nov. 1887.
[39]HA IX 5^v (p. 200).
[40]HA VIII 75^v (p. 165).
[41]HA IX 5^r (pp. 198–9).
[42]DE (Soeur Marie du Sacré Coeur) 29.7.1.
[43]P 3:30–2.
[44]P 17:9
[45] HA VIII 75^v (p. 165).
[46] P 31:4.
[47]Cf. Six, op. cit., pp. 84–91.
[48]P 31:5.
[49]HA IV 38^{rv} (pp. 82–3).
[50]DE 21/6.5.1.
[51]P 41:2
[52]HA I 10^{rv} (p. 27).
[53]HA IX 2^v–3^v (pp. 192–4).
[54]HA p. 316 (English tr. p. 276).
[55]P 13:12–13.
[56]HA I 7^r (p. 22).
[57]HA IV 36^r (p. 79), VII 69^v (p. 149).
[58]P 16:2
[59]HA V 45^v (p. 99), P 24:25.
[60]HA V 45^r (p. 98).
[61]HA V 44^v (p. 97).
[62]HA V 45^r (p. 99).
[63]HA VII 69^v (p. 149).
[64]LT 220.
[65]DE 31.7.5; cf. 21/6.5.7, 8.7.4, 18.7.1 etc.
[66]HA V 46^r (pp. 99–100); cf. Bernard Bro, *The Little Way* (London 1979), pp. 70–5.
[67]HA V 48^r (p. 104).
[68]HA X 5^v (p. 211).
[69]HA X 5^v (pp. 211–12).
[70]HA X 6^r, 7^r (pp. 212, 214).
[71]P 46:4.
[72]HA X 6^v–7^r (p. 213).
[73]HA X 6^r (p. 212).

[74]HA VIII 83ᵛ (p. 179).
[75]E.g. LT 143, 193, 196.
[76]HA XI 25ᵛ (p. 242), DE 20.8.16.
[77]Cf. HA XI 25ʳ (p. 242).
[78]*Acta Apostolicae Sedis* 17 (1925), p. 346.
[79]P 11:4.
[80]P 17:11.

Index

234   INDEX